NOVEL A FORUM ON FICTION

PUBLISHED IN MAY, AUGUST, AND NOVEMBER OF EACH YEAR

VOLUME 53   NUMBER 3   NOVEMBER 2020

NOVEL: A FORUM ON FICTION

NOVEL: A FORUM ON FICTION is published three times a year by Duke University Press, 905 W. Main St., Suite 18B, Durham, NC 27701, on behalf of Novel, Inc. A two-year individual membership ($90) or two-year student membership ($40) to the SNS includes a subscription to *Novel*. To obtain a membership, go to dukeupress.edu/sns.

Submissions/Correspondence All manuscripts must conform to the guidelines in the *MLA Handbook* (Seventh Edition), with in-text parenthetical documentation and a list of works cited. Manuscripts should be submitted electronically, along with a cover letter containing all relevant contact information (email, mailing address). Electronic copies of the manuscript and cover letter should be sent in both Word and PDF format to **novel.forum@duke.edu.** Further information is available at **novel.trinity.duke.edu.** *N.B.* Presses seeking book reviews in *Novel* must send books to our Brown office: Brown University, Box 1984, 70 Brown Street, Providence, RI 02912.

Online Visit Duke University Press at dukeupress.edu.

ISSN 0029-5132

Contents

Introduction: The Anagonist

TIMOTHY BEWES

> *protagonist* (Gk "first combatant") *The first actor in a play; thence the principal actor or character. In Greek tragedy, the playwright was limited to the protagonist (first actor), deuteragonist (second actor) and tritagonist (third actor). . . . The protagonist has come to be the equivalent of the hero.*
>
> —Cuddon

If "protagonist," from the Greek *proto-agonist*, meaning "first combatant," designates the first or primary actor in a play and "thence the principal actor or character" in any kind of narrative, "anagonist" would designate an actor or character who does not act, a nonacting hero. But this definition is still too simple, for action in the novel takes (at least) two forms: exterior and interior. E. M. Forster summarizes the distinction between exterior and interior action as that which is "observable" in a human being, on one hand, and his or her "romanceful or romantic side" on the other (56). Raskolnikov acts; but were he to have not acted he would still be a protagonist, and he is a protagonist even while he hesitates, for hesitation, too, is novelistic action. For an anagonist to count as such, he or she would not only not act, but would not feel, not think, not search, would not even hesitate. Or rather, the anagonist's feeling, thinking, quest, or hesitation would not have any organizing function with respect to the narrative. No object or event in a novel could account for its significance by reference to the consciousness of an anagonist; for the terms in which the anagonist narrates his or her impressions (should the anagonist happen to do so), the meanings he or she gives them, are not transferable to the perspective of the work. The sensorium of the anagonist is the site of a perception that is no longer predicated on a possible action, real or deferred.[1] This arrest of movement, actual or potential, represents a new chronotopic foundation for the novel, a break in the "intrinsic connectedness of temporal and spatial relationships" expressed in the classic chronotopes: the road, the salon, the threshold, the provincial town (Bakhtin 84)—a break, perhaps, in the structure of the chronotope itself. In fact, anagonists often seem to live and move outside time, or in what Erich Auerbach called a "symbolic omnitemporality of events" (545).[2]

---

[1] For example, for Robert Walser's narrator Jakob von Gunten, the fact that his friend Kraus "always writes home" is precisely as valid as the fact that Jakob himself never writes home. The two tendencies or habits coexist, equally eccentric and equally removed from any principle of action (20, 47–48).

[2] Auerbach names Leopold Bloom and Hans Castorp, among several others, as characters who fit this model. Readers will encounter many more as they peruse this issue of *Novel*, including Maggie Verver, Odradek, Bartleby (of course), Paul Rayment, Michael K, Nao Yasutani, and every first-person narrator of every novel by Kazuo Ishiguro.

Novel: A Forum on Fiction 53:3   DOI 10.1215/00295132-8624498   © 2020 by Novel, Inc.

Protagonism is the form in which the novel achieves centeredness, when the significance of every element is oriented through the hero's consciousness. Of course, it is impossible to conceive of a human being without "dreams, joys, sorrows and self-communings" (Forster 56), let alone one without actions, movements, and schemes. Nevertheless, it has become clear in recent years that the access the novel gives to an individual's dreams, self-communings, and movements is a sign of the form's limitations, not its "affordances"; for the novel's understanding extends only to that which meets the criterion of "a specific mode of causality" (Rancière 1). The difference between the novel and everyday life is that, as Forster puts it, "in daily life we never understand each other," whereas "people in a novel can be understood completely by the reader. . . . Their inner as well as their outer life can be exposed" (56–57). Jacques Rancière calls this the "surfeit of rationality" of the novel (1), and it is wrapped up in the fact of a protagonist. For the biographical individual is the novel's formal solution to the "'bad' infinity" of possible content, the horizon that every novel needs in order to hold at bay the "fissures and rents" that are always present on the periphery of the novel's understanding (Lukács, *Theory* 81, 60). "Most humans, properly speaking, do not act," says Rancière; "they make objects or children, execute orders or render services, and continue doing the next day what they had done the day before. Nowhere does any expectation or reversal arise, nor do any errors made enable one to pass from one condition to the opposite" (4).

The anagonist does not *represent* this community of nonactors; nor does the figure of the anagonist—as the later Georg Lukács understood inaction in Tolstoy—simply mirror a world, dominated by capitalism, in which "decent people can no longer find any opportunity for action" ("Tolstoy" 155, 166). (If either were the case, the anagonist would be nothing but a protagonist, whose inaction would serve as the work's horizon and fulcrum.) Rather, the anagonist is how the novel registers, in formal terms, something that it otherwise cannot acknowledge: "the empirical real's absence of cause" (Rancière 4). That is, the presence of an anagonist registers—and breaks—the novel's complicity with a world that seeks to convince us of the fundamental legibility of human motivations and of the exhaustion of behavior by narratives of material interest, sexual desire, emotional entanglements, and schemes of vengeance or expiation. The anagonist is alert—in a way the protagonist cannot be—to the holes and fissures in every such narrative and explanation; to the possibility that, for example, one day "the other can suddenly become a stranger," even when you know them so well that "you can read intentions behind their actions and calculate their responses to circumstances fairly accurately"; even when "you are sure there is not a single crease in them left unexplored" (Luiselli 21).

Thus one can say that an anagonist taking center stage is a rejection of the signifying economy and structure of the novel as conventionally conceived: of the completeness of represented actions, the meaningfulness of the hero's search or mission, the logic of centeredness itself—and is thus an opening to Lukács's "'bad' infinity." The critic Alex Woloch, citing Raymond Williams, talks of the "distribution of significance" proper to the "character system" of the realist novel, whereby a group of characters is "juxtaposed and concatenated within a closed and intricately organized discursive structure" (Woloch 51). The anagonist upends this structure, replacing the principle of knowability itself (of "people like this, relations like this," as Williams paraphrases it, calling this "the real achievement of most serious novels and plays") with unknowability; the principle of the novel's center of consciousness with a dispersal of consciousness; and the principle of the protagonist's enclosure within the diegesis with the possibility of an escape. By its means, the novel puts a fracture in that form of "hegemony" that Williams locates "in the fibres of the self" (Williams 209, 212).

*　　　*　　　*

To my knowledge, there is no established term for a hero who does not act, or whose action is nothing but an object of representation, framed at every moment by a larger condition of imperception or perception cut off from action—a nonsensorimotor perception. For the protagonist has long been held to be a defining element of the novel. The main tendencies of European novel theory (with the always remarkable exceptions of Bakhtin and the early Lukács) have seen no need to conceptualize a presence outside the positive relations of representation, identification, or recognition that accompany the logic of the protagonist, a presence alert to the fissures inherent in the "historical situation" of the novel (Lukács, *Theory* 60). On the contrary, scholars—from Ian Watt to Paul Ricoeur to Thomas Pavel—insist on the centrality to the novel of "human beings, the ideals and norms that guide their lives, the passions that drive them, and the action they take" (Pavel 19). As recent a work as Guido Mazzoni's *Teoria del Romanzo* (2011) has this to say: "For us as readers of novels, the destiny of characters is tremendously important; even when we do not agree with the goals that the heroes are pursuing, we are able to recognize ourselves in the schema of their existence. We are like them, thrown into a world, occupied in seeking a balance between desires and reality" (370–71).

But as the essays collected in this issue of *Novel* illustrate, the current critical moment demands an analysis that is attentive precisely to the "fissures and rents" that escape a conception of the novel based on action (and the ideals, norms, passions, and ambitions that guide it). For the novel, it turns out, and from as early as the beginning of the nineteenth century, has had not only minor characters but *heroes* who "fail to cohere as subjects around a clearly demarcated inner world" (Scribner, this issue, 317); who fall victim not only to other, more purposeful characters within the diegesis but to the narrative directionality of the novel itself; who, as such, lack "active imagination" and so find themselves caught up in other people's plots (Levin, this issue, 341). The implication, according to Abby Scribner in this issue, is an entirely different understanding of the subjective basis of the novel form; not (as Watt has it) "truth to individual experience . . . always unique and always new" (Watt 13), nor (in Mazzoni's terms) "the mimesis of the interior life" (Mazzoni 179)—propositions that accompany the long-assumed imbrication of the novel with liberalism—but, rather, "a self missing an interior world" (Scribner 329). Works such as Austen's *Mansfield Park* and Charlotte Brontë's *Villette*, Scribner argues, invent or discover "an incommensurability between internal experience and external world that renders inner life incommunicable" (328). Refusing the consensus of several generations of critics, for whom Austen's work confirms the constitutive relation between freedom and "interior experience,"

Scribner's essay reveals the possibility that the interior realm may be as "irrelevant" (323) to the subjectivity and political project of *Mansfield Park* as it seems to Fanny herself.

The articles in this issue of *Novel* do not necessarily subscribe to the principles outlined above. None, of course, uses the term *anagonist*. Nevertheless, the shift of perspective put forward in Scribner's article resonates across the essays featured in the issue, even when the focus remains on forms of "prenarrative" action that may be discerned beneath a character's hesitation and inaction, or when the theoretical basis of the reading remains something like Ricoeur's "inchoate narrativity" of human experience, or the necessary "entanglement" of consciousness in "untold and repressed stories" (Ricoeur 74–75). Janina Levin's essay "Temporality and the Unconfident Heroine in Henry James's *The Golden Bowl*" takes its point of departure from the "stalled beginning" of James's novel, a period of waiting and prevarication on the part of the protagonist, Maggie Verver, that extends at least through the work's first volume. In the second half of *The Golden Bowl*, Levin observes, Maggie passes almost indiscernibly "from anxiety to courage." For Levin, Maggie's earlier anxiety is best read—with Ricoeur—as the sign of a nascent entanglement in action that only needs "the configuring act of narrative" for its purposiveness to be revealed (Levin 342). Yet Levin is also alert to the ways in which anxiety or uncertainty might at any moment—such as in the extraordinary passage describing the "little timed silence" in which Maggie's husband Prince Amerigo looks at her from her drawing-room door—expand not into knowledge or recognition but, in the opposite direction, toward "an uncertainty in the very air," as the novel's narrator puts it (James 332, 335). At such moments, contra Ricoeur and despite the conceptual and compositional efforts of James himself, this work surely intuits the existence of something that its "biographical" organization cannot accommodate, a "script," perhaps, to which neither Maggie, nor James, nor the discourse of literary criticism "has access."

The phrase "a script to which he does not have access" appears in Maria Christou's essay "Kazuo Ishiguro's Nonactors," characterizing the experience of the celebrity pianist Ryder (the protagonist and narrator of Ishiguro's 1995 novel *The Unconsoled*) in the unnamed central European city where he is an honored guest (Christou, this issue, 372). Ryder moves around the city only passively, in response to pressing invitations, earnestly communicated expectations, and straight-up requests. He never receives a copy of the "schedule" that has apparently been prepared for him, and his every idea and narrative about his role and effectiveness are revealed as woefully at odds with the reality—all of which leads to Christou's claim that Ryder, like every Ishiguro protagonist, is "part of a broader turn against action" in the late twentieth-century literary imagination (378). This turn is closely allied to a cold war logic—analyzed, among others, by Hannah Arendt—in which human action begins to be experienced as risky and "dangerously unpredictable" (Christou 379). Christou distinguishes between "action" and "agency" as a way to hold onto the insights of critical rationality. Thus agency persists in Ishiguro's novels, but it is no longer located in their actors (or protagonists) but in—for example—the biopolitical rationality of the society depicted in *Never Let Me Go*, played out upon the bodies of the clones; in the technocratic theories of governance represented in *The Remains of the Day* by the views of the American senator Mr Lewis, urging the gentleman politicians of prewar Britain toward "professionalism"; and in "the absent yet somehow all-pervading schedule or 'script' that dictates Ryder's performance" in *The Unconsoled* (372). Ishiguro's nonacting protagonists, for Christou, retain a *critical* meaning and agency by their mobilization in the text as symptoms of "a broader condition or wider system of values." The nonaction she finds "center stage" in Ishiguro's work as a whole foregrounds nothing less than "the contemporary condition of the subject" (379).

Kate Wilkinson's essay "Letters and the Contemporary Novel: Materiality and Metaphor in Ian McEwan's *The Children Act*," by contrast, locates the silence and nonaction of the literary text—here, the 2014 novel by Ian McEwan—not in the characters, whose actions are all too legible and purposeful, but in the formal organization of the work itself. At the heart of *The Children Act* is a *differend*, a "place of silence" at the interstices of two discursive regimens: on one hand, the discourse of the legal ruling, inhabited by the High Court judge Fiona Maye (like every late McEwan hero, a virtuoso in her field); on the other, the declarative emotional letters sent to Fiona by a seventeen-year-old Jehovah's Witness, Adam, whose life she saved when she ruled against his petition that he be permitted, on religious grounds, not to undergo a medically necessary blood transfusion. Fiona's silence in the face of Adam's communications alerts us to the presence of something that "cannot yet" be put into phrases: an "intractable contemporary conflict between religious belief and the secular law" (Wilkinson, this issue, 383). Thus the differend—a concept developed by Jean-François Lyotard—is not only discursive, it is also chronological. The delayed action materialized in the novel by an unanswered letter (or indeed, as in Levin's essay, an unconfident heroine) gives a temporal quality to the differend. Both Levin's and Wilkinson's essays are attuned to the ways in which the differend has been present in the novel form from the beginning—whenever a letter goes unanswered or whenever a heroine is unable to make a decision. The anagonist lives and moves outside linear (narrative) time; her actions and utterances are never resolvable by reference to corresponding actions or utterances by other characters, however temporally or logically connected these are. In McEwan's novel this chronological dispersal—which we might justifiably call an omnitemporality of events—is found in the discrepancy (which is never closed or resolved) between a speech act and its response, which is to say, a duration in which it remains to be determined whether the letter is "not yet answered" or "not yet unanswered" (Wilkinson 393). We may also speak of a gap, or surplus, between an act of expression and its occasion or predicament; or in other words, of the "*wrong* at the heart of a fictional differend" (396; emphasis added).

In 1973, J. M. Coetzee began drafting a novel that he later abandoned, titled "The Burning of the Books." "Fiction," he wrote in his notes toward that work, "being a serious affair, cannot accept pre-requisites like (1) a desire to write, (2) something to write about, (3) something to say. There must be a place for a fiction of apathy toward the task of writing, toward the subject, toward the means" (qtd. in Attwell 59–60). The work of apathy that Coetzee is talking about here has not been realized—perhaps because what Coetzee was imagining at this moment was not an apathetic protagonist (a realizable, all too familiar fictional form) but an anagonist, a form that is inherently unrealizable.

This issue features two essays on Coetzee: Benjamin Lewis Robinson's "Fiction Cares: J. M. Coetzee's *Slow Man*" and Benjamin R. Davies's "Growing Up Against Allegory: The Late Works of J. M. Coetzee." Robinson makes no reference to Jean-François Lyotard, but a central concern of his article is the "fundamental irreconcilability" between the discourses of "justice" and "care" as it plays out across Coetzee's early work. But another differend appears in Coetzee's later "Australian" writings featuring Elizabeth Costello, including *Slow Man*, the main focus of Robinson's article. This second differend dramatizes the discursive limits of love as against care, nursing as against devotion, but also the real as against fiction. Robinson develops an ingenious distinction specific to *Slow Man* between realism and *vraimentism* (a play on the name of Coetzee's anagonistic hero Paul Rayment). Vraimentism is achieved when a fictional character establishes his fictionality by the very strength of his insistence that he is a real person. "Be a main character," his creator, Elizabeth Costello, implores Paul, meaning: "Do something. Do anything. Surprise me. . . . So that someone, somewhere, might put you in a book. So that someone might *want* to put you in a book. So that you may be *worth* putting in a book" (*Slow Man* 229). As he is, Paul is not "worth" putting in a book, and yet he is in one. The paradox presents us with another defining characteristic of the anagonist.

Like Robinson, Davies locates an epistemic break in Coetzee—one identified by Coetzee himself in a short essay from 1976, "The First Sentence of Yvonne Burgess' *The Strike*." The break that concerns Davies, however, does not divide Coetzee's body of work but defines its entirety. "To find what a sentence like 'Mr. Podsnap closed the book' or 'Philip Marlow [*sic*] closed the book' used to mean," writes Coetzee in 1976,

> is an archaeological endeavor. Included in its meaning, however, was certainly the following: that there was a social and characterological typology assumed and shared among the reading public; that the sign 'Mr. Podsnap' or 'Philip Marlow' in an initial sentence, empty to begin with, would in due course be filled with social and characterological details, some of them details of such fineness as to refine the typology, . . . the process of refining the typology being known as making the character individual just as adherence to the typology is known as making the character representative; and that the fit of 'Mr. Podsnap' or 'Philip Marlow' into the typological lattice would reciprocally reaffirm the typology and therefore the sociology and psychology of the reading public. ("First Sentence" 92–93)

In the wake of that shift—the historical disappearance of an entire "social and characterological typology"—what does it mean to attribute an action to a protagonist? One answer to that question informed an earlier generation of Coetzee criticism, according to Davies: the rejection of allegory—the literary form that is codependent with the "typological lattice." In place of allegory, argued Derek Attridge (that body of criticism's most prominent spokesperson), one should read Coetzee's works "literally"—for their capacity to engender "a strangeness, a newness, a singularity, an inventiveness, an alterity in what I read" (Attridge 40). Davies does not argue against Attridge so much as extend him. Thus in Davies's account,

Coetzee's recent "Jesus" series of novels (*The Childhood of Jesus*, *The Schooldays of Jesus*, *The Death of Jesus*) brings a new self-awareness to the unproductivity of allegorical reading. In the boy David—the series's enigmatic central character—Coetzee offers us a hero who not only subjectively refuses typology but is objectively inimical and immune to it. To his guardian and chronicler Simón, who will write a book about David's deeds when he is gone, David says: "But . . . you must promise not to understand me. When you try to understand me it spoils everything" (Coetzee, *Death* 103). The Jesus novels represent the coming of age of a literature "beyond allegory" (which is also to say, of a novel beyond *the* novel), with their hero David evolving the figure of the anagonist significantly beyond the state of a protagonist with issues.

Speaking of protagonists with issues, the form of action that is the focus of Joel Evans's essay "The Mob: J. G. Ballard's Turn to the Collective" is "meaningless action, the more violent the better" (Ballard 249). But is meaningless action the action of a super-protagonist or an anagonist? For Evans, the meaningless action that takes place in each of J. G. Ballard's last four novels, *Cocaine Nights* (1996), *Super-Cannes* (1996), *Millennium People* (2003) and *Kingdom Come* (2006)—a series of works set in closed or gated communities of various kinds—is both utopian and dystopian. Violence—action undertaken without an end in view—is a basis for community formation in a world without "transcendent structures and hierarchies" (Evans, this issue, 437). Such violence is as close as Ballard ever comes, argues Evans, to imagining a "flat collectivism"—an antihierarchical, revolutionary form of community that can shock the middle classes "out of their stupor" and "stop the universe in its tracks" (444). Evans claims that in conceiving the unifying principle of this "flat formation" in terms of violence, Ballard refuses any possibility or role for literature in imagining what a collective "might lead to in any positive, lasting, or rational sense" (445). Ballard's imagination enacts the disastrous consequences of presenting the anagonist not as a character who, though central, exists peripherally alongside his or her fellows but as one who configures a plot, cast of characters, and world around his vision of meaningless action and thereby founds a community upon it. The problem with Ballard's anagonists is simply that they step forth as such, subordinating the narratives in which they appear to the principle of their own existence.

The limits of the novel form are highlighted in a very different way in Alison Glassie's essay on Ruth Ozeki's 2013 work *A Tale for the Time Being*. Set in the aftermath of the 2011 Tōhoku earthquake and tsunami, Ozeki's novel is the story of a schoolgirl's diary that washes up as flotsam at a beach on Cortes Island, British Columbia, a few months after the disaster and is discovered by Ruth, a novelist, and her husband Oliver. We read the diary as Ruth and Oliver do—in diegetic real time. The anagonist principle is *thematically* present in Ozeki's work in at least two forms: the character of the "famous anarchist-feminist-novelist-turned-Buddhist-nun" Jiko Yasutani, who instructs her great-granddaughter Nao, the diary's author, in the ways of "time being"—a concept Ruth traces to the thirteenth-century Zen master Dōgen (Ozeki 30); and second, the ocean—the work's "most important narrative agent," writes Glassie, on account of its ability to undercut Ruth's own "narrative preferences" (Ozeki 33), such as her desire that the tsunami be the explanation for the diary's oceanic passage. In Glassie's reading, Ozeki's work strives for a "not-knowing" that might be conceived as proper to the novel form, in opposition to both the views of the novelist Ruth and the novel theory tradition alluded to earlier. To come to terms with not-knowing is to awaken to our own nature as "time beings." This formulation—time being—is yet another plausible definition of the anagonist.

*   *   *

A journal issue—like a tree or a whale, according to Ozeki, or like a letter, according to Wilkinson—is a time being. Its essence is durational in the way that a "blog," for example, is not (Ozeki 26). By the time you read this, says Nao in the diary entry that opens Ozeki's novel, "everything will be different" (3). Like the articles in the issue, this introduction will be read by its addressees at least six months after the issue is sent to production.

Begin where you are, Jiko tells Nao (15). I am writing this at my home in Providence, Rhode Island, on April 3, 2020. The university where I work is off limits; the library and offices have all been closed. My partner is with her parents, under curfew, in Bangalore, India. The official death toll from the coronavirus in the United States has just passed 7,000 ("Coronavirus Map"). The count has been doubling every three days. In Italy the figure is 14,681; in India the official number is 72. What seems certain is that the world will be unimaginably altered in six months' time. What better lesson in the futility of traditional models of novelistic agency, and the need for a new conception of narrative action, than the coronavirus pandemic. "You don't make the timeline, the virus makes the timeline," said Anthony Fauci, director of the National Institute of Allergy and Infectious Diseases, in March.[3] But the novel has known this all along. The novel has never been (only) what Amitav Ghosh, quoting John Updike, damningly characterizes as an "individual moral adventure" (Ghosh 127). Looking back at the long epoch of "surging carbon emissions," Ghosh notes that "very few . . . of the literary minds of that intensely *engagé* period were alive to the archaic voice whose rumblings, once familiar, had now become inaudible to humanity: that of the earth and its atmosphere" (124). This may be true of the period's "literary minds"; but the novel has always included a dimension of not-knowing and nonaction, a dimension that is sometimes even found occupying the narrative space of the work's central characters. This principle of limitation is as intrinsic to the novel's being and thought as the consciousness and action of the protagonist. The nonaction attests to everything that escapes human motivations and human narratives; the not-knowing knows all about such archaic rumblings.

*   *   *

TIMOTHY BEWES is professor of English at Brown University and associate editor of *Novel: A Forum on Fiction*. His books include *Cynicism and Postmodernity* (1997), *Reification, or The Anxiety of Late Capitalism* (2002), and *The Event of Postcolonial Shame* (2011). His latest book, *Free Indirect: The Idea of Twenty-first Century Fiction*, is forthcoming.

---

[3]   Fauci was speaking to Chris Cuomo on *Prime Time*, CNN, 25 March 2020. See Budryk.

Works Cited

Attridge, Derek. *J. M. Coetzee and the Ethics of Reading: Literature in the Event*. Chicago: U of Chicago P, 2004.

Attwell, David. *J. M. Coetzee and the Life of Writing: Face-to-Face with Time*. New York: Penguin, 2015.

Auerbach, Erich. *Mimesis: The Representation of Reality in Western Literature*. Trans. Willard R. Trask. Princeton: Princeton UP, 2013.

Bakhtin, M. M. "Forms of Time and of the Chronotope in the Novel: Notes toward a Historical Poetics." *The Dialogic Imagination: Four Essays*. Trans. Caryl Emerson and Michael Holquist. Austin: U Texas P, 1981. 84–258.

Ballard, J. G. *Millennium People*. London: Flamingo, 2003.

Budryk, Zack. "Fauci: 'You Don't Make the Timeline. The Virus Makes the Timeline.'" *Hill* 26 March 2020 < thehill.com/policy/healthcare/489636-fauci-you-dont-make-the-timeline-the-virus-makes-the-timeline >.

Coetzee, J. M. *The Death of Jesus*. London: Harvill Secker, 2020.

Coetzee, J. M. "The First Sentence of Yvonne Burgess' *The Strike*." *Doubling the Point: Essays and Interviews*. Ed. David Attwell. Cambridge, MA: Harvard UP, 1992. 91–93.

Coetzee, J. M. *Slow Man*. London: Secker and Warburg, 2005.

"Coronavirus Map: Tracking the Global Outbreak." *New York Times* 3 April 2020 <www.nytimes.com/interactive/2020/world/coronavirus-maps.html>.

Cuddon, J. A. *A Dictionary of Literary Terms*. Rev. ed. London: Deutsch, 1979.

Forster, E. M. *Aspects of the Novel*. New York: Penguin, 2005.

Ghosh, Amitav. *The Great Derangement: Climate Change and the Unthinkable*. Chicago: U of Chicago P, 2016.

James, Henry. *The Golden Bowl*. Notes by Patricia Crick. New York: Penguin, 1987.

Luiselli, Valeria. *Lost Children Archive*. New York: Knopf, 2019.

Lukács, Georg. *The Theory of the Novel: A Historico-philosophical Essay on the Forms of Great Epic Literature*. Trans. Anna Bostock. Cambridge, MA: MIT P, 1971.

Lukács, Georg. "Tolstoy and the Development of Realism." *Studies in European Realism*. Trans. Edith Bone. New York: Fertig, 2002. 126–205.

Mazzoni, Guido. *Theory of the Novel*. Trans. Zakiya Hanafi. Cambridge, MA: Harvard UP, 2017.

Ozeki, Ruth. *A Tale for the Time Being*. New York: Viking, 2013.

Pavel, Thomas G. *The Lives of the Novel: A History.* Princeton: Princeton UP, 2013.

Rancière, Jacques. *The Edges of Fiction.* Trans. Steve Corcoran. Cambridge: Polity, 2020.

Ricoeur, Paul. *Time and Narrative.* Vol. 1. Trans. Kathleen McLaughlin and David Pellauer. Chicago: U of Chicago P, 1984.

Walser, Robert. *Jakob von Gunten.* Trans. Christopher Middleton. New York: New York Review Books, 1999.

Watt, Ian. *The Rise of the Novel: Studies in Defoe, Richardson, and Fielding.* London: Hogarth, 1987.

Williams, Raymond. *Marxism and Literature.* Oxford: Oxford UP, 1977.

Woloch, Alex. *The One vs. the Many: Minor Characters and the Space of the Protagonist in the Novel.* Princeton: Princeton UP, 2003.

Liberalism and Inner Life: The Curious Cases of *Mansfield Park* and *Villette*

ABBY SCRIBNER

Though not often read together, both Jane Austen's *Mansfield Park* (1814) and Charlotte Brontë's *Villette* (1853) have regularly provoked dissatisfied responses in readers. Austen recorded her mother's well-known reaction in her collection of "Opinions of *Mansfield Park*": "My Mother—not liked it so well as P. & P.—Thought Fanny insipid" (231). Similarly, Matthew Arnold famously wrote in an 1853 letter, "Why is *Villette* disagreeable? Because the writer's mind contains nothing but hunger, rebellion, and rage, and therefore that is all she can, in fact, put into her book" (33–34). Critical responses to both texts remain polarized into the twenty-first century. Various critics have described *Mansfield Park* as "dispiriting," "unlikable," and Austen's "oddest work" (Stout 58; Auerbach, *Romantic Imprisonment* 22; Johnson, "What" 62). *Villette* has received similar treatment, being described as "obsessive and disturbing," "claustrophobic," "despairingly feminist," and an "ambiguous exception" among Brontë's other novels (Auerbach, *Communities* 78; Ablow 80; Gilbert and Gubar 399; Eagleton 18, 45).

This essay argues that the two texts elicit such strong responses because their protagonists do not fit the model of the liberal subject. An influential strain of literary criticism links the nineteenth-century novel to liberal politics through a shared emphasis on the subjective interior. However, neither Fanny nor Lucy presents a legible interior realm to the reader. *Mansfield Park* gives us glimpses of Fanny's interior only to spatially and rhetorically circumscribe it. It ultimately defers to exterior social structures to such an extent that the individual interior becomes unusable for constructing the subject. *Villette* shows an analogous conflict. It depicts several of Lucy's attempts to communicate her interior self to an exterior social world, all of which take the form of failed architectural constructions. It thereby displays anxiety around the threat of solipsism. Both protagonists fail to cohere as subjects around a clearly demarcated inner world. The two texts read together thus indicate that our understanding of the link between liberalism and the nineteenth-century novel, by way of a shared emphasis on interiority, is incomplete. As a result, they provide opportunities to reconsider each of three terms, both separately and together: the nineteenth-century novel as form, liberalism as political paradigm, and interiority as a space supposedly essential to both.[1]

Many thanks to my mentor, Deborah Elise White, and to the other members of my dissertation committee: Lynne Huffer, Paul Kelleher, and Elissa Marder. Thanks also to Tamsin Kimoto and Will Parshley for help with earlier drafts, to my anonymous reader for an exceptionally thoughtful engagement with my writing, to Alian Teach and Kathy Ly-Nguyen for keeping me sane, and to Jason Walsh, for all this and everything else.

[1]   Though I tend to refer to the novel as a "form" and liberalism as a "program" or "paradigm," they could both be called forms. I take seriously Caroline Levine's argument that forms "mov[e] back and forth across aesthetic and social materials" and that aesthetic and political forms

Liberalism, the Novel, and the Subjective Interior

Subjective interiority has long been considered essential to the nineteenth-century novel. Critics of the nineteenth-century novel often argue that the texts they analyze posit and affirm a new model of subjectivity concomitant with modernity that takes many features of an "outside" and moves them inward. Sally Shuttleworth, for example, describes how, in the nineteenth-century novel, "Selfhood no longer resided in the open texture of social act and exchange, but within a new interior space" (9). Similarly, Nancy Armstrong traces the historical movement through which "the intricate status system that had long dominated British thinking" is replaced via the nineteenth-century novel with a system that "began to represent an individual's value in terms of his, but more often in terms of *her*, essential qualities of mind" (*Desire* 4). By emphasizing personal experience and psychologizing political conflicts to convert them into emotional ones, the story goes, the nineteenth-century novel affirms a subject model that privileges the interior realm. It takes exterior structures like status and social exchange, individualizes them, and moves them into an essentialized inner world.[2]

In a complementary way, political theorists have posited a connection between subjective interiority and liberal politics. In *Identity and Difference*, for example, Etienne Balibar argues for a reading of classical liberal thinker John Locke as the inventor of consciousness. By linking Locke's epistemological claims in *An Essay Concerning Human Understanding* with his sociopolitical claims in the *Two Treatises of Government*, Balibar shows how Locke's political project necessarily entails a theory of the subject. As Nancy Armstrong explains, Balibar finds two different origin stories in Locke's two texts: "[T]he first, a story of the individual's extension through labor into the world of property, and the second, an account of that individual's appropriation of sensory information from the world, as he transformed that information into a separate domain of personal experience" ("Just" 288). Around the domain of personal experience, the interior realm of consciousness, Locke creates the modern subject. Balibar's reading of Locke brings out the parallelism between the two stories, thus showing, as Stella Sandford describes in her introduction to *Identity and Difference*, how "identity [is] an *effect* of appropriation and the inalienable rather than its (logical, ontological, or social) condition of possibility" (xl). A politico-economic structure generates a subjective form around an internal space.

If, as Balibar argues, Locke creates the modern subject by enabling "the possibility of an interior experience with direct access to 'mental reality,'" John Stuart Mill confirms and elaborates on such a subjective model as the grounds for his

can therefore interact directly (5). See the introduction to *Forms: Whole, Rhythm, Hierarchy, Network* 1–23.

2   For other works that advance this critical claim, see Mary Poovey, and see my account of D. A. Miller's *The Novel and the Police* below. Georg Lukács also memorably argues in *The Theory of the Novel* that "the novel tells of the adventure of interiority" (89). Contemporary critics most often evoke this tradition in order to argue against it. See, for example, Kramnick 2; Ward 2, 11–12; Schaffer, *Romance's Rival* 20–23.

political liberalism two centuries later (Balibar 1–2). In "On Liberty," Mill attempts to circumscribe the "appropriate region of human liberty" to which his Principle of Liberty applies—the realm that "affects only himself, or, if it affects others, only with their free, voluntary, undeceived consent and participation" (14). Mirroring Locke, Mill first defines the realm of human liberty as "the inward domain of consciousness" that merits liberty of conscience, thought, feeling, opinion, and sentiment. From the inward domain, Mill derives the outward-directed liberties of "expressing and publishing opinions," "of tastes and pursuits," and "of combination" (14).[3] Mill's interior realm of human liberty, in other words, founds his politics. The subject for both Locke and Mill congeals around a constitutive interior space, the domain of consciousness that serves as the seat of the self.[4] Wendy Brown argues that such a model of the liberal subject based on "fixed boundaries, clearly identifiable interests and identities, and power conceived as generated and directed *from within the entity itself*" remains dominant until well into the twentieth century (10; emphasis added).

Both the nineteenth-century novel and liberalism, then, supposedly depend on a subject that coheres around a constitutive inner realm. D. A. Miller's *The Novel and the Police* is perhaps *the* paradigmatic account that links the nineteenth-century novel to liberalism based on a shared reliance on a particular subjective form. He argues that the function of the nineteenth-century novel "is to confirm the novel-reader in his identity as 'liberal subject,' a term with which I allude not just to the subject whose private life, mental or domestic, is felt to provide constantly inarguable evidence of his constitutive 'freedom,' but also to, broadly speaking, the political regime that sets store by this subject" (x). The interpellative function of the novel that Miller describes, in other words, operates primarily through confirmation of a constitutive internal realm, the same essential realm of liberty we find in Mill and of interior experience we find in Locke. Miller's account connects all of the dots: by confirming the novel-reader as a subject constituted around an interior realm (as Shuttleworth and Nancy Armstrong argue), the nineteenth-century novel also necessarily conscripts the reader into a political regime that operates through and thus depends on that same vision of the subject (as Locke and Mill argue). The novel constructs a subject who is also the subject of a liberal politics.

Mansfield Park and *Villette* both resolutely refuse the series of connections that Miller describes. In a historical period—that of nineteenth-century liberalism—and an aesthetic form—the novel—in which interiority is supposedly dominant, both novels build up spaces of interiority only to foreclose them. They thus challenge any straightforward connection, through a shared subject model that privileges

---

[3] Elaine Hadley 70–73 explains how Mill's three types of liberty move progressively outward, corresponding respectively to mind, action, and society.

[4] My spatial understanding of subject formation, though it takes its cues from Locke's and Mill's texts, is indebted to Michel Foucault's notion of subjectivation. In *The History of Sexuality, Volume 2*, Foucault describes subjectivation as "self-formation as an 'ethical subject,' a process in which the individual *delimits that part of himself* that will form the object of his moral practice, defines his position relative to the precept he will follow, and decides on a certain mode of being that will serve as his moral goal" (28; emphasis added). See also *Security, Territory, Population* 184; and for an early elaboration without the term *subjectivation*, see *Discipline and Punish* 29–30.

interiority, between the nineteenth-century novel as form and liberalism as political program. The influential argument of critics like Miller cannot account for the transformed subjectivities and foreclosed interiorities of Austen's and Brontë's strangest novels. These two famously disliked texts thus reveal that our understanding of the link between liberalism and the nineteenth-century novel is incomplete. They demonstrate the necessity of revising our understanding of the nineteenth-century novel, of liberalism and its subjective forms, or of both.

Exterior Stasis: *Mansfield Park*

Numerous critics have noted *Mansfield Park*'s persistent externality. Marilyn Butler describes it as a work in which Austen "gives her external world a solidity and scale which eventually belittles individual characters" (228). Daniel Stout argues that it is primarily interested in "the way characters are circumscribed by and identified with (and the one because the other) the circumstances in which they happen to fall" (54). Such a novel, as Stout identifies, ends up having a "glancing (at most) interest in interior life" (60). Protagonist Fanny Price, especially, seems to readers a resolutely moral character (often annoyingly so), but we do not often see the workings of her interior. Stout describes how Fanny's inner life "is registered as kind of low-level white noise rather than the detailed transcript of a score" (69).

However, there are moments in the novel in which the "white noise" of Fanny's inwardness explodes into a cacophony. These moments are persistently associated with the space of the east room, a derelict room in the upper part of the house of which Fanny gradually takes possession. Despite the scant critical attention it has received, the east room is one of the only places in the novel in which Fanny's inner life is displayed.[5] In depictions of the east room, then, we might expect to find the constitutive internal realm of consciousness, Locke's "interior experience with direct access to 'mental reality,'" Mill's "region of human liberty," and so on. We might even expect to find a more essentialized interior in order to allow the specifically feminine novelistic subject to perform her function of "depoliticiz[ing] class relations . . . partly by translating class difference into psychological or moral difference" by moving them into an interior world (Poovey 9).[6] And we do find an inner world represented through the east room, for a moment.

---

[5]   Both Duckworth and Butler briefly discuss the east room as a straightforward space of self-examination and moral improvement, but neither recognizes how strange it is (Duckworth 73–74; Butler 231). See Isobel Armstrong's "Theories of Space" for another reading of the east room as the novel's exceptional space (19).

[6]   It could be objected that Fanny, and later Lucy, do not have interiors corresponding to those of the classic liberal subject model because that subject was always implicitly masculine. While I agree that the supposedly neutral liberal subject is coded masculine, the most common mode of understanding women's exclusion from full subjectivity is that the woman is confined to an interior realm—domestic, affective, material, or psychological—in order to shore up the full subjectivity of her male counterpart. Thus feminine exclusion from liberal subjectivity is often accounted for by showing not the absence of an interior realm for women but the absence of an interior realm that is constitutive of or in fundamental relation to the exterior. This is why someone like Brontë can argue for the inclusion of women in an implicitly male subject model

In the end, though, each display of inner life attached to the east room is smoothed over. Again and again the text explores the dynamics of the interior only to reject them for the immobility of the exterior. The process of its closure occurs as the discrepancy between two distinct levels of narration of these moments of inwardness—Fanny's dissimulated relationship to her own inward space and the narrator's skepticism about Fanny's perspective. We perceive the distinct levels through Austen's use of free indirect discourse. As the novel progresses, the gap in between these two narrative registers closes, resolving into a unitary, external perspective. This movement serves as a rhetorical marker of the novel's foreclosing of the spaces of inner life. The text thus ultimately refuses to construct Fanny's subjectivity around an interior space. Instead, it affirms purely external structures of status in which individual subjectivity and interiority are inconsequential, refusing the link between the nineteenth-century novel and liberalism.

Inside I

Mansfield Park introduces the east room following a scene in which Fanny is again pressured to take part in the production of *Lovers' Vows* that her cousins are putting on. She retreats to the east room to contemplate her moral dilemma: should she capitulate to her cousins and participate, or stick to her guns and refuse? As the narrator tells us, "The little white attic, which had continued her sleeping-room ever since her first entering the family, proving incompetent to suggest any reply, she had recourse, as soon as she was dressed, to another apartment more spacious and more meet for walking about in, and thinking, and of which she had now for some time been almost equally mistress" (105). This "other apartment" is the east room. Our first scene in the east room, then, stages a moment of deliberation meant to alleviate moral confusion.

However, rather than being a neutral container for contemplation, the east room is a space overflowing with junk. The narrator describes the objects of the east room lovingly enough—there are some books, a writing desk, and Fanny's works of charity. However, the exhaustive list quickly begins to encompass items of more questionable value: broken furniture that has "suffered all the ill-usage of children," a badly done "faded footstool" made by Fanny's cousin Julia, three once fashionable but now passé transparencies, and a motley collection of family profiles "thought unworthy of being anywhere else" (106–7). Such a profusion of objects, rather than suggesting a tidy scene of pleasant domesticity, evokes a cramped, claustrophobic space. The narrator's additional details about the space endorse such a reading—there is "never [to be] a fire in it on Fanny's account" and it is a space that "nobody else wanted," giving the space a grim aspect indeed (106).

merely through a mechanism of greater inclusivity: "[W]omen feel just as men feel; they need exercise for their faculties and a field for their efforts as much as their brothers do" (*Jane Eyre* 93). Women have interiors like men do. They are just not allowed to connect their interiors to exteriors. Such an explanation, however, does not account for Fanny's and Lucy's strange relationships to their interiors.

Fanny attempts to seclude herself in the east room, to retreat into her interior in order to check in with her conscience, which, according to Mill, should reside there. The scene, however, quickly becomes wild and destabilizing. Rather than "catch[ing] any[one's] counsel" or "inhal[ing] a breeze of mental strength," the narrator describes Fanny's "doubts . . . increasing" as she walks around, eventually growing "bewildered" at "the sight of present upon present" from her cousins (107). Far from providing moral guidance, then, the east room makes Fanny even more confused.[7] The confusion is heightened when Fanny is finally startled from her reverie by a tap at the door, which the narrator describes as rousing Fanny "in the midst of this attempt to find her way to her duty" (107). Fanny's confusion here is also spatialized, joining with the description of the cramped space of the east room to suggest a maze out of which Fanny is physically unable to find her way.

The text, therefore, strongly associates the east room with Fanny's inward-facing activity of contemplation, correlating it to Locke's "interior experience with direct access to 'mental reality'" and creating it as a spatial analogue of her "mental reality." The text thus designates the east room as an interior space around which Fanny could cohere as a subject of liberalism. However, the scene in the east room quickly presents an interiority only to circumscribe it. Fanny's internal reverie is described in the familiar form of free indirect discourse. The profusion of questions ("Was she *right* . . . ?" "What might be so essential . . . ?" "Was it not ill nature . . . ?"), the steadily lengthening syntax, and the repetition ("present upon present") indicate to us that although we are in the third person grammatically, we are inhabiting Fanny's increasingly panicked perspective (107). Interiority, however, is dramatically cut off with Edmund's "tap at the door," after which the style shifts back to the matter-of-fact, external format of dialogue (107). Fanny's interiority is revealed briefly in conjunction with the space, only to be remanded *to* the space when she leaves it at the end of the chapter.

The space of the east room is not only physically circumscribed. Closer attention to the scene reveals a complex narrative structure in which the text, following Fanny's perspective on the east room, rhetorically relegates its scenes of suffering to the past in order to insist on a passive acceptance of the present. By tracing this rhetorical separation, we can catch a glimpse of the text's foreclosure of inwardness. After this scene, the rhetorical separation between Fanny and the narrator progressively diminishes, eventually disappearing completely. Its disappearance is what allows the text to affirm exteriority and efface its own traces of inner life, thereby refusing to allow Fanny to cohere around an interior as a liberal subject.

The narrator tells us that the east room functions for Fanny as a "nest of comforts" (107). Many critics take the narrator at her word, and this is the point at which critical accounts often stop.[8] However, the passage continues:

---

[7] Marilyn Butler notes this as well when she archly remarks that Fanny's attempts at contemplation in the east room "do not in fact throw much light on the general issue" (231). However, this failure of resolution does not at all affect Butler's account of the east room as a successful space of inwardness.

[8] See, for example, Kirstyn Leuner 51 and Henna Marian Messina 206.

> *. . . and though there had been sometimes much of suffering to her—though her motives had been often misunderstood, her feelings disregarded, and her comprehension under-valued; though she had known the pains of tyranny, of ridicule, and neglect, yet almost every recurrence of either had led to something consolatory. . . . Edmund had been her champion and her friend;—he had supported her cause, or explained her meaning, he had told her not to cry, or had given her some proof of affection which made her tears delightful—and the whole was now so blended together, so harmonized by distance, that every former affliction had its charm.* (106)

The passage describes events that take place outside the range of the narrative, in the past tense. Hence it is a scene of remembering. It stays in the grammatical third person point of view of the omniscient narrator throughout. However, the passage uses the structures of free indirect discourse to take us through the process of Fanny's remembering. Parallelisms and winding syntax (the entire quoted passage is a single sentence) indicate that we are traveling with Fanny's thoughts as they occur to her. These formal features generate a reading that we can align to a limited extent with Fanny's perspective—that the east room is a nest of comforts, that it serves a consolatory function, as the passage makes explicit.

However, another interpretive register is generated through a more ironic mode. Taken as a whole, it is clear that within this passage, the descriptions of pain and suffering far outweigh the recollection of any consolation. Although Fanny describes her "friends," their actions include misunderstanding, disregarding, under-valuing, tyrannizing, ridiculing, and neglecting her, causing her to suffer so much that she has to seek the east room for consolation. The ironic tone achieved through the prevalence of negative words, the immense space that is given to descriptions of pain compared to the quick insistence that everything turned out fine, generates a contrasting reading of the passage. This reading is more aligned with a distanced narrative perspective, unavailable to Fanny at the level of character. These two perspectives match what Miller calls the two "poles of Austen style, narration and character" (*Jane Austen* 69). The first perspective suggests a proximity to Fanny's point of view, tending toward the pole of character. The ironic distance of the second tends more toward the pole of narration. The text is able to inhabit both at once through free indirect discourse, in which it hovers between the third person omniscient and the first person perspectives.

The space in between the two narrative levels—the initially apparent level of acceptance masking another level of irony—is where we can perceive Fanny's disavowal of interiority. Though we as readers can see Fanny's clear association of pain and suffering with the space, these sensations have been smoothed over with the memory of blandly positive "comfort" and "consolation" by the time of the narrative. The negative excess is reigned in and covered up with the passive complacency dictated by Fanny's social position in relation to the others in the household. The text here begins to train us to consider Fanny's interiority as irrelevant, as Fanny does herself. Although it has given us a glimpse of the makeup of her "mental reality," it denies the effect of this reality on how we should think of her as a character. Her pain and suffering, though given significant narrative space, end up as concerns secondary to a system of values that aligns the worth of characters almost precisely with their social status. *Mansfield Park* begins to construct Fanny as a liberal subject through the east room as an analogue for her inner world only to reveal to us that this is not the logic of the subject that governs the novel.

Inside 2

A second scene in the novel follows a similar pattern—it associates the east room with the interior space of the liberal subject but then effaces this inwardness through another instance of dissimulation at a disparate textual level. In contrast to the scene above, though, in which Fanny's dissimulated perspective and the narrator's ironic one are given simultaneously through the use of free indirect discourse, the second scene represents an effacing of the separation between these two perspectives, a disavowal of interiority not just from Fanny's point of view but from the narrator's as well. Thus not only Fanny as a character but the text itself begins to consider Fanny's interiority as irrelevant. It renders its creeping disavowal visible by dropping the marks of free indirect discourse and relating to its protagonist through the detached form of quoted dialogue.

In this scene, Mary Crawford gives Fanny a necklace chain in preparation for the ball being held in her honor. Fanny correctly suspects that Henry is behind Mary's gift, and she goes to deposit "this doubtful good of a necklace, in some favorite box in the east room which held all her smaller treasures" (179). Upon reaching the east room, the narrative continues, "what was [Fanny's] surprise to find her cousin Edmund there writing at the table! Such a sight having never occurred before, was almost as wonderful as it was welcome" (179). The use of an exclamation mark immediately alerts us to the narrator's ironic tone. Once again, we are inhabiting Fanny's perspective, but we are also able to see how excessive such a perspective is. It turns out Edmund has been writing a note to Fanny, but since she has appeared, he can communicate his message to her in person. Another painful scene for Fanny follows in which Edmund presents Fanny with his own gift of a necklace chain, only to counsel her to accept Mary's chain instead. He waxes poetic on Mary's charms, calling her and Fanny "the two dearest objects I have on earth" (181). Edmund thus reveals what Fanny has tried to avoid acknowledging all along—that he is in love with Mary. He then leaves her alone in the east room to contemplate this new information, surrounded by her "treasures."

After Edmund leaves, the narrative describes how Fanny "shed many tears" and prayed "fervent[ly]" in an attempt to subdue her "agitation" (181). It slips into the familiar marks of free indirect discourse, signifying that we have slipped partially into Fanny's interior realm. There are more exclamation marks and many short sentence fragments ("But the other!—The first!"), and the narrator repeats the description of Edmund's confession as "a stab" several times (181). Within the same formal register, the negative affect quickly transitions to ecstatic excess, as Fanny seizes "the scrap of paper on which Edmund had begun writing to her, as a treasure beyond all her hopes, and reading with the tenderest emotion these words, 'My very dear Fanny, you must do me the favor to accept'—locked it up with the chain, as the dearest part of the gift" (182). The narrator's equivocal tone is heightened by the reproduction of the contents of the letter itself—we as readers can see that it is merely twelve perfectly conventional words, highlighting the distance between the reality that we perceive and the one in which Fanny exists.

Thus we get a split narration once again—the ecstatic exaggerations of Fanny's perspective on the letter, coming to us seemingly directly from Fanny's inner world, and the narrator's ironic distance, conveying an exterior perspective. The text embodies both points of view together through free indirect discourse. As such, we are able simultaneously to access Fanny's interior experience and view it from the outside with a mix of humor and irony. However, unlike the earlier scene of Fanny's pleasant sufferings in the east room, this scene is followed by a quick effacing of the narrative gap and a convergence of the two disparate perspectives into a single one, indicating that the disavowal of interiority has progressed to the narrative level. We see the text enact this convergence when, comically, Fanny becomes wistful about Edmund's presence in the east room on the very next page. We have moved forward only a single day in the time of the narrative, yet the narrator already describes Fanny's "fond indulgence of fancy"—"Suppose I were to find him there again to-day!" (183). In this subsequent scene, the marks of free indirect discourse have disappeared. Fanny's "fancy" is confined within quotation marks rather than being represented fluidly as part of the narration. Rather than giving us the telltale signs of interiority, the narrative rehearses the moment once again in order to be able to move on from it quickly.

A purely external style, therefore, quickly replaces the free indirect style, and the sensation of direct access to Fanny's interior is cut off. The narrative registers its shift by dropping the marks of performative internality and rendering Fanny's thoughts instead through the fully realized detachment of quotation marks. The quotation marks, like the east room itself, displace and contain Fanny's interiority, though in this case within a grammatical space rather than a physical one. From two clearly disparate perspectives on a scene of strong affect, embodying both Fanny's and the omniscient narrator's perspectives together through its two poles, the narrative moves to a single unified perspective, casting Fanny's interiority aside as something that we can now access only indirectly through quoted thought or speech. Thus it is not just Fanny's example we follow in finding interiority irrelevant but the example of the structure of the narrative itself. Again, the text produces an interior realm around which we expect Fanny to cohere as liberal subject, only to snatch it away and cover it over with an external perspective.

Inside to Outside

The full triumph of the exterior over spaces of interiority in the novel occurs when Fanny leaves Mansfield Park to visit her immediate family in Portsmouth. Her family's loud, messy cottage is described in stark contrast to Mansfield's pristine space. Tellingly, Fanny metonymically substitutes her east room for the entirety of Mansfield. As she and her sister Susan sit upstairs to avoid the chaos of their family, the narrator remarks that the lack of a fire in the room does not bother Fanny because she is "reminded by it of the east-room. It was the only point of resemblance. In space, light, furniture, and prospect, there was nothing alike in the two apartments, and she often heaved a sigh at the remembrance of all her books and boxes, and various comforts there" (270). Here we see the full contrast between the initial description of the east room and Fanny's memory of it: the furniture recalls the "ill-us[ed]" furniture and Julia's "faded footstool," and the boxes are the same "present upon present" that caused Fanny to spin out into her bewildered state. The text replaces the picture of Fanny's chaotic inner world that we were given earlier in the novel with suspiciously positive memories.

Such fond remembrances should caution us once again against automatically accepting Fanny's evaluations of Mansfield: "At Mansfield, no sounds of contention, no raised voice, no abrupt bursts, no tread of violence was ever heard . . . every body had their due importance; every body's feelings were consulted . . . and as to the little irritations, sometimes introduced by aunt Norris, they were short, they were trifling, they were as a drop of water to the ocean, compared with the ceaseless tumult of her present abode" (266). The passage displays clearly the narrative's powers of reinscription. Just as Fanny's dilapidated furniture and anxiety-inducing gifts—the objects that made up Fanny's bewildering interior realm, of which we were given just a glimpse—have become her "comforts," her painful experiences have transformed into the simple assertion that "every body had their due importance; every body's feelings were consulted." Claudia Johnson reminds us to be skeptical of this assertion: "The stately household [Fanny] pines for from afar is about to explode; as we well know, it has never been 'cheerful' or orderly, and 'every one's' feelings there are *not* consulted, Fanny's least of all" (*Jane Austen* 116). The disavowal has a retroactive structure: Fanny's moments of interiority in the east room did not matter at all, even when the text made it seem as though they did, because what they communicated to us of Fanny's inner world was always going to be disregarded in favor of an exterior system of status.

Thus the irony that is present in the narration of the first scene in the east room and that is at least initially present in the scene with Edmund and his letter has all but disappeared here. The first description of the east room clearly shows two disparate narrative perspectives: Fanny's earnest one and the narrator's ironic one. Next, the two perspectives are displayed but quickly disavowed in the second scene of Fanny's "fancy." By this third scene, Fanny's perspective and the narrative's have merged, and the gap between the two discrepant levels has been effaced; to return to Miller's vocabulary, we have moved from the "performance" of interiority to its "notation" (*Jane Austen* 64–65). In notation, we are not given access to Fanny's interior but merely reassured that it exists somewhere. We thus do not consider Fanny a coherent liberal subject because the text ultimately does not allow us to consider the interior realm that is the constitutive space of that subject. Instead, the narrative reaffirms the positions circumscribed by external factors: Sir Thomas has authority, Fanny's total subservience is correct, Edmund is above her. Everything at Mansfield Park, and in *Mansfield Park*, is fine. There are no more scenes in the east room for the remainder of the novel.

The east room, in effect, teases its readers by displaying a spatial analogue for Fanny's interior realm only to gradually close it off. The novel identifies Fanny as its protagonist by giving us glimpses into her inner life and suggesting that we will eventually get to experience her as a full subject of liberalism, but instead it rehearses its moments of interiority only to supersede them and retroactively cover them over, as if it wishes they had not been visible at all. In the place of a robust interior around which a liberal subject could cohere, it directs readers elsewhere, rhetorically and spatially nudging them to affirm a system based on exterior status rather than consider the individual people within such a system.[9] *Mansfield Park* refuses to display what Talia Schaffer calls "the interiority so fundamental to the novel form," thereby calling into question how fundamental interiority actually is to the novel form ("Why" 84). Without the interior as a linking device, the connection between the nineteenth-century novel and liberalism also becomes tenuous. Indeed, the structure of *Mansfield Park* ends up looking not liberal but reactionary, almost neo-feudalist, disregarding individual interiority because its characters are essentially interchangeable.[10] If there is a fundamental link between liberalism and the novel, *Mansfield Park* shows that we need to look to something other than interiority to establish it.

Interior Incommunicability: *Villette*

If *Mansfield Park*'s primary feature is its externality, *Villette*'s might be its spatialization. The text is full of intricately rendered interior spaces—the Bretton household (represented twice), Lucy's dorm, the *allée* at the pensionnat where Lucy paces and buries Graham's letters, the garret in which M. Paul locks her. Suzanne Keen describes Lucy as Brontë's "most mobile" protagonist and argues that "the novel is structured around Lucy's entrances into strange houses" (96, 98). Likewise, Eva Badowska summarizes how "*Villette* places interiority in an intimate connection with object-filled interiors" (1510). The novel has no shortage of spatialized interiors for Lucy, ranging from the space of her desk, on which M. Paul constantly intrudes to leave her various texts, to the entire city of Villette as an allegory for her psyche. However, for the purposes of this essay I focus on three particular moments in the text in which Lucy herself explicitly characterizes her own interior—her own thoughts and ideas, her feelings, her dreams—rather than on moments in which the text produces spaces that can be analyzed as interior analogues for Lucy.

As moments in which Lucy offers images of herself to the reader, these three examples counter a persistent critical trend of reading Lucy as uniformly hostile toward sociality. Following Shuttleworth's influential account, critics often read Lucy's resistance to the social world as a necessary move to protect herself from the outside forces of surveillance by which she is constantly besieged.[11] However, these types of readings only provide one side of the story. Lucy's isolation is not

---

[9]   Stout summarizes, in an analysis that concurs with my own, "If *Mansfield Park* is a dispiriting novel, it is dispiriting not because of how the characters are (looming, indolent, trivial, trivial, trivial, weak, dissipated, flat, etc.) but because it doesn't really matter how they are" (58).

[10]   Though it is beyond the scope of this essay to elaborate, I am hesitant to call *Mansfield Park*'s outlook truly feudal. William Galperin's reading describes its strange temporality as a "recognition of what the future, in Austen's dystopic reckoning, has *already* foreclosed upon" (161).

[11]   For a more recent account in the tradition of Shuttleworth's reading, see Joseph A. Boone. For a slight twist on the tradition, see Rachel Ablow 78.

completely a choice, and she does bristle against it at times. Leila S. May concurs, arguing that "Lucy's attitude toward her own highly valued privacy is surprisingly uneven" and that "she sometimes seems to invite the very kind of intrusion she normally struggles against," especially in the case of M. Paul (56, 53). Against the overwhelming critical tendency to read Lucy's preference for isolation, therefore, I want to examine the moments in which Lucy displays the opposite tendency, the moments in which she attempts outward communication of self.

Twice in *Villette*, Lucy tries to share with readers a picture of her interior realm using images of dwellings, what I will call her "houses." However, every attempt to externalize an interior realm results in a transformation. In response to Ginevra Fanshawe's attempts to discern her mental space, Lucy imagines a lopsided house that is ambiguously related to her own body. Then, in an attempt to compare her feelings for Graham Bretton to his feelings for her, she constructs a mythical structure that defies the laws of space and again cannot quite be connected to her physical body. Finally, when M. Paul tries to display his successful understanding of Lucy's interior by setting up a physical home for her, the objects of Lucy's mental space shrink to a diminutive size.

Each of the three moments shows Lucy representing her inner self in the form of architectural structures. However, the text characterizes each attempt at external communication as a failure. It thus cuts off our access to Lucy's subjective interior not by covering it over and retroactively disavowing it, as *Mansfield Park* does for Fanny's, above, but by suggesting an incommensurability between internal experience and external world that renders inner life incommunicable.[12] Instead of a coherent liberal subject that forms around a legible inner world, *Villette* "produces a character who morphs in ways that might bewilder a reader accustomed to a more stable idea of character" (Schaffer, "Why" 93). The text creates Lucy as a subject who cannot quite localize her interior realm and thus cannot create herself as a liberal subject in the way Locke and Mill describe. Her example complements Fanny's by again prompting us to reconsider any straightforward relationship between the novel and the interior and, by extension, any relation between either term and the subject of liberalism.

Lucy's Third-Class Lodgers

Like Fanny's east room, Lucy's houses make use of a common metaphor for the interior world of the individual subject. Gaston Bachelard, in *The Poetics of Space*, describes the house as "one of the greatest powers of integration for the thoughts, memories and dreams of mankind" (6). In "Theories of Space and the Nineteenth-Century Novel," Isobel Armstrong clarifies this sentiment, arguing that Bachelard's "lyrical poetics of the house reads this as a primal space, a '*vital space*,' in which consciousness and the body is fused with it as a physical container . . . Bachelard's point is that this primal phenomenological space of dreams and images is the vital source of an image-making capacity that is *integrating*" (15). Its training of the

---

12   Schaffer similarly finds Lucy's true interior inaccessible, in her case because of Lucy's status as a care worker whose job is to commodify her inner world ("Why").

capacity for integration, then, is concerned with bridging the gap between the realm of consciousness and that of the body. Thus in addition to offering us a privileged image of interiority, the house-as-image is supposed to train our capacity to integrate the worlds of the interior and the exterior.

It is notable, then, that our first scene of Lucy's houses is itself concerned with the problem of integrity, a term that shares its etymological root with Bachelard's function of integration. In this scene, Ginevra puzzles at Lucy's being invited to the same social event as her, asking Lucy, "Who *are* you, Miss Snowe?" (307). Lucy deflects the question, responding, "Who am I indeed? Perhaps a personage in disguise" (308). But Ginevra persists in her attempts to find out the key to Lucy's hidden nature: "But *are* you anybody? . . . Do—*do* tell me who you are! I'll not repeat it" (309). Lucy's outward response is again to laugh and dismiss Ginevra. However, she gives a lengthier narrative to the reader. In a direct address, she tells how Ginevra adhered "with ludicrous tenacity to the wise notion of an incognito she had got hold of" (309). Ginevra, in other words, takes seriously Lucy's suggestion that she might be a personage in disguise. Rather than reading Lucy's opacity as hiding a secret interiority that must be discovered, Ginevra reads it on the model of romance, as hiding a secret background or identity. Already characterized through her name and her relationship with the Count de Hamal as an embodiment of romantic tropes, Ginevra can only come up with "fanciful" charges to explain Lucy's impenetrability, "proving, by her obstinate credulity, or incredulity, her incapacity to conceive how any person not bolstered up by birth or wealth, not supported by some consciousness of name or connection, could maintain an attitude of reasonable integrity" (309). The text construes these external status markers as distinct from those externalizations that would reveal Lucy's inner world because, for Ginevra, they would signify not the true essence of the liberal self but other facts of external status that are, for whatever romantic reason, hidden from view.

The image Lucy provides in the course of narrating Ginevra's perspective is the start of one of the text's plentiful "architectural internalization[s]," a term that Molly Ryder defines as a technique through which "an interior aspect of the mind or body is described metaphorically in architectural terms, allow[ing] authors to provide spatial extension to the intangible, housing thoughts and emotions within a material organ" (328). Though it becomes clearer later in the passage, this introduction to the image already conceives of the subject in spatialized, architectural terms. The self in Ginevra's view, according to Lucy, is an architectural entity that needs to be "bolstered" or "supported," thus physically held up, by external attributes. This image suggests a self missing an interior world, something that would collapse into itself without the structures propping it up. The narrator's use of the word "attitude" enriches the architectural metaphor—"attitude" can mean both a mental habit and a physical posture. Thus maintaining an "attitude of reasonable integrity," as Lucy describes, can ambivalently mean both an external pose implying integrity (to others) and an interior disposition toward integrity (knowable only to the self).

Lucy continues by setting up her distinct view of the self in contrast to Ginevra's: "[T]he rest sat on me easily: pedigree, social position, and recondite intellectual acquisition, occupied about the same space and place in my interests and thoughts;

they were my third-class lodgers—to whom could be assigned only the small sitting-room and the little back bedroom" (309). She supposedly draws us away from Ginevra's romantic view of subjectivity in order to display her own, presumably one constructed around an inner realm that she represents as the house in which her interests and thoughts "lodge." However, close attention to the narrator's language reveals a persistent spatial ambiguity. The external qualities are Lucy's "third-class lodgers," not inside her self-as-house, but inside her "interests and thoughts." In the traditional picture of the "mental realm" or the constitutive interior "realm of liberty" à la Locke and Mill, we would expect to find interests and thoughts inside the clearly demarcated inner sphere of self. In the case of Lucy's third-class lodgers, however, we find an architectural space—a house with "pedigree, social position, recondite intellectual acquisition" as lodgers—carved out *inside* several mental concepts—interests and thoughts—which are themselves only ambiguously tied to a physical body—both inside Lucy's mental realm and stacked on top of her. Instead of a clearly circumscribed inner realm from which the essence of the liberal self can emanate, we find something more like a *mis en abyme* structure of the subject in which the addition of layers of interiority, rather than clarifying the space, only carves it out more.[13]

The Tent of Peri-Banou

Later in the novel we find another striking example of a subjective-architectural embodiment. Describing her feelings toward Graham Bretton, Lucy tells us, "I kept a place for him, too—a place of which I never took the measure, either by rule or compass: I think it was like the tent of Peri-Banou. All my life long I carried it folded in the hollow of my hand—yet, released from that hold and constriction, I know not but its innate capacity for expanse might have magnified it into a tabernacle for a host" (457). Lucy thus narrates in a second direct address what should be another feature of her inner realm—her feelings for Graham—and locates it within an architectural structure.[14] However, like the architectural structure within Lucy's "thoughts and feelings," the tent-space for Graham is only ambiguously linked to Lucy's physical body. Despite critical persistence in labeling this tent as a space within Lucy's heart (see, for example, the quote from Jenkins below), Lucy describes it as existing "folded in the hollow of my hand," thus characterizing it as an external space. The hand connotes the ability to affect the outside world, to externalize. However, in locating her interior space outside herself, Lucy skips the formation of

[13]   Hadley emphasizes the importance of the move from inside to outside for Mill's liberal subject: "[I]ndividual freedom [for Mill] is located not primarily in the liberal public sphere, nor mostly in the process of opinionated exchange among diverse peoples. These practices are in fact *enabled by rather than constitutive of individuality.* Instead, they emerge from 'the inward domain of consciousness' . . . " (80–81; emphasis added).

[14]   Both this passage and the one above are direct addresses and yet fail to produce a coherent picture of Lucy as a subject. They should thus prompt us to question Schaffer's assertion that "through the novel's forty-four direct addresses . . . we can begin to intuit the character of the narratee" ("Why" 101). In a novel famous for its narrator's unreliability, Lucy's direct addresses are baffling as often as they are productive.

an interior space that is then communicated to an outside and instead imagines her interior space *on* the outside. Such a complicated localization problematizes the neat partition of the liberal self into a constitutive inner world and an exterior world to which essential features of the self can be communicated.

Additionally, the tent functions as a poor exterior manifestation of an interior realm because its physical dimensions are impossible to discern. Although it gives the suggestion of a physical space through comparison to a physical object—a tent—the space, like the tent of Peri-Banou in *The Thousand and One Nights*, shrinks and grows as necessary. The image plays on an additional linguistic ambiguity to further stretch the limits of what we might want to consider a concrete space. As Keith A. Jenkins points out, the passage shifts between two different uses of the term *tabernacle*. The first is associated with another tent, continuing the image that Lucy has begun to build through comparison to the tent of Peri-Banou: "During the period Israel spent in the wilderness, God dwelt among them in an elaborate tent called the Tabernacle" (Jenkins 134). Lucy's use of the term *host*, though, suggests an additional interpretation. Jenkins continues, "Graham's space in Lucy's heart is . . . rather the tabernacle on the Christian altar, the repository for the Eucharistic elements (i.e. the 'host') after they have been transformed into the body and blood of Christ" (134). The space, then, seems to be simultaneously the expanding and shrinking tent from *The Thousand and One Nights*, an elaborate tent housing Graham as God, and a box holding Graham as a figure of Christ. Its contours are again difficult to articulate: it is two tents, one of which is spatially impossible, and a box, all three of which represent Lucy's inner world but are located outside her body, something that Lucy can hold in her hand. In attempting to externalize an internal space through description, Lucy has once again only produced impossible architectural structures. Our inability to access Lucy's ambiguous interior correlates with Lucy's unwillingness to "take the measure of it." Without a clear picture, it is difficult for us to imagine how such a space would serve as the foundation for Lucy's liberal subjectivity.

I consider the text's particular impossible space akin to the mirror that Michel Foucault describes in his 1967 lecture "Different Spaces." Foucault starts from the premise that space has its own history and that it has existed in various forms according to the conditions of its world. He aims to retrace this history beginning in the Middle Ages, which consisted of a "hierarchized ensemble of places" in which space could be localized (176). With the discoveries of Galileo, space became "infinite, and infinitely open. . . . A thing's place was no longer anything but a point in its motion" (176). According to this change, he says, localization was replaced with the concept of extension. In our contemporary era, extension is subsequently supplanted by the notion of "emplacement," which Foucault defines as "the relations of proximity between points or elements" (176). In contrast to the localization within a hierarchy or the extension of a point to a movement, contemporary space can best be understood through its "emplacement" within a larger network of other emplacements.

Foucault is especially interested in particular spaces that are "connected to all other emplacements, but in such a way that they suspend, neutralize, or reverse the set of relations that are designated, reflected, or represented . . . by them" (178).

These spaces tend to come in two types: utopias, which are "emplacements having no real place," and what he terms "heterotopias," which are "real places . . . in which . . . all the other real emplacements that can be found within the culture are, at the same time, represented, contested, and reversed" (178). In other words, while both of these spaces are defined through their relationality to other spaces and the way they are able to do something to these related spaces, utopias have no real place, while heterotopias are localizable—they exist in physical space.

The division between utopias and heterotopias, however, is not definite, as Foucault goes on to describe the space of a mirror as both at once:

> The mirror is a utopia after all, since it is a placeless place. . . . But it is also a heterotopia in that the mirror really exists, in that it has a sort of return effect on the place that I occupy. . . . The mirror functions as a heterotopia in the sense that it makes this place I occupy at the moment I look at myself in the glass both utterly real, connected with the entire space surrounding it, and utterly unreal—since, to be perceived, it is obliged to go by way of that virtual point which is over there. (179)

The place/non-place of Lucy's tent has a similar status to the mirror space. It too is a "placeless place," embodying the fantastic attributes of three unreal images at once. However, it does perform a reflex action on the spaces with which it is connected. The relationship it has to the space of Lucy as subject might be one of suspension or reversal: in her attempt to move outside herself, to communicate her interior world, she encounters only a return to the isolated space of self. It thus characterizes the subjective place she occupies as "both utterly real . . . and utterly unreal." The space of self and the space of house-subject exist through their relations to one another. Like Foucault's mirror, Lucy's interior world "is obliged to go by way of that virtual point which is over there." These virtual points, these subject-houses, remain stubbornly "un-emplace-able," defying attempts to localize them in physical space. Lucy's interior space remains simultaneously utopia and heterotopia—both there and not, rendering the communication between self and society that is requisite for the liberal subject impossible.

Faubourg Clotilde

The text makes clear its anxiety about the communicability of the interior in one of its final scenes, in which M. Paul attempts to represent his recognition of Lucy's interior world by transposing it into the exterior world. *Villette* consistently characterizes M. Paul as the sole character who sees Lucy for who she really is. As Schaffer describes, in contrast to Graham, who "correlates to Lucy's specious performative cover," M. Paul "matches her own fiery secret core self" ("Why" 97). In the well-known first interaction between him and Lucy, M. Paul performs a physiognomic reading of her in which he supposedly deciphers her character, concluding simply, "I read it" (66).[15] Throughout the action of the novel, M. Paul

---

[15]   May points out, despite Shuttleworth's reading to the contrary, that the text specifies this as a scene of physiognomic rather than phrenological reading (50).

continues to insist that Lucy's cold exterior houses a fiery, defiant nature: "Other people in this house see you pass, and think that a colorless shadow has gone by. As for me, I scrutinized your face once, and it sufficed" (155). Through his recognition, he functions as a means of drawing Lucy's inner world out into the open.

Thus it is unsurprising that when the text finally brings the two together in a love relationship, it characterizes their union as two internal worlds reaching one another. One way it attempts this characterization is through M. Paul's gift to Lucy of the schoolhouse she has been dreaming of.[16] The text insists that his gift is in response to a conversation they have had: "I had talked once, he reminded me, of trying to be independent and keeping a little school of my own: had I dropped the idea?" (484). Lucy's assertion, however, reads to us as compensatory, a "reminder" instead for the reader, since the conversation is never represented within the text. Instead, Lucy's description of her dream of owning a school comes in yet another narrative aside, locating it firmly within the interior space of her imagination. She says "to [her]self . . . [w]hen I shall have saved one thousand francs, I will take a tenement with one large room, and two or three smaller ones, furnish the first with a few benches and desks, a black tableau, an estrade for myself; upon it a chair and table, with a sponge and some white chalks" (361). The amount of detail in this interior picture is noteworthy, emphasizing again Lucy's attraction to architectural images.

When M. Paul gives Lucy his architectural gift, it follows Lucy's interior image very closely. Though it is larger than her imagined three or four rooms, the school-room itself contains "two rows of green benches and desks, with an alley down the centre, terminating in an estrade, a teacher's chair and table; behind them a tableau" (486). Only the sponge and chalk are missing, presumably to be acquired later when Lucy starts using the room. Though the text insists that M. Paul has been paying attention to what Lucy says, within the world of the text this episode strikes us as further evidence of his instinctive discernment of Lucy's interior world. He is able to reproduce almost exactly the school that Lucy represented textually only within the bounds of her imagination. The text thus correlates M. Paul's value as a lover with his ability to successfully reach Lucy's interior world and bring it outside into the realm of the physical.

Despite how critics tend to read M. Paul's gift, though, the text does not allow him full success in his endeavor.[17] From the beginning, Lucy's praise of it is qualified. The house, she notes, is located in a Faubourg in which "the houses were small, but looked pleasant" (484). As Lucy enters the house, she immediately assesses, "No servant appeared." She describes the vestibule as "small, like the house, but freshly and tastefully painted." The repetition of the "small, but . . . " structure is so excessive

[16]   Eve Kosofsky Sedgwick makes a similar point (146).

[17]   Schaffer, for example, argues that M. Paul's gift allows Lucy to "fulfill[] the immigrant dream" by "start[ing] her own business," thereby cuing a shift in the narrative that "allow[s] us to read all of *Villette* as a long thank-you letter to Paul . . . not just for his love but for the life he gave her, the career that allows her to escape the *pensionnat*" ("Why" 101–2). For additional critical accounts that read M. Paul's gift as a happy ending, see Judith E. Pike 182; Terry Eagleton 73; and Keen 98. For another account that notes its insufficiency, see Cohen 68.

that it quickly dominates the descriptive passage—the salon is "very tiny, but . . . very pretty," it houses a "small round table . . . a little couch, a little chiffonnier," it has a "single" but "ample window"; the "little kitchen" has a "little stove and oven, with few but bright brasses," a "small cupboard" that holds "a diminutive but commodious set of earthenware"; the staircase is "narrow but clean," and so on. (485). Though Lucy insists on remaining cheerful, graciously accepting the tiny house as her own, the text marks its insufficiency over and over. When we finally reach the schoolroom, which otherwise matches the image of Lucy's imagination perfectly, the sense of narrative disappointment continues. The apartment is "scrupulously clean, though bare," "carpetless," and houses only a "few hardy plants" (486). Lucy responds in the next section with ecstatic happiness, but these descriptive passages belie such ecstasy. As M. Paul tries to show Lucy that he has accessed and understood her interior world, he reflects back to her a miniaturized, distorted version of it. He thus causes us to wonder whether he has actually accessed anything at all.

Villette thus renders Lucy's inner world inaccessible by repeatedly highlighting the treacherous journey it would have to undertake to be communicated to the outside. In each of Lucy's attempts to display her inner world to the reader, and in M. Paul's final attempt to reflect such communication back to Lucy, we find only spatial ambiguity. We are not sure if Lucy's inner world is like a house in a thought on top of her head, like two tents and a box inside her hand, or like a miniature house more appropriate for the doll-like Paulina Home than for Lucy and her "fiery secret core self." The text ultimately denies us access to it. With M. Paul's ambiguous death at sea, Lucy ends the novel as isolated as she began it. *Villette* concludes with accounts of others: the fates of Madame Beck, Père Silas, and Madame Walravens (496). Lucy, the text implies, remains sealed off in her diminutive cottage, unable to communicate any clear inner life to others and therefore unable to appear in our eyes as a liberal subject.

Whither Interiority?

Neither *Mansfield Park* nor *Villette* supports the idea of an affinity between interiority and the nineteenth-century novel. The story of the link, therefore, between liberalism and the nineteenth-century novel through a shared emphasis on interiority does not account for *Mansfield Park*'s quasi-feudal exterior stasis nor for *Villette*'s anxious solipsism. Why does it matter that the two novels fall outside the purview of this oft-repeated critical account? Is it possible that these two strange novels are merely aberrations, exceptions to a generalized theory of the nineteenth-century novel that is not meant to be totalizing? To investigate this claim further, we would need to turn to additional nineteenth-century novels and analyze their treatment of interiority. In their respective ways, novels like *Jane Eyre*, *Bleak House*, and *Persuasion* all foreground the vexed relationship between the interior of the subject and the exterior world and would thus be worth examining more closely. Given Austen's and Brontë's central status within the nineteenth-century canon, too, it is likely important not to simply write off two of their major novels as exceptions.[18] If we take them seriously as suggesting that the association between the nineteenth-century novel and liberalism via interiority is incomplete, there are three possible options for explaining why.

The first option is that our understanding of the relationship between the novel and interiority is incomplete. Such an argument is advanced by Schaffer, for example, who uses Lucy's status as a care worker to argue that the putatively universal association of the novel and the interior in fact "depends on class privilege" ("Why" 84). Stout, too, demonstrates the surprising predominance of collective subjects in eighteenth- and nineteenth-century fiction and therefore casts doubt on the supposedly central role of the individual interior. Schaffer, Stout, and others are undoubtedly right that our critical story of the nineteenth-century novel is in need of additional nuance.[19] A second option is that our understanding of the relationship between the novel and liberalism in general is incomplete. In other words, once the link between the two via a shared emphasis on interiority is called into question, we might want to suggest that there is in fact no necessary link between the aesthetic form of the novel and the political form of liberalism. Isobel Armstrong, whose *Novel Politics* takes issue with "[a] belief that the novel indelibly registers bourgeois ideology and morality . . . that the novel's default position [is] conservative and hegemonic," advances such a view (1). She instead finds the nineteenth-century novel to be "deeply experimental" when viewed in light of its engagement with the concept of illegitimacy (7). Her position also merits careful consideration, especially if we can no longer use the interior as a linking device between the two forms.

There is a third option, however, that literary critics often fail to consider.[20] While it is not possible to argue for it definitively within the space of this article, I will outline why it is the most crucial of the three options. It assumes that there is a fundamental link between liberalism and the novel. However, it does not assume that the link occurs through a shared emphasis on interiority but through some other shared strategy or investment. As a result, if *Mansfield Park* and *Villette* have a vexed relationship to interiority *but still* sustain a fundamental relationship to liberalism, it should cause us in turn to reconsider the centrality of the subjective

---

[18]   Jesse Rosenthal comically suggests that Austen and Brontë are two members of the "big eleven" out of the only "about twenty-six" Victorian novelists who make up our shared field of reference in Victorian studies, although he notes that Austen is not even a proper Victorian (192).

[19]   For additional analyses critical of the tradition linking the novel to interiority, see Megan Ward and Pamela K. Gilbert.

[20]   Stout is a notable exception. He argues that "however individualist it may be in theory, liberalism does not, once deployed, simply reduce the social field to a set of isolated actors subjecting one another to the instrumental logic of atomic self-interest" and that "we have understood liberalism to be a more monolithic ideological contender than it actually was" (2, 6). He intervenes in the name of showing the persistence of collectivity in a liberalism that is supposedly individualist; I do so in the name of showing how a liberalism that is supposedly dependent on an interior functions through novels that foreclose such interiority. While other thinkers—Hadley, Lauren M. E. Goodlad, Amanda Anderson, and Nathan K. Hensley among them—likewise complicate our understanding of nineteenth-century liberalism, they do not question its reliance on a particular version of subjective interiority.

interior to a theory of liberalism. Although the subject model we find in Locke, Mill, and Brown above conforms to one particular picture of the subject in which the interior is the seat of the self, *Mansfield Park* and *Villette* might show us that such a picture of the subject is not the only one that liberalism is able to accommodate. This is not to say that *no* subjective form poses an effective challenge to liberalism. But perhaps liberalism is capacious enough to encompass many more variations in subjective form than is often thought.[21]

The third option is important to consider because thinkers who are interested in developing critiques of liberalism, among whom I number myself, often argue that de-emphasizing the interior and shifting the form of the subject will lead to something other than a liberal politics. Dianna Coole and Samantha Frost's introduction to *New Materialisms*, for example, asserts, "[O]ver the past three decades or so theorists have radicalized the way they understood subjectivity . . . Yet it is on subjectivity that their gaze has focused. Our motivation in editing this book has been a conviction that it is now time to subject objectivity and material reality to a similarly radical reappraisal" (2). Jane Bennett's work likewise calls on us to "[p]ostpone for a while the topics of subjectivity or the nature of human interiority" (120). Contemporary political exigencies, such critics claim, demonstrate that a picture of the subject cohering around an interior realm has lost its explanatory power. These critics argue that in order to understand the crises amid which we live and to develop a new politics effective for addressing them, we need to revise our understanding of the subject by shifting our attention to what have traditionally been considered objects. I argue that such a stance makes unwarranted assumptions about the relationship between subjective form and political paradigm and is therefore incomplete as an effective critique of liberalism. It posits a liberalism that has not changed since the twentieth century, and it relies on a surprisingly static picture of the subject of politics. *Mansfield Park* and *Villette* show us that such an understanding of the subject of politics was likely overly reductive even in the nineteenth century, in which it was supposedly dominant. If we are interested in opposing the logic of liberalism, we will need to continue to investigate whether liberalism actually depends on one specific model of the subject.

I conclude, somewhat ironically, with another idea from John Stuart Mill. In his argument in favor of diversity of opinion in "On Liberty," he explains that free expression of opinion is important for the sake of the common case in which "conflicting doctrines, instead of being one true and the other false, share the truth between them" (47). While *Mansfield Park* and *Villette* suggest that something is incomplete about the traditional association between the nineteenth-century novel, interiority, and liberalism, it is unlikely that a single revision to the critical account will give it totalizing explanatory power over all nineteenth-century novels or all liberal thought. Rather, each element of the account is deserving of further nuance:

---

[21]   The third option is, additionally, the one I explore in the larger project of which this essay is a small part. In the rest of the project, I read additional works by Austen and Brontë as well as novels by Dickens and Eliot to argue that there is a fundamental connection between liberalism and the novel but that it is not achieved through a shared view of interiority precisely because liberalism does not depend on one definitive form of the subjective interior.

the association between the novel and interiority, between liberalism and the novel, and between liberalism and interiority. In the complex interaction between a historical period, a political paradigm, an aesthetic form, and a theory of the subject, there are not likely to be any easy explanations. *Mansfield Park* and *Villette* provide two additional opportunities to rethink the connections between social, political, literary, and subjective forms.

*   *   *

ABBY SCRIBNER is a PhD candidate in the Department of Comparative Literature at Emory University. Her dissertation project, "Robots, Corpses, and Plants: Subjectivity and Its Alternatives in the Nineteenth-Century Novel," analyzes literary experiments in subjective form and their relationship to both Victorian and contemporary incarnations of liberalism.

<h2 align="center">Works Cited</h2>

Ablow, Rachel. *Victorian Pain*. Princeton: Princeton UP, 2017.

Anderson, Amanda. *Bleak Liberalism*. Chicago: U of Chicago P, 2016.

Armstrong, Isobel. *Novel Politics: Democratic Imaginations in Nineteenth-Century Fiction*. New York: Oxford UP, 2016.

Armstrong, Isobel. "Theories of Space and the Nineteenth-Century Novel." *19: Interdisciplinary Studies in the Long Nineteenth Century* 17 (2013): 1–21.

Armstrong, Nancy. *Desire and Domestic Fiction: A Political History of the Novel*. New York: Oxford UP, 1987.

Armstrong, Nancy. "Just Like a Woman: Balibar on the Politics of Reproduction." *Balibar and the Citizen Subject*. Ed. Warren Montag and Hasan Elsayed. Edinburgh: Edinburgh UP, 2017. 284–308.

Arnold, Matthew. *Letters of Matthew Arnold 1844–1848*. Vol. 1. Ed. George W. E. Russell. London: Macmillan, 1895.

Auerbach, Nina. *Communities of Women: An Idea in Fiction*. Cambridge, MA: Harvard UP, 1978.

Auerbach, Nina. *Romantic Imprisonment: Women and Other Glorified Outcasts*. New York: Columbia UP, 1985.

Austen, Jane. *Mansfield Park*. Ed. Claudia L. Johnson. New York: Norton, 1998.

Austen, Jane. "Opinions of *Mansfield Park*." *Later Manuscripts*. Ed. Janet Todd and Linda Bree. New York: Cambridge UP, 2008. 230–34.

Bachelard, Gaston. *The Poetics of Space*. Trans. Maria Jolas. Boston: Beacon, 1994.

Badowska, Eva. "Choseville: Brontë's *Villette* and the Art of Bourgeois Interiority." *PMLA* 120.5 (2005): 1509–23.

Balibar, Etienne. *Identity and Difference: John Locke and the Invention of Consciousness*. Ed. Stella Sandford. Trans. Warren Montag. Brooklyn: Verso, 2013.

Bennett, Jane. *Vibrant Matter: A Political Ecology of Things*. Durham, NC: Duke UP, 2010.

Boone, Joseph A. "Depolicing *Villette*: Surveillance, Invisibility, and the Female Erotics of 'Heretic Narrative.'" *Novel* 26.1 (1992): 20–42.

Brontë, Charlotte. *Jane Eyre*. Ed. Richard J. Dunn. New York: Norton, 2001.

Brontë, Charlotte. *Villette*. Ed. Margaret Smith and Herbert Rosengarten. New York: Oxford UP, 2008.

Brown, Wendy. *Politics Out of History*. Princeton: Princeton UP, 2001.

Butler, Marilyn. *Jane Austen and the War of Ideas*. New York: Oxford UP, 1975.

Cohen, Monica F. "Homesick: The Domestic Interiors of *Villette*." *Professional Domesticity in the Victorian Novel: Women, Work, and Home*. New York: Cambridge UP, 1998. 44–69.

Coole, Diana, and Samantha Frost, eds. *New Materialisms: Ontology, Agency, and Politics*. Durham, NC: Duke UP, 2010.

Duckworth, Alistair. *The Improvement of the Estate: A Study of Jane Austen's Novels*. Baltimore: Johns Hopkins UP, 1971.

Eagleton, Terry. *Myths of Power: A Marxist Study of the Brontës*. London: Macmillan, 1975.

Foucault, Michel. "Different Spaces." *Aesthetics, Method, Epistemology: Essential Works of Foucault 1954–1984, Volume 2*. Ed. James D. Faubion. Trans. Robert Hurley. New York: New Press, 1998. 175–85.

Foucault, Michel. *Discipline and Punish: The Birth of the Prison*. Trans. Alan Sheridan. New York: Vintage, 1995.

Foucault, Michel. *The History of Sexuality, Volume 2: The Use of Pleasure*. Trans. Robert Hurley. New York: Vintage, 1990.

Foucault, Michel. *Security, Territory, Population: Lectures at the Collège de France 1977–1978*. Ed. Michel Senellart. Trans. Graham Burchell. London: Picador, 2007.

Galperin, William. "Jane Austen's Future Shock." *The Historical Austen*. Philadelphia: U of Pennsylvania P, 2003. 154–79.

Gilbert, Pamela K. *Victorian Skin: Surface, Self, History*. Ithaca: Cornell UP, 2019.

Gilbert, Sandra M., and Susan Gubar. *The Madwoman in the Attic: The Woman Writer and the Nineteenth-Century Literary Imagination*. 2nd ed. New Haven: Yale UP, 2000.

Goodlad, Lauren M. E. *Victorian Literature and the Victorian State: Character and Governance in a Liberal Society*. Baltimore: Johns Hopkins UP, 2003.

Hadley, Elaine. *Living Liberalism: Practical Citizenship in Mid-Victorian Britain*. Chicago: U of Chicago P, 2010.

Hensley, Nathan K. *Forms of Empire: The Poetics of Victorian Sovereignty*. New York: Oxford UP, 2016.

Jenkins, Keith A. *Charlotte Brontë's Atypical Typology*. New York: Lang, 2010.

Johnson, Claudia L. *Jane Austen: Women, Politics, and the Novel*. Chicago: U of Chicago P, 1988.

Johnson, Claudia L. "What Became of Jane Austen? *Mansfield Park*." *Persuasions: The Jane Austen Journal* 17 (1995): 59–70.

Keen, Suzanne. *Victorian Renovations of the Novel: Narrative Annexes and the Boundaries of Representation*. New York: Cambridge UP, 1998.

Kramnick, Jonathan. *Actions and Objects from Hobbes to Richardson*. Stanford: Stanford UP, 2010.

Leuner, Kirstyn. "'The End of All the Privacy and Propriety': Fanny's Dressing Room in Mansfield Park." *Bodies and Things in Nineteenth-Century Literature and Culture*. Ed. Katharina Boehm. New York: Palgrave Macmillan, 2012. 45–65.

Levine, Caroline. *Forms: Whole, Rhythm, Hierarchy, Network*. Princeton: Princeton UP, 2015.

Lukács, Georg. *The Theory of the Novel: A Historico-philosophical Essay on the Forms of Great Epic Literature*. Trans. Anna Bostock. Cambridge, MA: MIT P, 1971.

May, Leila S. "Lucy Snowe, a Material Girl? Phrenology, Surveillance, and the Sociology of Interiority." *Criticism* 55.1 (2013): 43–68.

Messina, Henna Marian. "Fanny Price's Domestic Assemblages in Austen's *Mansfield Park*." *Persuasions: The Jane Austen Journal* 38 (2016): 205–12.

Mill, John Stuart. "On Liberty." *The Basic Writings of John Stuart Mill*. Ed. Dale E. Miller. New York: Modern Library, 2002. 3–119.

Miller, D. A. *Jane Austen, or The Secret of Style*. Princeton: Princeton UP, 2003.

Miller, D. A. *The Novel and the Police*. Berkeley: U of California P, 1988.

Pike, Judith E. "'How English is Lucy Snowe'? Pink Frocks and a French Clock in Jane Eyre and Villette." *Time, Space, and Place in Charlotte Brontë*. Ed. Diane Long Hoeveler and Deborah Denenholz Morse. London: Routledge, 2017. 169–83.

Poovey, Mary. *Uneven Developments: The Ideological Work of Gender in Mid-Victorian England*. Chicago: U of Chicago P, 1988.

Rosenthal, Jesse. *Good Form: The Ethical Experience of the Victorian Novel*. Princeton: Princeton UP, 2017.

Ryder, Molly. "Dwelling in the Heart-Shrine: Lucy Snowe's Creative Architectural Metaphors in Charlotte Brontë's *Villette*." *Brontë Studies* 40.4 (2015): 328–33.

Sandford, Stella. Introduction. *Identity and Difference: John Locke and the Invention of Consciousness*. By Etienne Balibar. Ed. Stella Sandford. Trans. Warren Montag. London: Verso, 2013. xi–xlvi.

Schaffer, Talia. *Romance's Rival: Familiar Marriage in Victorian Fiction*. New York: Oxford UP, 2016.

Schaffer, Talia. "Why Lucy Doesn't Care: Migration and Emotional Labor in *Villette*." *Novel* 52.1 (2019): 84–106.

Sedgwick, Eve Kosofsky. *The Coherence of Gothic Conventions*. New York: Arno, 1980.

Shuttleworth, Sally. *Charlotte Brontë and Victorian Psychology*. Cambridge: Cambridge UP, 1996.

Stout, Daniel M. *Corporate Romanticism: Liberalism, Justice, and the Novel*. New York: Fordham UP, 2017.

Ward, Megan. *Seeming Human: Artificial Intelligence and Victorian Realist Character*. Columbus: Ohio State UP, 2018.

Temporality and the Unconfident Heroine in Henry James's The Golden Bowl

JANINA LEVIN

In fictions, perhaps more than in life, a time lag represents an opportunity. Deception plots have traditionally depended on characters skilled at capitalizing on the slowness of others, since slowness—comparative slowness—generally marks the dupe. Historically, the literary dialectic between victim and duper also endows the duper with the ability to create a plot, while the victim lacks an active imagination and is therefore caught within someone else's plot.[1] In comic versions of a successful deception, victims exist not only for the opening they provide for transgression but to reveal the workings of a mind that can shape the future.[2] Nineteenth-century realism marks a transition from this pattern in world literature, since realism emphasized characters who had not attained mastery over their own lives or even found a clearly defined personal narrative. In his three-volume *Time and Narrative* (1983–85), Paul Ricoeur synthesizes critical work on the realist tradition by referring to a "prenarrative quality of experience" that produces latent plots (1: 74). Our "being entangled" demands narrative art just as much as human mastery does (1: 75).[3] I build on this attention to the intersection between life and art by closely examining Henry James's *The Golden Bowl*, which emphasizes how Maggie Verver comes to grips with being caught in an adultery plot. She pulls herself out of this situation in the second half of the novel and wins back her husband's affections, but the stalled beginning of their marriage—as well as the effects of stalled beginnings in general—has not received adequate attention as a narrative problem. Although *The Golden Bowl* has inspired many fine close readings, it deserves a closer look given recent thinking about temporal scale and pacing in literary history (see Sachs).

---

[1] I refer to the long tradition of deception plots in realistic folktales, some of which have entered the European literary tradition. Mary Jane Schenck's *The Fabliaux: Tales of Wit and Deception* (1987) discusses the duper's power of manipulating plots. Stith Thompson's *The Folktale* (1946) points out the mutual relations between oral and literary cultures, including how deception plots flourished in world literature.

[2] Discussing folktales that highlight the victim/duper dynamic, Thompson describes the appeal of "realistic moods in which they [audiences] are particularly interested in stories of deception, cheats, swindles and clever thefts . . . [that show] an interest in the workings of a keen mind" (152–53).

[3] I extrapolate a nascent form of the deception plot from Ricoeur's analysis of being "entangled." As some critics have pointed out, James's deception plots express a general state of human entanglement, not merely stupidity. See Matthew Sussman's "Henry James and Stupidity." Although deception plots are ubiquitous narratives, they have not been adequately theorized, as Svetlana Rukhelman suggests in describing her book in progress, *The (Dis)pleasures of Being Cheated*.

Novel: A Forum on Fiction 53:3   DOI 10.1215/00295132-8624534   © 2020 by Novel, Inc.

Ricoeur defined three levels of mimesis in narrative representations; I draw on the first two to describe Maggie's change of role in *The Golden Bowl*.[4] Mimesis$_1$ is the raw material for narrative, the level at which imaginative fictions intersect with life, or how the field of narrative leads back to a phenomenology of action (1: xi). Mimesis$_2$ is the power of "grasping together" events in a meaningful sequence, the configuring act of narrative that pulls from the diversity of life's events a purposive order (1: 66). These two elaborations of mimesis in narrative art are of interest for Henry James's fictions because, first, James questions the stereotypes attached to passive characters—that they are weak, stupid, and, for the purposes of fiction, merely fodder for others' narrative machinations. So James revisits the material of human subjective activity (Mimesis$_1$) and follows the path of many realist writers in presenting more seriously unexceptional characters that are nonetheless coaxed into significance as bearers of an action. As Peter Brooks has put it, the "motor" of a Jamesian plot belongs to characters "driven by something occult, mostly hidden even to themselves" (173). Second, such characters also become, unexpectedly, plot makers (Mimesis$_2$). Maggie is a particular instance of an underdog plot maker, a "sleeper" character whose powers of configuring a narrative have been underestimated in her world (by herself and others).

Ricoeur's emphasis on the intersections between narratology and the phenomenology of action clarifies the high point in Maggie's journey as she moves from passive victim to fictional agent. Ricoeur identifies a doubled, reflective present that expresses a narrative agent's confidence-in-practice: "*Now* I am doing it, because *now* I can do it" (1: 60).[5] This simplified grammar frames, in temporal terms, the satisfaction Maggie experiences when she finally takes on agency. Yet *now I can do it* implies release from a stalled beginning. Maggie's low point should interest critics as a problem with beginnings. Her estrangement from her husband follows her slowness to express her desire for him, even after four years of marriage. As the one relatively impartial observer in the novel, Bob Assingham notes that Maggie has not "had four [years] of the Prince," at least not "undividedly" (319).[6] Her slowness to establish an intimacy with Amerigo also becomes her rival Charlotte's advantage, allowing Charlotte to assert her own designs upon him.

For an analysis of stalled action, I turn to Jacques Lacan's 1945 essay "Logical Time and the Assertion of Anticipated Certainty," which explores both the logical and the affective dimensions of mistiming, of being too fast or too slow. Narrative theory has not highlighted this contrast in characters' pacing—when characters

---

[4]   Mimesis$_3$ is the rhetoric of narrative, its entry into the field of communication and thus its reception by audiences (Ricoeur 71). Since I am concerned here with reading closely how Maggie navigates deception by way of temporality, I am not engaging with the reception of *The Golden Bowl*, except as it relates to my reading of her as an unconfident heroine. There is an extensive literature on Maggie as a protagonist, which has been covered in R. B. J. Wilson's *Henry James's Ultimate Narrative: "The Golden Bowl"* (1981).

[5]   Ricoeur follows upon work by Algirdas Julien Greimas on narrative actors but also integrates into Greimas's rather rigid narrative sequence Augustine's formulation of a doubled present.

[6]   Penguin's 1987 edition of *The Golden Bowl*, referenced here throughout, is based on Scribner's 1909 New York edition of the novel.

that are too fast and too slow are pitted against each other, although some James critics and one theorist have noted it.[7] Lacan's essay also inspired an extended analysis by Alain Badiou in *Theory of the Subject* (1982). Badiou expands Lacan's affective analysis of mistiming (by way of anxiety) in referencing courage. For Badiou, courage cannot be understood without anxiety. Lacan and Badiou thus give us tools to understand how Maggie passes from anxiety to courage—deepening our understanding of her underdog appeal—as well as how her rival Charlotte's courage falls in value and becomes an experience of anxiety.

Psychoanalytic readings of James's late novels have productively illustrated the extent to which the deceiver and the deceived are not stable subject positions—the two often switch roles.[8] Yet such focus on the complexities in James's fiction comes at the expense of pinpointing his narrative solutions. As Ricoeur argues, narrative fictions are a form of productive imagination in the realm of temporal experience (2: 3). They "re-figure . . . temporal experience[s]" that would otherwise be prey to the "aporias of philosophical speculation" (1: xi). I read Maggie's developing temporal know-how as a narrative solution that refigures her previously unformed temporal experience. Having been too slow, she becomes attuned to mistiming and notices that her rival Charlotte responds too quickly when Maggie puts pressure on her. This attunement generates a discovery—her husband prefers a slower pace in a romantic partner. Thus instead of capitalizing on a time lag, as a traditional duper character would, Maggie gains advantage by noticing a time of haste. Maggie's and Charlotte's contrasting temporal modalities express different styles of failure, but since Maggie's failure comes first, it is a form of apprenticeship. She gives us a properly realistic representation of the affective investments involved in human action: the passage from anxiety to courage when readers witness a buildup of confidence and from courage to anxiety when courage becomes merely haste.

The Kairotic Heroine

When Charlotte Stant comes to London shortly before her former lover's marriage to an American heiress, she seems to be saying goodbye to him. But the ambiguity surrounding her return creates a mood of mystery at the beginning of the novel, as the opening pages are heavy with foreshadowing. Impoverished Prince Amerigo broods on the stakes of his marriage to the wealthy Maggie, and when he goes to talk over his anxiety with his friend and matchmaker Fanny Assingham, he finds that she too is "not at ease" (63). Fanny announces, "She's back" and that this is "a

---

[7] Adeline R. Tintner's analysis of James's short story "The Great Condition" (a story that focuses a woman's choice between two men, one who is always rushing and another who takes his time) points to James's conception that how these men handle time "determines the happiness of each" (Tintner 113). In this story, the patient man wins. Michael Snediker's "Stasis and Verve" discusses the dialectic between patience and impatience in *Portrait of a Lady* and *The Golden Bowl*. Theorist Avital Ronell notes that stupidity has a "subtle history of literary sightings" and that most of them focus on the "aporetic snags" connecting stupidity to both slowness and speed (68–71).

[8] Two effective psychoanalytic readings are Lucy La Farge's "Caught in the Snare of Deception" (2011) and Slavoj Žižek's "Kate's Choice, or The Materialism of Henry James" (2006).

complication" (70). Readers learn what they probably already suspected: Amerigo has a past with another woman, and the lovers' prior relationship still lingers on and demands something. But what exactly? Closure? Self-sacrifice? Intervention? Restitution?[9]

Not long after her arrival, Charlotte makes a moving speech in a London park that testifies to their former bond. Amerigo clings to the theme of closure as he listens, but for an attentive reader her speech presents more levels of intention:

> *I don't care what you make of it, and I don't ask anything whatever of you—anything but this. I want to have said it—that's all; I want not to have failed to say it. To see you once and be with you, to be as we are now and as we used to be, for one small hour—or say for two—that's what I've had for weeks in my head. I mean, of course, to get it before—before what you're going to do . . . it was a question for me if I should be able to manage it in time. If I couldn't have come now I probably shouldn't have come at all—perhaps even ever . . . it was either this or nothing . . . I had to take the risk.* (107)

Dorothea Krook has pointed out that *The Golden Bowl* should be read in relation to James's long literary development, taking into account his previous novels and tales in which the key themes of his career had already been elaborated (233–34). Charlotte's speech has specific details in common with Caspar Goodwood's quarrel with Isabel in *The Portrait of a Lady* (1881). When Goodwood comes to see Isabel after hearing of her engagement to another man, she tells him that his timing is off, that she would have appreciated a visit from him after her marriage. The drift of his conversation is a plea for closure on their relationship: "I came because I wanted to see you once more—even just as you are . . . I wished to hear the sound of your voice . . . I've done what I wished. I've seen you" (381–82). Goodwood's talk presents a useful contrast to Charlotte's speech because, although their line of reasoning is similar, their mode of expression is not. Goodwood's words are uncalculated and of the present; they are not rhetorically effective.[10] But Charlotte speaks in a monologue that Amerigo reads as a set piece, without the need for commentary and with admiration for the manner in which she carries it off:

> *What she gave touched him. . . . She really renounced—renounced everything, and without even insisting now on what it had all been for her. . . . He let himself accordingly be guided; he so soon assented, for enlightened indulgence, to any particular turn she might wish the occasion to take. . . . [After] her demonstration was*

---

9   Amerigo actually asks Fanny, speaking of Charlotte, "What has she come *for*?" (67). They run through various motives, some more sinister than others: to celebrate the Prince and Maggie's marriage, to cure her "loneliness," to plot "designs" upon Amerigo (67–68). In a later scene, Fanny and her husband Bob continue the debate; their most striking interpretation, given the novel's attention to the stalled beginning of Maggie and Amerigo's marriage, is that Charlotte has come back to give Maggie "lessons" on how to relate to her future husband (98).

10   The narrator suggests Charlotte's speech is performative: "She had paused as if her demonstration was complete . . . as if in fact to give it a few minutes to sink in; into the listening air, into the watching space, into the conscious hospitality of nature . . . or even for that matter into her own open ears rather than into the attention of her passive and prudent friend" (108).

complete . . . [h]is attention had done all that attention could do. . . . She let him off, it seemed, even from so much as answering . . . (106, 108)

Amerigo treats Charlotte as a performer and sees himself as an attentive audience, not expecting to pay more for her performance than an appreciative theatergoer. Yet Charlotte's timing is uncanny and has the potential to break through this aesthetic bubble. Like Goodwood, she explicitly tells her lover she wants this moment together *before* the impending marriage, that getting it afterward is out of the question. But in contrast to Goodwood's transparent plea to Isabel that he must speak now because "you'll be different then" (i.e., after her marriage) (381), Charlotte's reference to the future concerns her own timing, which is a theme in her speech. She mentions timing at the beginning of the speech and at the end. At the end, she brings attention to the fact that this moment with him is a "risk" that she "had to take." Charlotte sees herself as a risk-taker, even in her abjection. And why does one take a risk, if not for some hope of a future benefit? Charlotte's art, although it seems on the surface to plead for closure—for an ending that Amerigo interprets as "the full tune of her renouncing" (106)—highlights her future-oriented stance. But this interpretation can only be verified *in the future*, an implication Amerigo clearly misses. We know he has to, even though he does sense something "disconcerting in such an appeal at such an hour" (105) and in her condition that he keep their rendezvous a secret from Maggie.

Although readers will notice nothing indicating that Charlotte has a concrete plan at the moment, the calculated pressure she exerts as well as the foreboding and suspense surrounding her arrival generate a future out of so much uncertainty. A nascent plot forms when Fanny suggests to Amerigo that they owe it to Charlotte to arrange a good marriage for her. Both of them implicitly believe that securing Charlotte's financial future is the best way to bury the past. And since Maggie and her father Adam are anxious about Adam's future as a wealthy bachelor with an empty nest who must fight off "ravening women" (312), Charlotte's charm and social graces will become valuable and, eventually, seductive qualities. It turns out that all the major characters want Charlotte to marry well. So why not marry her wealthy friend's father? Simply by inserting herself into the thick of these conflicting motives at the right time, Charlotte plays an important role as a heroine who seizes timely moments to her advantage. But only the short interval before Amerigo's wedding carries the potential to create the combination of guilt, fear, and desire necessary to solicit Amerigo and Fanny to work on her behalf. And their willingness to help Charlotte paves the way for Maggie and her father to help later. Ruth Bernard Yeazell has noted that "characters in the late James seem to possess something of the artist's own power" (*Language* 6). We can see Charlotte's power in the way she seizes a present moment and pushes it into the future. By the time the rendezvous between her and Amerigo is over, Charlotte's last words to him augur their future adultery: "Well, I would marry, I think, to have something from you in all freedom" (125).[11]

---

[11]   An equal marriage would create the conditions for Charlotte and Amerigo to pick up their relationship in an adulterous mode; thus Charlotte could receive his affections again "in all

Maggie "Takes the Field"

The well-known opening to volume 2 of *The Golden Bowl* dramatizes Maggie's anxiety about her marriage. She has made a small gesture to let her husband know that *she* knows they have been estranged—waiting for him at home alone in their house at Portland Place rather than with her father at his house in Eaton Square. She calculated this act to gain Amerigo's attention—as a sign for him that she misses him and recognizes that something is amiss between them—and the narrative gains momentum from her "departure from custom" (331). This act also gives her a practical sense of her own power and its use. But both the scale of the act (it is a small change of routine) and its mode (Maggie calls it a "poor thing") indicate her lack of confidence (332). Since readers traditionally associate the risks of heroism with confidence in one's abilities, an unconfident heroine seems to be an oxymoron. One of the few precedents for the attention James gives to an unconfident heroine's mode of action is Jane Austen's Fanny Price, whose passivity led to many readings for and against Austen's decision to focus on her character in *Mansfield Park* (1814).[12] James's Maggie has generated a similar divisiveness in the critical literature.

Yet James's narrative interest in her case goes farther than Austen's because Maggie becomes a plot maker. James demonstrates that she has the capacity to be an effective actor, even though she does not fully believe in her own power. I read Maggie as a special case within the underdog character type. She surprises readers with the pleasure of a "win," but James's realistic art painstakingly dramatizes the incremental steps she takes, not only to make this win possible but to develop a know-how or knowing-how-to-do.[13] This latter process highlights her specific temporality, as Maggie's reflections about time are integrated into the dramatic texture of the narrative, becoming a source of insight for her as she searches for a solution to her problems. But Maggie emerges as a new type of heroine only in contrast with Charlotte.

We saw a time-value attached to Charlotte's act—it had a "now or never" quality that highlighted her risk. She clearly faces the prospect of a mercenary marriage, and she must believe that when she does make one, Amerigo will not only meet her on equal terms financially but will also risk adultery himself. Thus Charlotte fulfills the reader's traditional sense of heroic action as courage in the face of risk. Additionally, we do not see that she has any anxiety in making these choices, which constitutes her strength—also adding to her heroic stature. Yet James did not create Charlotte as a caricature of heroism—all strength and no weakness. R. B. J. Wilson's

---

freedom." In context, the "something" Charlotte refers to is a present Amerigo offers her during their rendezvous, which she refuses.

[12] Two articles (for and against Fanny as a novelistic heroine) are "In Defense of Dullness, or Why Fanny Price Is My Favorite Austen Heroine" (2008), by Dawn Potter; and "The Puzzle of Fanny Price" (2006), by Joyce L. Jenkins.

[13] I borrow the terminology "knowing-how-to-do" from A. J. Greimas's modalities of acting in *On Meaning* (138). Greimas developed a "performative series" categorization of possibilities for action in narrative actors, which Ricoeur discusses in some detail in the second volume of *Time and Narrative* (38–50).

description of her is perhaps the most accurate in the context of the novel: "[Charlotte has no] divided state of mind . . . . She knows precisely what she wants to do, why she wants to do it, how she believes she can do it . . . [although] [t]here is in her characterization . . . no gradual development to depict, merely a sustained singleness of purpose and a crisis with painful consequences" (96). Charlotte appears to us fully developed and ready to act; however, this position does not hold the highest value in *The Golden Bowl*.

In this particular narrative world, an understanding of the power to act cannot be gauged without an understanding of anxiety, which stalls action. We may borrow from Lacan's analysis of anxiety the formula "not without having it," which means that one's "resources are obscure" but not necessarily nil (*Anxiety* 89). So, as we follow James into this territory, we should keep in mind that Maggie's resources are obscure because she has not taken stock of her own power to act. She only begins to do so in volume 2. The narrator informs us, "The Princess . . . hadn't wished [to act] till now—such was the odd case" (327). And when Amerigo responds to her design to make him return home to see her alone and not with her father in Eaton Square, Maggie awakens and her detective work begins:

> *The great moment, at any rate, for conscious repossession, was doubtless the first: the strange little timed silence which she had fully gauged, on the spot, as altogether beyond her own intention. . . . [H]e had come back, had followed her from the other house,* visibly *uncertain—this was written in the face he for the first minute showed her. . . . Why* first?—*that had later on kept coming to her; the question dangled there as if it were the key to everything. . . . [A]t the end of a moment, he had taken in what he needed to take—that his wife was* testifying, *that she adored and missed and desired him. . . . He held her close and long, in expression of their personal reunion*
> (332, 335, 337)

In retrospect, then, Maggie stretches out Amerigo's "little timed silence" and places it in a sequence with a specific temporal tension. First Amerigo looks at her, hesitates, and is speechless. He then quickly follows with an interpretation that Maggie wants more intimacy from him. Seemingly, he has made the right interpretation. Yet the interval between his bewilderment and his confidence strikes her as "historic," despite his quick recovery (336). Did he guess her desire, or is he afraid of her? If he is afraid of her, she has to wonder why, since she had never given him any cause for fear.

The small temporal anomaly that Maggie notices in Amerigo becomes for her an objective thing, and the narrator gives this interval various images as Maggie attempts to solidify the experience; for example, a drama: "some scene so acted as to have left a great impression on the tenant of one of the stalls"; a portrait: "a great picture hung on the wall of her daily life for her to make what she would of"; a string of pearls: "those [moments] . . . she could feel again most, count again like the firm pearls on a string, had belonged more particularly to the lapse of time before dinner" (332). This interval is an event that she must, at all costs, retain: "living over and over again any chosen minute . . . she could choose them, she could fix them"

(332). We experience her slow-motion replays as the emergence in her of an "analytic consciousness" (338). She has finally "taken the field" (349).

Taking the field, Maggie begins to measure her husband's pacing, noticing a pattern of hesitation followed by haste. After Amerigo's first hesitation/haste sequence, when she suddenly changes her routine, she notices two more. Before he goes upstairs to dress for dinner, Maggie asks him if she can help him dress. The pattern repeats: "[H]e had met her asking him, in hesitation first, then quickly in decision . . . but he had declined her offer . . . he should go straighter and faster alone" (338). Finally, after Amerigo emerges, dressed and ready for dinner, "There was still for the instant something in suspense, but it passed more quickly than on his previous entrance. He was already holding out his arms" (342). Three times, Maggie—and the reader along with her—notes the same sequence: hesitation, born of some kind of uncertainty, and Amerigo's quick recovery of his bearings. Maggie's "field of action" (342) and her awakening confidence as an actor happen as she analyzes these relatively fleeting sequences of hesitation and then haste to act.

Untimeliness: Moving from Anxiety to Courage

Hilary Schor expresses very well the reversal readers may experience in the second half of *The Golden Bowl*: "James pulls the rug out from under us . . . unexpectedly, after a half-novel in which she has been placid, quiet, and good, even . . . 'stupid,' Maggie Verver comes to curious life" (240). But to understand how Maggie comes to life—and comes to defend herself—it is more accurate to ask not how she becomes smart after having been stupid but how she passes from anxiety to courage, since these two affective states have distinctive temporal qualities that give us different narrative tonalities. To solidify an answer to this question, I would like to turn to Lacan's and Badiou's efforts to express qualitative differences in temporal experience.

At the end of his first published seminar (1953–54), Lacan discusses two existential-temporal modes. He gives the familiar Hegelian master-and-slave dialectic an individualized narrative dimension by expressing the time consciousness of the master vs. the time consciousness of the slave. The one who posits mastery exhibits an "abrupt" relation to conflict, seeking to get ahead of it, while the much less confident "slave" waits indefinitely for a time to act, a time that may not come without outside intervention (*Freud's* 286–87). In this seminar Lacan also mentions his "Logical Time" essay in which he elaborated on the "quality" of different temporal tensions, using a well-known prisoner's dilemma (166). I am reading both Lacan's initial analysis of this prisoner's dilemma and Badiou's interpretation of it as a way to think about Maggie's untimeliness and how it contributes to her underdog status in *The Golden Bowl*.

The terms of the prisoner's dilemma are as follows: three prisoners are shown five disks, two black and three white. The prison warden declares that the first to guess the color of the disk affixed to them "between the shoulders" (thus outside their "direct visual field") will be freed ("Logical Time" 161). No verbal communication between the prisoners is allowed, so the only information they have about each other's deliberations is their timing. All three prisoners receive white disks; no use is made of the two black ones, as this would establish the limiting condition that gives immediate clarity to the situation, for any prisoner who sees two black disks would head for the door. No one moves because none of them actually sees the limiting condition directly, but this is clear only to the warden. What is the situation like inside the game? Lacan stresses that the two combinations that remain in play (three white disks or one black disk and two white disks) warrant a temporal analysis.

Badiou points out that the trick to this problem—its "algebra"—requires recognizing that the one black/two white disk combination is "inclusive" to the limit condition, leading to the same result—one cannot be wearing a black disk (252). The difference between the two is that the one black/two white combination takes an extra step—Badiou calls this step R2 (reasoning 2)—because it requires inferring the limit condition (R1) from what one does not immediately see. The logic of inclusion—R2 goes back to R1—is complicated by an unseen virtual scenario, which each prisoner must entertain and then abandon. To clarify—the problem involves recognizing a "law" twice, once as a given (only two black disks) and a second time as an inference (moving back to the law based on what is not readily visible). For Badiou and Lacan this indicates an excess of the law, and for literary theory, it should indicate the presence of a narrative complication. Is not narrative complication in excess of a lawful movement toward a conclusion? Why bother to tell a story when the path is so straight that it is obvious?

Badiou picks up his exposition by entirely agreeing with Lacan's attempt to subject this anecdote to a narrative analysis (253). Timing is the unknown variable that creates a complication. How much time does it take each prisoner to realize the extra step leads straight back to the limit condition? Lacan asks, "How can we measure the limit of this time . . . ? The time for comprehending can include the instant of the glance, but this glance can include in its instant all the time needed for comprehending. The objectivity of this time thus vacillates within its limit" (168). The prisoners have no guidance, no algebra, for exactly how long it should take for each one of them to move from R2 back to R1. All they know is that it cannot take too long—that would suspend the game altogether—and that it might take more than a "glance." Lacan insists that this "sophism" shows "a very peculiar misrecognition on the part of [human] subjects of the reality of other people" (163). We must recall that the limiting condition involves a detour inferring what the others are thinking and thus taps into what today we would call Theory of Mind.

I would like to point out that Lacan was attuned to the untimeliness of subjective processes and sometimes called this untimeliness failure, but with an emphasis on the irony of the word *failure* in particular contexts.[14] In "Logical Time," the success (or failure) of being too fast, of displaying an abrupt relationship to conflict, takes

---

[14]   In *The Ego in Freud's Theory* (1954–55), Lacan engages with game theory to point out that winning or losing the first round of a game "has no meaning whatsoever . . . except purely conventionally . . . all you have to do is invert this game into *who loses wins*" (182). Jonathan Freedman's analysis of *The Golden Bowl*, "What Maggie Knew," also employs game theory as a methodology. Freedman admirably clarifies some of Maggie's tactics, although he discusses temporality only implicitly. I differ from him regarding Maggie's success in the novel. Freedman views Maggie's tactics instrumentally, arguing they do little to distinguish her from Charlotte (perhaps game theory alone, without an affective component, encourages this view).

center stage in his analysis of the prisoner's dilemma in "Logical Time" because the test of mental agility creates a challenge to be "first." So for the pause to have a meaning (other than that they do not want to play this game), someone has to move first. Moving first, however, does not mean one is right about what the others think. Without any stable reference point about the others' timing, the only measure the subject (the *I*) has is one's own timing, which could be off target. If they go faster than I do, it could mean they may not complete the reasoning process and act based on faulty reasoning (leading me astray), or I may be slow to act on what I conclude (thus missing the time to conclude). So being first does not mean one is wrong, but simply that one pushes the situation out into the open—lays one's cards on the table—and puts down the first signifiers of the game.

In his 1962–63 seminar on anxiety, Lacan argues that anxiety is "that which deceives not" (*Anxiety* 76). Stalling narrative development, anxiety references the need to be "entirely free of doubt" (76). Lacan also points out that "all activity opens out onto certainty" and therefore that human activity is an effort "to snatch from anxiety its certainty. To act is to bring about a transfer of anxiety" (77). Thus Lacan places anxiety and action into a dialectic, one in which acting, even in an untimely way, narrativizes what would otherwise be kept in suspense. Clearly the need for haste in the prisoner's dilemma is a way of transposing the certainty that someone must move to get the game going into an act in which *I am the one to move*, the one to snatch from this immobile moment a push forward and therefore create an opening for certainty through time and narrative. This one move does not necessarily end the game, since it is not clear that anyone gets the right answer. In fact, doubt can clearly follow the initial push forward. I can doubt I have made the right move and stop soon afterward. According to Lacan, doubt is the other side of haste, following it closely in a narrative trajectory (171). But the first move left a trace. Two sequences of pauses are needed to "desubjectify" the situation and end the game (172). However, the "reference of the '*I*'" plays a role in "temporalizing" the situation (173).

Although Lacan does not refer to courage in his essay, Badiou interprets courage as implied within the dialectic between anxiety and action but not as the confirmation of an immobile law, a predefined certainty; rather, as an opening—sideways—toward the new. In this particular problem, if we recall, R2 merely goes back to R1 (the limit condition, the law that regulated the game). It is just an extra step referring back to what would have been obvious if presented in a clearer form. So Badiou points out that "there must be something that Lacan does not say" if he is concerned with temporal unfolding (253). The different speeds of reasoning, or different forces of thinking in action, show us the other side of anxiety, which is courage to see the new (253). Badiou also insists the prisoner's dilemma goes beyond logic, or supplements logic, by referencing human freedom (it is about prisoners vying for their freedom) (253). My analysis of Maggie's discovery of adultery asserts a similar trajectory: Although Maggie finds the inevitable consequence (the law) of her neglect of her husband—his adultery—she makes a sideways discovery, finding in her situation an unexpected opportunity for self-transformation.

I see Maggie as happy at being able to act (something Charlotte takes for granted), a qualitative difference I believe gives significance to Maggie's story.

As Daniel Brudney has pointed out in his analysis of *The Golden Bowl*, adultery is less about detecting the act of betrayal than about "the hopeless question of how your lover feels . . . what is wanted is *certainty*, an incision into your lover's head or heart" (410). This is what Maggie refuses when she seeks, beyond blame—even beyond blaming herself—to grasp in what way she is different from Charlotte and how this difference might draw her husband back to her. She finds this difference in her approach to timing.

What Maggie Knows

Slowness does not necessarily indicate the dunce or the fool in a narrative, which is precisely what James dramatizes the moment Maggie "takes the field" and begins to read temporal tensions in *The Golden Bowl*. She does it by counting and comparing how much time it takes the three people in her and her father's life whom they trusted the most—Amerigo, Charlotte, and Fanny—to respond to her as she makes small but unexpected changes to her usual behavior. She learns from this process that Charlotte is clearly the decision maker among the three, the one who responds most quickly to the probings. The other two lag behind Charlotte in confidence, Fanny recovering her composure more slowly than Amerigo (396–97). Maggie finally understands that Charlotte needs to be the first, and this is both her weakness and her strength. To defend herself, she reconsiders Charlotte's courage, which fascinated her before.

The value of Charlotte's courage must fall for readers as well. The one chapter that gives us an inside glimpse into Charlotte's consciousness, if readers pay close attention to it, presents her as capitalizing on creating moments of "crisis" (214). We meet her in the novel's action of an official party, as Adam's wife, where she drops a bomb on Fanny by telling her she plans to commit adultery: "Maggie thinks more on the whole of fathers than of husbands. And my situation is such . . . that this becomes . . . a thing I have to count with" (221). As we can see, a strong offense disarms her opponent. Fanny finds herself "heaving" and "panting" at Charlotte's words (221). In this context, the risk is small that Fanny will expose her friend's adulterous intent. As Charlotte's matchmaker, Fanny herself will be exposed. Charlotte simply wants Fanny out of the way so that she herself can be Amerigo's sole influencer. She tells Amerigo, "Oh Fanny. . . . We're beyond her" (257).

Now we can understand much better the well-known scene, late in the novel, in which Charlotte confronts Maggie about what has been going on with Amerigo, who has suddenly turned cold on her, refusing any communication but the most polite. Charlotte knows his coldness can be traced to Maggie, but how will she discover exactly how much Maggie knows? Now Maggie knows much more than the fact of adultery; she knows Charlotte's weakness. So she waits for Charlotte to drop her bomb. But the only bomb Charlotte can drop is to show her need for haste: "I've been wanting . . . to put a question to you for which no opportunity has seemed to me quite so good as this. It would have been easier perhaps if you had struck me as in the least disposed to give me one. I have to take it now, you see, as I find it. . . . Have you any ground of complaint of me?" (495–96). We now see Charlotte's strategy more clearly because she has no disarming effect on Maggie, who recognizes

Charlotte's move it for what it is, hastening an event to take control of the situation. Critics have traditionally focused on what follows Charlotte's attempt to disarm Maggie in this scene—Maggie's lie. She assures Charlotte that she has no quarrel with her; they even kiss on it (499). But Maggie's lie is coupled with her understanding of Charlotte's temporal framing, which is an act of control. Yet Charlotte is not in control because her strategy has fallen in value for Maggie, who does not read it as courage. The only crisis is the one Charlotte now has with herself: "try[ing] to look as if she weren't afraid" (496). The pattern Maggie sees is the reverse of her own: Charlotte's movement from courage and confidence to anxiety.

Maggie's Success

For Amerigo, too, Charlotte's value begins to fall in the course of the novel. Ironically, the process begins when Maggie resists his sexual advances. She resists his attempts at sexual charm in the days and months following his first anxious hesitation at Eaton Square, fearing this "shortest way with her" will blot out the anxiety she noticed on his face before he made the decision to embrace her (422). Maggie's temporal resistance to him serves multiple purposes, but the one purpose that stands out as she works on saving her marriage is that this temporal tension shows him that her desire for him is strong:

> [S]ince she had given to him as yet no moment's pretext for pretending to her that she had either lost faith or suffered by a feather's weight in happiness, she left him, it was easy to reason, with an immense advantage for all waiting and all tension. She wished him for the present to "make up" to her for nothing. Who could say to what making-up might lead, into what consenting or pretending or destroying blindness it might plunge her? She loved him too helplessly still . . . [yet] [s]he was keeping her head for a reason, for a cause; and the labour of this detachment . . . held them together in the steel hoop of an intimacy compared with which artless passion would have been but a beating of the air. (422–23; emphasis added)

Clearly Maggie does not want the accusations that would come with the exposure of his infidelity. She believes, she hopes, that keeping this moment of accusation in suspense indicates to him how much she loves him. And the metaphor of a "steel hoop of intimacy" suggests that Maggie's self-control on this matter expresses her passion, since it reflects a dynamic conflict between her desire for Amerigo and her need for self-respect. As she encourages Amerigo to understand this conflict, her resistance communicates to him that there is an intensity in her desire, which he had missed before.

It is tempting to see "artless passion" in Maggie's meditation as representing Charlotte. It obviously does not, since Charlotte's passion for Amerigo is also a labor. But the word *artless* does express Amerigo's experience of Charlotte when they were most attuned to each other, and it is precisely this kind of attunement that the narrative exposes as false. In the shadow of Charlotte's artlessness, Amerigo feels that she is a bit ahead of his thought process:

> *They had these identities of impulses—they had them repeatedly before; and if such*
> *unarranged but unerring encounters gave the measure of the degree in which peo-*
> *ple were, in the common phrase, meant for each other, no union in the world had ever*
> *been more sweetened with rightness. What in fact most often happened was that her*
> *rightness went . . . further than his own; they were conscious of the same necessity at*
> *the same moment, only it was she who as a general thing most clearly saw her way to*
> *it.* (290)

Amerigo often feels that he and Charlotte are in sync, and this experience creates their emotional and erotic connection. Yet the narrator's conventional phrase, "meant for each other," indicates an ironic distance on the idea of being completely in sync. And the truth is that Charlotte is one step ahead of Amerigo's thoughts. In the end, Amerigo chooses Maggie's slowness. The erotic implication of Maggie's bond with Amerigo is that she gives him time to catch up with himself, clearly symbolized in the confrontation scene between Maggie and Amerigo with the broken bowl:

> *He stood with his hands in his pockets; he had carried his eyes to the fragments . . . and*
> *she could already distinguish the element of relief, absolutely of succor . . . [in] every*
> *added inch of reflexion and delay . . . by her helping him, helping him to help*
> *himself . . . , she should help him to help* her. *Hadn't she fairly got into his labyrinth*
> *with him? . . . She offered him thus assuredly the kind of support that could not have*
> *been imagined in advance and that moreover required . . . some close looking at before*
> *it could be believed in and pronounced void of treachery.* (454)

From Maggie's attempt to give Amerigo "reflexion and delay," we can see that she is trying to forge a new bond with him, one she could not have predicted or expected to be founded on her patience. By the end of the novel, giving him time begins to take on an erotic charge for both of them.

Maggie's waiting develops erotic implications but is also open to other productive possibilities between her and her husband. She creates suspense when she discovers the golden bowl and what it means, keeping it in a drawing room, hoping he might see it but willing to wait long enough for some sign from him without forcing a response. In fact, Fanny breaks the bowl and takes on the role of the precipitating agent. Given the novel's attempt to rethink precipitating agents and their place in a sequence of narrative action (through Charlotte's characterization), it is fitting that James delegates the act of breaking the golden bowl to a comic character. After this dramatic scene, contrived so that we see another dramatic scene—Maggie and Amerigo confront the bowl—we encounter a new meaning behind the force of Maggie's patient waiting. Amergio asks her why she waited to tell him about the bowl, and her response is, "To see what difference it would make for myself" (463). So waiting also gives her time to decide if she still loves him enough to forgive him. And when she decides the answer is yes, waiting helps her to help *him* save face as she confronts him with evidence.

"These Three Months"

Gérard Genette poses a question for narratological analysis when he notes the relationship between a story's duration (its actual clock time) and the length of the telling—that is, how much narrative attention a writer gives to the temporal interval. He asks, does a page cover minutes, months, or years? And what does this indicate about writers' modulations between acceleration and deceleration? (35) Genette also asks whether (and when) a longer narrative will inform readers of how much time has passed, thus allowing readers to measure the writer's pacing preferences for a particular section (34). James clearly favors deceleration in *The Golden Bowl*, although this varies by section. Volume 2 is known for being particularly slow going, but some notable James critics—Dorrit Cohn and Ruth Bernard Yeazell—have pointed out the grammars of tense that bring the reader closer to Maggie and thus to her lively activity in this section of the novel. I would like to close this essay by synthesizing Cohn's and Yeazell's focus on the particular grammars of time in volume 2—which help to express how Maggie comes alive in *The Golden Bowl*—with Genette's observation about duration's relationship to narrative attention. To understand James's portrait of an unconfident heroine, we must recognize both the internal grammars of time that critics have noted and the actual time that has passed. In volume 2 of the novel, Maggie's detective work takes approximately three months and 138 pages.[15] It is not easy to pinpoint the clock time, and it may surprise readers that she solves her marital problem in three months, given Maggie's strategy of patience. Thus our narrative attention has been intensely focused on a fairly narrow time scheme. As I read James's pacing, Maggie's build-up of confidence actually cuts down on a time that could have otherwise been longer.

Cohn and Yeazell have both identified a temporal mode that James uses when he wants to establish an especially intimate relationship between narrator and protagonist—a mode that expresses "a future moment when the experience described will have come to lie in the past for the remembering consciousness" (Cohn 5). A formal name for this time scheme is *analeptic prolepsis* (Cohn 5). More descriptively, it could be called the "future time in the past" (Yeazell, "Remembrance" 237n1). Yeazell points out that the technique should be familiar to readers of late James, citing phrases such as "he was to remember" (referring to Strether in *The Ambassadors*), he "was to measure after" (Densher in *Wings of the Dove*), and "she was to remember afterwards" (Maggie in *The Golden Bowl*) ("Remembrance" 231–32). Such phrases indicate an "anticipated recollection" (232). According to both critics, James uses this technique to give readers a realistic impression of delays in the mind's processing of mental events (Cohn 6; Yeazell, "Remembrance" 231). Cohn

[15]   When they both confront the broken bowl that reveals Amerigo's betrayal, Maggie tells Amerigo that the time that Fanny Assingham has gained for her "these three months, don't you see? has been everything" (456). In terms of pages, I am counting from the beginning of volume 2 (book 4, chapter 1) to the end of book 4, chapter 10, when Maggie and Amerigo both confront the broken bowl and its meaning for their relationship.

further emphasizes James's attempt to heighten the reader's sense of Maggie Verver's "inner life" (8). Clearly James's dramatic use of analeptic prolepsis facilitates readers' understanding of Maggie's developing analytic powers in *The Golden Bowl*, which I have pointed to earlier.

Additionally, in my reading, James's realistic presentation of Maggie's developing know-how aligns with later insights by Lacan and Badiou regarding delayed beginnings. A human act, as experienced by the actor, is never perfectly timed. Yet the extent of untimeliness—the length of delay in mental processing—may determine personal happiness or personal tragedy. In an earlier novel, *Washington Square* (1880), James dramatizes an innocent heiress (Catherine Sloper) who suffers from her father's and her lover's cruel judgments that she is an inevitable victim, someone too slow to spot trickery. Yet Catherine learns to see the two men in her life for what they are through the "retribution of time" (183). Her waiting in the novel serves an analytic function, although James had not yet developed the technique of analeptic prolepsis to concentrate on her thought process. While a decade for Catherine to process what happened to her is too much time for most readers to credit her with transcending the victim's role, in *The Golden Bowl* James gives Maggie better odds to develop a productive form of temporal retribution. James's use of analeptic prolepsis in his later novel projects a future time that is already in the past for her to analyze. But the projected future is not a very distant future, and the past moment not a very distant past. Thus Maggie's process does not take up most of her adult life, and her awakening analysis helps her find a middle ground between the two positions she negotiates—the complacent wife and the enraged victim. This technique reflects how the future and the past can come close without actually reaching an instant of simultaneity in the present.

James's double time scheme complements the narrowing duration (relatively speaking) of Maggie's activities. Both techniques express her emerging temporal discipline. The opening of volume 2 of *The Golden Bowl* begins: "It wasn't till many days had passed that the Princess began to accept the idea of having done, a little, something she was not always doing" (327). We do not know exactly how many days, but the detailed narration has distended this fairly narrow time frame, so that we may actually forget it is so narrow.[16] Yet we have some temporal markers. The Matcham party in volume 1, where Amerigo and Charlotte consummated their adultery, is our most obvious one, so the "many days" period counts down from this event. Another marker is Fanny's analysis of the party, when she reveals to her husband that Maggie has somehow changed since Amerigo and Charlotte returned late from Matcham (their conversation concludes volume 1). These narrative clues keep readers informed and give us some grounding for what is to come, which is

---

16   This problem of gauging proper temporal proportions is incorporated into certain scenes of the novel. One example is when Maggie begins to ignore Charlotte and Amerigo during a party: "[She was] sticking to her policy of giving the pair no look. There were thus some five wonderful minutes during which they loomed . . . larger than they had ever loomed before, larger than life, larger than thought, larger than any danger or any safety. There was thus a space of time in fine, fairly vertiginous for her, during which she took no more account of them than if they weren't in the room" (362).

that Maggie will come to knowledge and will act in her own way. As Michael Snediker has pointed out in his analysis of Maggie's temporality, her patience does not mean a "disrecognition of time" but exists in a temporal tension with impatience: "Is it possible . . . to say to someone 'I'm being patient,' without being construed as . . . imminently becoming . . . impatient?" (26). When she confronts Amerigo with the golden bowl, we learn (because she tells Amerigo) that the dense and seemingly slow-going sections we have been reading have only spanned three months.

What exactly has happened during these three months? We may recall that Maggie's first clue that Amerigo has something to hide from her is a slight hesitation—suggesting anxiety—and a (possibly) hasty attempt to embrace her to recover from the anxiety. Maggie attends to her husband's anxiety, and as in any mystery, its function as a clue forms a narrative, something to be clarified later. For Maggie, future moments of clarity emerge around a seemingly banal series of summer plans for the family—a trip to Europe with her father, which she abandons to continue watching Charlotte and Amerigo; a dinner party at her house for the Matcham people—those people who must have witnessed Charlotte and Amerigo's intimacy; a plot to get everyone together at Fawns, the summer house where they all resided when Adam and Charlotte began their "courtship." Beneath her seemingly boring, domestic plans, Maggie retraces the steps that led to her father's marriage to Charlotte, and even before then, to Charlotte and Amerigo's rendezvous. She does all this by simply waiting to see how Amerigo and Charlotte will respond to her small but disruptive behaviors. As Fanny puts it: "[She wants] to see what . . . time may do for her" (416).

Clearly, Maggie has felt incredibly alive these three months, as if she is living from moment to moment, even if the moments seem to consist mainly of waiting. She compares herself to an actress "quite heroically improvising" (348), and the narrator follows her small steps while giving us the sense that each one, while novel and surprising, has a material meaning and a cumulative logic. She has cut down the four years (since her marriage) of malingering to three months of soul searching and conscious strategy. The narrator's involvement in this narrowing time scheme suggests that Maggie's analysis is a lively and courageous mental process with its own intense affective investments.

Therefore, despite Maggie's success in winning her husband back, readers can sense that her real desire lies in a beyond of love, and so does the novel's. *The Golden Bowl*'s force comes from its close attention to Maggie's strategic thinking but also from the premise that any successful strategy has a backstory, a "thrilling tale" that deepens our appreciation of narrative unfolding (James, "Roderick Hudson" 1040).[17] Strategies begin with an aim before developing a plan of action. In fact, clarifying one's aim precedes any good strategy. In the twists of a Jamesian plot, the strategists whose aim has no backstory, no wavering narrative, are not privileged. The novelist's business is to unfold time in ways that are not entirely predictable, so

---

[17]   In his preface to *Roderick Hudson*, James discusses his "addict[ion] to stories" (1040). The particular story he wants to develop in this preface is the artist's composition behind the novel. Yet, as I read it, the context belies the novelist's continuous search for new narratives.

for James the characters whose aims are not clear to themselves are the ones who need the space for narrative unfolding. Maggie's purpose emerges gradually, and she is not fully conscious of it until Charlotte tests her intelligence. In the end, we find that Maggie is an Enlightenment heroine seeking the satisfaction of applying her intelligence. She learns on her own to fashion a workable and effective action by analyzing her competitor's speed in the same way as her own slowness was an object of analysis for Charlotte. And when she finds her object, "Maggie went, she went—she felt herself going" (348). She comes alive to a sense of her own mental power, and James gives her process authenticity, even if—especially as—it is the story of an arrested development.

*   *   *

JANINA LEVIN currently teaches in the Writing and Rhetoric Program at University of the Sciences in Philadelphia. Her main interests are narrative strategies of slowness and how they affect literary fiction, the relationship between literature and life, empathy, and deception narratives. She has published articles on Henry James, James Joyce, and literary modernism. Her work has appeared in *Journal of Modern Literature*, *Review of Communication*, and *James Joyce Quarterly*.

Works Cited

Badiou, Alain. *Theory of the Subject*. Trans. Bruno Bosteels. London: Continuum, 2009.

Brooks, Peter. *The Melodramatic Imagination: Balzac, Henry James, Melodrama, and the Mode of Excess*. New Haven: Yale UP, 1976.

Brudney, Daniel. "Knowledge and Silence: *The Golden Bowl* and Moral Philosophy." *Critical Inquiry* 16.2 (1990): 397–437.

Cohn, Dorrit. "'First Schock of Complete Perception': The Opening Episode of *The Golden Bowl*, Volume 2." *Henry James Review* 22.1 (2001): 1–9.

Freedman, Jonathan. "What Maggie Knew: Game Theory, *The Golden Bowl*, and the Possibilities of Aesthetic Knowledge." *Cambridge Quarterly* 37.1 (2008): 98–113.

Genette, Gerard. *Narrative Discourse Revisited*. Trans. Jane E. Lewin. Ithaca: Cornell UP, 1988.

Greimas, Algirdas Julien. *On Meaning: Selected Writings in Semiotic Theory*. Minneapolis: U of Minnesota P, 1987.

James, Henry. *The Golden Bowl*. Harmondsworth: Penguin, 1987.

James, Henry. *The Portrait of a Lady*. Harmondsworth: Penguin, 1986.

James, Henry. "Roderick Hudson." *Literary Criticism, Volume Two*. New York: Library of America, 1984. 1039–52.

James, Henry. *Washington Square*. New York: New American Library, 1964.

Jenkins, Joyce L. "The Puzzle of Fanny Price." *Philosophy and Literature* 30.2 (2006): 346–60.

Krook, Dorothea. *The Ordeal of Consciousness in Henry James*. New York: Cambridge UP, 1962.

Lacan, Jacques. "Logical Time and the Assertion of Anticipated Certainty." *Ecrits*. Trans. Bruce Fink. New York: Norton, 2012. 161–75.

Lacan, Jacques. *The Seminar of Jacques Lacan: Book I, Freud's Papers on Technique 1953–1954*. Ed. Jacques-Alain Miller. Trans. John Forrester. New York: Norton, 1991.

Lacan, Jacques. *The Seminar of Jacques Lacan: Book II, The Ego in Freud's Theory and in the Technique of Psychoanalysis*. Ed. Jacques-Alain Miller. Trans. Sylvana Tomaselli. New York: Norton, 1991.

Lacan, Jacques. *The Seminar of Jacques Lacan: Book X, Anxiety*. Ed. Jacques-Alain Miller. Trans. A. R. Price. Cambridge: Polity, 2014.

La Farge, Lucy. "Caught in the Snare of Deception: An Exploration of the Psychology of Being Deceived through Two Novels of Henry James." *Psychoanalytic Quarterly* 80.1 (2011): 91–210.

Potter, Dawn. "In Defense of Dullness, or Why Fanny Price Is My Favorite Austen Heroine." *Sewanee Review* 116.4 (2008): 611–18.

Ricoeur, Paul. *Time and Narrative*. Vol. 1 and 2. Trans. Kathleen McLaughlin and David Pellauer. Chicago: U of Chicago P, 1984.

Ronell, Avital. *Stupidity*. Urbana: U of Illinois P, 2002.

Rukhelman, Svetlana. Curriculum Vitae, Harvard University < https://scholar.harvard.edu /srukhelman/home > (accessed 1 Nov. 2019).

Sachs, Jonathan. "Slow Time." *PMLA* 134.2 (2019): 315–31.

Schenck, Mary Jane. *The Fabliaux: Tales of Wit and Deception*. Amsterdam: Benjamins, 1987. Proquest Ebook Central, < https://ebookcentral.proquest.com/lib/templeuniv-ebooks /reader.action?docID=805786 > .

Schor, Hilary. "Reading Knowledge: Curiosity in the Golden Bowl." *Henry James Review* 26.3 (2005): 237–45.

Snediker, Michael. "Stasis and Verve: Henry James and Fictions of Patience." *Henry James Review* 27.1 (2006): 24–41.

Sussman, Matthew. "Henry James and Stupidity." *Novel* 48.1 (2015): 45–62.

Thompson, Stith. *The Folktale*. Berkeley: U of California P, 1946.

Tintner, Adeline R. "'The Great Condition': Henry James and Bergsonian Time." *Studies in Short Fiction* 21.2 (1984): 111–15.

Wilson, R. B. J. *Henry James's Ultimate Narrative: "The Golden Bowl."* St. Lucia: U of Queensland P, 1981.

Yeazell, Ruth Bernard. *Language and Knowledge in the Late Novels of Henry James.* Chicago: U of Chicago P, 1976.

Yeazell, Ruth Bernard. "Remembrance of Things Present in *The Ambassadors.*" *Henry James Review* 38.3 (2017): 231–37.

Žižek, Slavoj. "Kate's Choice, or The Materialism of Henry James." *The Parallax View.* Cambridge: MIT P, 2006. 125–44.

Kazuo Ishiguro's Nonactors

MARIA CHRISTOU

The human being, Hannah Arendt observes, has been described as the speaking/ rational animal (*zoon logon echon*), the political animal (*zoon politikon*), the fabricating animal (*homo faber*), and the laboring animal (*animal laborans*); but in the twentieth century, she suggests, it becomes possible "for the first time in our history" to think of it primarily as *the acting animal* (*Between Past and Future* 62–63). Action, like all the other capabilities listed above, is an inherent human capacity for Arendt, but in the twentieth century it comes to assume center stage. Twentieth-century achievements like Ernest Rutherford's "splitting" of the atom, Arendt claims, show that the powers of the human capacity to act are significantly amplified, its consequences extending far beyond the human world. Action, she concludes, can now be considered to be the most prominent and the most consequential of all human capacities (60, 63).

Given Arendt's intellectual debt to Aristotle, her elevation of action to a position of prominence invites associations with the latter's famous declaration that the best literature constitutes "primarily" [*archi*] an imitation of action (*Poetics* 1450a38–39; *Arte Poetica* 1450a38–39)—so much so that the characters, or "agents" [*prattontes*], are understood to be needed mainly in order to act [*prattein*] (1450b3–4). If, as Aristotle has it, good literature ought to imitate only human beings who act, then this is a prescription that Arendt's reflections imbue with renewed, even magnified, significance. Coming as it does from one of Aristotle's most prominent disciples, the claim that action becomes the dominant human capacity in the twentieth century raises the question of whether, in the literature of the period, we might accordingly expect to find an amplified adherence to Aristotle's dictum on the primacy of action.

Rather than characters who act, however, I want instead to flag up a crucial preoccupation with the figure of the nonactor. Around the time Arendt advances her argument about the centrality of action, in the 1950s,[1] we encounter characters like Arsene from Samuel Beckett's novel *Watt* (1953), who talks about the bliss of finding oneself "in a situation where to do nothing" constitutes "an act of the highest value" (33). In John Barth's *The Floating Opera* (1967), nonaction is at center stage. The narrator, Todd Andrews, tells the story of how one day he decides to act and then changes his mind. The action in question, it transpires, is suicide, and Barth's novel turns out to be a rewriting of *Hamlet*—albeit one in which the protagonist manifests an attitude toward action that is fundamentally different from Hamlet's. Though the latter has been described as "the paradigmatic figure of the 'man of inaction'" (Wagner 24), he in fact betrays a belief in the *value* of acting: his hesitation to act is the source of much inner torment throughout. Andrews's decision, by contrast, rests on the insight that action lacks "intrinsic value"; he decides to commit suicide because "there's no final reason for living," as he puts it, but then

---

[1] Portions of Arendt's essay were first published in *The Review of Politics* 20.4 (1958): 570–90.

Novel: A Forum on Fiction 53:3   DOI 10.1215/00295132-8624552   © 2020 by Novel, Inc.

changes his mind because, as he comes to assert, there is no value in opting for not living either (Barth 223, 228). In short, even if "doing nothing" does not exactly constitute "an act of the highest value" for Andrews, as it does for Beckett's Arsene, it ultimately emerges as the preferable option. The question concerning the value of action (or, to be precise, the lack thereof) is also at the heart of *The Floating Opera*'s companion novel, *The End of the Road* (1967), where the central character and narrator, Jacob Horner, suddenly realizes that there is "no reason to do anything," and immediately becomes paralyzed on a bench for days, unable to perform even the most minimal of actions (Barth 323). The trend continues, and appears to be intensified, in the twenty-first century, with novels like Ben Marcus's *Notable American Women* (2002) presenting us with a scenario in which everyday actions such as simple bodily movements are seen not just as lacking in value but as having extortionately harmful consequences, while nonaction features as something worth striving for. "[P]eople" are said to be "slaughter[ing]" the sky "when they move," the theory being that if they were to "cease" the "world might begin to recover" (46). In fact, the "perfect world" is here conceptualized as one in which "nothing would have happened," and indeed, the "notable women" of the title undertake "voluntary paralysis," vowing to abide by "ever-diminishing motion quota[s]" in pursuit of an ideal state of stillness and actionlessness (53, 65, 109).

Another remarkable example of this turn to nonaction that straddles the twentieth and twenty-first centuries is found in Kazuo Ishiguro's oeuvre, and it is on a selection of his novels that this essay focuses. Ishiguro's first novels, *A Pale View of Hills* (1982) and *An Artist of the Floating World* (1986), tell the stories of characters whose past actions turn out to be regrettable, while in *When We Were Orphans* (2000) we have a protagonist who acts in the present in order to "fix" the past but whose actions are delusional and are doomed to fail. In what follows, I examine *The Remains of the Day* (1989), *The Unconsoled* (1995), and *Never Let Me Go* (2005), where at center stage is the figure of the nonactor—a figure which, as the examples above suggest, constitutes a wider preoccupation in the literary imagination from the mid-twentieth century onward, but whose presence would, at least at first glance, appear to be somewhat enigmatic in the light of Arendt's comments.

Jacques Rancière's work in the past two decades demonstrates that there has been a broader revival of interest in the problem of action in literature—a problem that, of course, stretches further back. In *The Politics of Literature* (2006) and in *The Lost Thread* (2014), Rancière examines a departure from Aristotle's prescriptions—one that, as he says, begins in the Romantic tradition, constitutes the principle that "brings the so-called realist novel into play," and culminates in the "absolutization of style" in the aesthetics of the protomodernist and modernist novel (*Politics of Literature* 15, 11). This departure, Rancière argues, signals a democratizing process evident not only in the shift away from the Aristotelian model of great actions performed by great men ("princes, generals, or orators") and toward "ordinary human beings" and the everyday (*Politics of Literature* 12, 11) but also in "fiction's new proportions and disproportions," as he puts it, whereby "description[s]" become more expansive than before and are not subjugated to the "dynamics of action" (*Lost Thread* xxx). Rancière's take on this is different from that of Georg Lukács, who, far from identifying a democratizing impulse, criticizes modernist literature for its emphasis on subjective interiority—an emphasis, he argues, that hinders the possibility of action in the external world. For Rancière, on the other hand, this is not a case of "dethroning . . . action" (*Lost Thread* xxxiii), but one of demolishing the "hierarchies that had governed the invention of subjects [and] the composition of action" (*Politics of Literature* 10)—hierarchies, that is, that elevate certain *types* of action and consequently divide "humanity [into] an elite of active beings and a multitude of passive ones" (*Lost Thread* xxxiii). Rancière, then, views this democratizing turn as consisting in a shift from one type of, or from one way of conceptualizing and composing, action to another and not in a questioning of the value of action as such.

In examining the figure of the nonactor in Ishiguro's work, this essay begins where Rancière stops, offering a glimpse into how the problem of action manifests itself in the contemporary novel. As we have seen, Rancière discovers in the modernist novel the culmination of a process whereby Aristotelian action is replaced by a reconfigured understanding of action. Richard Halpern addresses this question in his recent study *Eclipse of Action* (2017), albeit from a different angle. Here, Halpern identifies an interplay between action [*praxis*] and production [*poiesis*], between doing and making, which, he says, becomes "particularly transformative" with the advent of capitalism and of political economy (12). In promoting the idea that what really "matters" is production (which, unlike action, enables accumulation), capitalism and the discourse of political economy, Halpern argues, form a material and intellectual context where we witness "a relative . . . devaluation of action" (7)—a devaluation that he traces in literature up until the mid-twentieth century. Notably, when Halpern briefly turns to the mid-twentieth century and beyond at the end of his book, he accepts that the model according to which action is "in the process of being eclipsed by production" seems to break down (242), and indeed, the trend I identify here is distinct from this model. Ishiguro's novels present us with a devaluation of action that cannot be adequately captured by the shift from action to production under capitalism. In *The Remains of the Day*, *The Unconsoled*, and *Never Let Me Go*, this is a devaluation of action in its own right; the worthier alternative to action here is not, as is the case in Halpern's study, something other than action (like production and accumulation) or, as is the case in Rancière's studies, a more democratic reconfiguration of action. And neither is it a matter of devaluing action in the external world by focusing too much on an individual's internal world, as is, according to Lukács's criticisms, the case with modernist literature. Instead, the preferable alternative to action in Ishiguro's novels is nonaction.

And yet, far from contradicting Arendt's diagnosis of the status of human action in the twentieth century, the understanding of action that emerges from these novels in fact betrays an affinity with it. A closer look at Arendt's claims serves to indicate how this is so. In *The Human Condition* (1958) she writes that action is the human capacity that has "the closest connection with natality"—a concept that, stripped to its bare bones, expresses the idea that a human birth bespeaks new beginnings, not so much because it introduces a new being to the world but "because the newcomer possesses the capacity of beginning something anew, that is, [the capacity] of acting" (9). Through this association with natality, then, the capacity to act is posited as an inherent quality that enables human beings to bring about something new to the world, effect change, or cause disruption—for better or worse. This is precisely what underlies Arendt's claims about action in *Between Past and Future*: namely, the *unpredictability* of the "better" or the "worse" that defines the consequences of human action. Here Arendt says that no one can ever have "the wisdom of knowing what one does" (*Between Past and Future* 60) because, as she puts it elsewhere, "the results" of human action "can never be reliably predicted" (*Violence* 4). As we saw, Arendt suggests that the inevitably unpredictable consequences of human action become more expansive than ever before with Rutherford's "splitting" of the atom in the early twentieth century—a claim that resonates more loudly at the time Arendt is writing this essay, the 1950s, by which point Rutherford's discovery of the nucleus had been channeled into the development of nuclear weapons. Clearly, then, human action becomes not only the most prominent of all human capacities but also, as Arendt points out, "the most dangerous" (*Between Past and Future* 63). Against this backdrop of human action coming to be seen as extraordinarily risky, we witness a turn toward nonaction. Ishiguro's novels, as we will see in what follows, can be understood as the legacy, and indeed the mutation, of this broader turn in the contemporary novel.

It is just such a concern about the dangers and unpredictable consequences of action that defines much of the narrative in *The Remains of the Day*. As will become apparent by the end of this essay, Ishiguro's hierarchy-conscious novel presents us with a certain demolition of hierarchies—a demolition, however, that does not add up to a process of the sort that Rancière identifies, whereby a shift from "great men" to "ordinary human beings," or an emphasis on the mundane instead of the monumental, can be seen as amounting to a democratization of action. Rather, this is a demolition of hierarchies that ultimately bespeaks a wholescale devaluation of any individual's (be they a "great" or a merely "ordinary" human being) capacity to act because of the expansive risks that any action (be it monumental or merely mundane) entails. Even in scenarios where action is both contemplated and planned, as in *The Unconsoled*, there is a sense in which this is less a plan of action and more a strategy of nonaction; what this plan aims to achieve, it seems, is not change, which would be disruptive and therefore potentially dangerous, but a prevention of the worsening of the problems being faced and, as such, the preservation of the status quo. As for *Never Let Me Go*, the possibility of change is here hardly contemplated. More so than in *The Remains of the Day* and *The Unconsoled*, the central characters in this novel find themselves in a truly dire situation which would otherwise appear to mandate action; indeed, the strongest element of surprise is not that these characters turn out to be clones but that they never even think of acting to escape a system under which their organs are harvested until they die, or "complete."

Even such a brief overview serves to point us toward one of the features shared by Ishiguro's characters in these novels: namely, that they do not pursue their best interests. It is, in this sense, clear that these characters can, to different extents, be seen as complicit in the fact that their circumstances are far from ideal. Addressing the central problem of action in these novels with the sole aim of flagging up the characters' complicity or their various delusions, however, as has been the case in much of the scholarship,[2] ends up leading us to view them as strange, or as outsiders, and puts us in danger of, in Nancy Armstrong's words, either "patronizing" them or losing patience with them (451). Ishiguro, in fact, points out that he is "not sure" that his characters "are really outsiders as much as people say" (Matthews 115); indeed, a reading aimed at exposing their complicity or their delusions would end up bypassing the call for understanding that is at the heart of their narratives. All three novels, after all, confront us with first-person narrators who put us in the place of the *you* that they explicitly or implicitly address, and in so doing, as Armstrong argues via Émile Benveniste and Roberto Esposito, they issue a call for identification: as in a dialogue, the *you* can theoretically change places with—"can imaginatively become"—the *I* (454). The fact, however, that our circumstances differ significantly from the circumstances of a character like *Never Let Me Go*'s Kathy, Armstrong stresses, means that this character's attempt to communicate with us on the basis of an *I-you* relationship makes us all the more aware that the *I* that addresses us keeps "sliding from the first person . . . to a third person" with whom we cannot fully identify (454). As opposed to a complete separation, though, this *sliding* implies a process both of distancing and of affiliation, and this, I want to suggest, enables us to understand as well as to assess critically Ishiguro's characters and their marked aversion to action. In what follows, then, rather than treat this devaluation of action merely as proof of a character's complicity or dismiss it as a peculiarity of sorts, as something "other" that cannot be comprehended, I seek to understand it.

There is, however, a sense in which such a preference for nonaction in the literature of the late twentieth century and beyond is particularly difficult to understand. If, as Lukács has it, modernist literature emphasizes subjective interiority to the extent that the possibility of action in the external, objective world all but disappears from the horizon, this tendency would appear to have been reversed by the end of the century, in the post–Cold War world: a world marked by the entrenchment of neoliberalism and thus by a persistent promotion of the worthiness of individual action in the pursuit of one's interests. In S. M. Amadae's words, "the close of the twentieth century" effectively coincides with the abandonment of the "no harm principle at the root of classical liberalism," the hunt for individual gain "despite others" becoming the very principle that "animates the action of rational actors" (Amadae xvi). In light of this, it appears all the more significant that the protagonists of Ishiguro's novels—novels published in the very era that Amadae is describing here—opt for nonaction even when they would stand to gain more from acting. The apparent strangeness of these characters could, then, be partly attributed to the fact that their behavior is at odds with some of the key principles that define the context within which the novels appear and within which we, their addressees, whose understanding they seek, find ourselves.

This state of being at odds with the present is also explored in various ways within the novels themselves. In *The Remains of the Day* and *Never Let Me Go*, for instance, the employment of the frame narrative brings to the forefront the notion

---

[2]   A notable exception here is Rebecca L. Walkowitz's reading of *The Remains of the Day*, which I address below.

of a past with which, though it is far from ideal, the characters seem more at ease than with the present, while *The Unconsoled* confronts us with a situation in which the narrator's past becomes merged, in strikingly literal ways, with the present of the story he relates—a present that is further complicated by the fact that the story is told in the past tense, the story's present thus also featuring as part of the past. In one way or another, then, the present circumstances of Ishiguro's protagonists remain inextricably bound to their pasts—pasts to which they repeatedly hearken back. Similarly, it is through such hearkening that I attempt here to make sense of these characters. As my references to Arendt already suggest, I seek to examine their aversion to action in relation to a broader twentieth-century intellectual context in which human action comes to be seen as riskier than ever before: a context that speaks to, and helps reveal an underexplored aspect of, our present condition.

One of the most important manifestations of this broader intellectual development outside the realm of literature is game theory, which, from the mid-twentieth century onward, in a world defined by the nuclear threat, was hugely impactful in promoting the principle of the fail-safe system, according to which rational methods of operation should seek to minimize risks. Crucially, the end of the Cold War and the de-escalation of nuclear tensions do not result in the abandonment of game theory; on the contrary, many thinkers identify significant affinities between fundamental game theoretic principles and the neoliberal ideologies that prevail in the post–Cold War world. As we saw with Amadae, what defines the period from the end of the twentieth century onward is the ruthless attempt to maximize individual gain despite others, which she flags up as one of the central elements of orthodox game theory. In Ishiguro's novels, though, we are confronted with a vision that is different from this: far from witnessing characters in such profit-maximizing pursuits, we are introduced to characters whose behaviors are geared toward risk aversion or manifest the spirit of nonaction, even if this contradicts their best interests. It is just such a mindset that they exhibit whenever they are, for example, seen to expand the significance of even the most minimal of actions; when they worry about the "catastrophic possibilit[ies]," as one of them puts it, that such actions could theoretically bring about (*Remains* 16–17); and when they refer to their employment of "strategies" or their devising of "plans" to avert possible risks or unspecified crises. Read as part of an intellectual constellation that includes Arendt's reflections on the status of human action in the twentieth century as well as game theoretic principles of risk aversion, Ishiguro's nonactors serve to carve out an aspect of the post–Cold War era that is different from, though no less pernicious than, that encapsulated in the received neoliberal ideal of the hyperindividualistic, self-serving actor. These character types reveal the persistence, expansion, and transformation of a legacy that posits the unpredictability of human action as particularly dangerous and from which nonaction (even against one's best interests) emerges as a rational imperative.

The Butler Didn't Do It

In *The Remains of the Day*, the protagonist and narrator, Mr. Stevens, introduces himself in the 1950s, when he tells us about his life as a butler at Darlington Hall and gradually reveals that Lord Darlington, whom he had proudly served for many years, was a Nazi sympathizer. Even when Darlington's sympathies become explicit, though, Stevens carries on. When Darlington dismisses two members of staff because they are Jewish, Stevens fails to voice his opposition. As for his personal life—on matters that directly and immediately affect him—Stevens does not act here either. Although he evidently has feelings for the housekeeper, Miss Kenton, he never confesses his love. At center stage in this novel, in short, is a man whose life is defined by nonaction.

Crucially, this attitude does not seem to stem from a disbelief in the potential effectiveness of action. On the contrary, Stevens is time and again seen to magnify the importance of even minor actions. He begins his story, for example, by borrowing the language of the adventure narrative in telling us of an "expedition" that he is about to "undertake" (3), before it becomes clear that what he so meticulously prepares for is nothing more than a six-day holiday in the surrounding area. At one striking point in his narrative Stevens goes as far as to suggest that his polishing of the household silver before an important meeting at Darlington Hall "comprise[d] a contribution to the course of history" (147). As Rebecca Walkowitz says, Stevens ascribes to action an "unimaginable largeness," extending the consequences of seemingly isolated actions both "beyond the individual" and "beyond the local" (218). As will become apparent in the course of my reading, it is this "largeness" that is at the heart of Stevens's aversion to action. Precisely because he believes that even seemingly minor actions can have expansive consequences, whenever he has a choice he opts for nonaction instead.

Stevens's tendency to magnify the importance of action is obvious in the way he structures his narrative—that is, as a list of anecdotes, which allows him to place marginal actions such as his polishing of the household silver alongside central ones, such as Darlington's political decisions. In doing so, of course, Stevens does not simply extend the importance of the former but diminishes that of the latter. In a sense, then, the structure of Stevens's story instantiates something akin to Rancière's "new proportions and disproportions," but the effects here are different from those that Rancière extrapolates. Stevens's narrative has been seen not as indicative of a democratizing impulse (whereby a butler's tasks are elevated and placed alongside a lord's actions) but as an exercise in self-deception. Indeed, the actions whose significance Stevens diminishes—most notably, Darlington's dismissal of his Jewish staff—are actions that, in the present of the narrative, are seen as clearly mistaken, and so Stevens's way of telling his story has been read as an attempt to conceal from himself the complicity of his own nonaction in these matters (Cooper). The fact, however, that Stevens appears to engage in such an attempt only retrospectively suggests that he does not immediately see his nonaction as problematic, and so the question of why he does not act in the first place resurfaces.

Ishiguro seems to offer a hint as to what the answer might be in his recent Nobel lecture, where he says that *The Remains of the Day* is about a character who "has lived his life by the wrong values" (*My Twentieth Century* 19). In light of this, it would appear that it is neither ignorance nor lack of courage that prompts Stevens's nonaction but something deeper and broader: a set of values. Stevens's definition of the "great butler" is especially revealing in this respect; the aspiration to be a great butler, after all, is what directs his existence, and so his idea of what this consists of offers a glimpse into what he really values:

> It is sometimes said that butlers only truly exist in England. . . . I tend to believe this is true. Continentals are unable to be butlers because they are as a breed incapable of the emotional restraint which only the English race is capable of. Continentals—and by and large the Celts, as you will no doubt agree—are as a rule unable to control themselves in moments of strong emotion . . . and it is for this reason that when you think of a great butler, he is bound, almost by definition, to be an Englishman. (Remains 44)

This passage shows just how much Stevens values consistency and "dependable" service (7); great butlers, he says, guarantee stability by behaving in the same way in every situation. This is why he looks down on the Continentals and the Celts, who, in his evidently essentialist/racist view, are prone to being emotional, and, as such, are liable to respond differently under different circumstances. Since emotions arise when one finds oneself in a situation that somehow deviates from the norm, experiencing emotions means registering often subtle differences that can affect one's behavior, thus risking a disruption of stability. It is for this reason that emotional proclivity is anathema to Stevens, as are any other practices that inject a given situation with unpredictability.

Banter is one such practice that is of particular concern to Stevens. As he confesses, his suspicion that his new employer expects him to engage in banter fills him with anxiety: "How would one know for sure that at any given moment a response of the bantering sort is expected?" (16). Since opportunities for banter arise unexpectedly, allowing no time for preparing what one might say, they give rise to what Stevens describes—without irony—as "catastrophic possibilit[ies]" (16–17). True to his conviction that a great butler ought to strive for consistency, then, Stevens devises a strategy that will enable him to banter in the least unpredictable way: whenever an "odd moment" arises, he tells us, he looks at his "immediate surroundings" and formulates three possible bantering comments (139). And, given that Stevens's surroundings remain unchanged—he has not left Darlington Hall for many years—this strategy comes down to building an archive of safe responses that he can retrieve whenever needed. For Stevens, it seems, to engage in banter spontaneously rather than by sticking to a fail-safe strategy is to be like those individuals who cannot "control themselves"—individuals whose actions are unpredictable and who, therefore, cannot be great butlers (44).

If, however, as both Stevens and Arendt have it, action bespeaks the possibility of change and has potentially expansive consequences, then all actions entail the unpredictable; indeed, for Arendt, this is so to the extent that "only the total abolition of action can ever hope to cope with unpredictability" (Between Past and Future 60). And if unpredictability is inextricable from human action, then Stevens's clear attempt to oust even the smallest possibility of the unpredictable effectively constitutes an attempt to banish action from the realm of the butler. We might, then, say that the long-standing cliché that "the butler did it" is here revised through a butler who cannot be (rightly or wrongly) accused of doing "it," but a butler who is fundamentally *averse* to doing or acting and who opts instead for mechanical-like models of behavior that seek to do away with unpredictability. Stevens's nonaction, in short, does not stem from a failure to recognize how he might stand to gain from acting; his focus, in other words, is not on the potential gains of action but on its potentially unwelcome consequences, and so the capacity to act and bring about change is, for him, best left unactualized. The continuity and stability ensured by nonaction are his preferable alternatives.

The Ideal of Nonaction

In his reading of Stevens, Kwame Anthony Appiah argues that this illiberal character unwittingly promotes liberal principles in that he is asking to be understood as an individual, on the basis of his own values: the values that he has chosen for himself and by which he has lived his life (313–16). Stevens's values, though, are not as individual or idiosyncratic as Appiah seems to be suggesting; rather, his concern with stability, his aversion to the unpredictable, and his advocacy of emotionless, mechanical-like, and risk-free behaviors are all in alignment with a wider proclivity for models of operation that seek to marginalize human action. Such a proclivity is seen in the work of leading game theorists, which began rising to prominence around the time when Stevens tells his story, in the 1950s, and which, by the time *The Remains of the Day* was published, had become hugely influential. In *Theory of Games and Economic Behavior* (1944), the foundational text of game theory, John von Neumann and Oskar Morgenstern suggest that their "game" scenarios can evaluate in advance all the possible outcomes in a given situation and can point out the most rational behavior in each case—a behavior that typically seeks to avert risks. Their aim, they say, is to provide "a complete set of rules of behavior in all conceivable situations" (33). The *raison d'être* of their theory, in this sense, is ultimately to oust unpredictability and, in so doing, in effect to minimize or eliminate human action as defined by Arendt. Indeed, Arendt herself writes that the "trouble" with game theoretic strategies is that, far from enhancing proper, thoughtful decision making on the subject's part, they in fact *preclude* it (*Violence* 6): they dictate behaviors "so thoroughly" that the player "never" really has to "make a decision" (Poundstone 48). In this sense, the human subject-as-agential-actor is essentially removed from the picture; the fallibility of such actors and the dangers entailed in any actions they might have otherwise carried out are replaced by behaviors whose outcomes are "known" and evaluated in advance—by, as such, behaviors that Arendt would regard as amounting to nonaction.[3]

---

3   As Arendt goes on to say, game theory's devaluation of action is manifested not only in its replacement of human action with rigid models of operation that preclude thinking but also in its disregard for the actual in favor of the potential. "The logical flaw in [game theory's] constructions of future events," she writes, is that "what first appears as a hypothesis . . . turns immediately, usually after a few paragraphs, into a 'fact,' which then gives birth to a whole string of non-facts, with the result that the speculative character of the whole enterprise is forgotten" (*Violence* 6–7).

Player A / Player B	B: acts collaboratively	B: acts individualistically
A: acts collaboratively	**0 years** / 0 years	**−4 years** / −2 years
A: acts individualistically	**−2 years** / −4 years	**−2 years** / −2 years

Figure 1. The Prisoner's Dilemma. The matrix shows losses depending on whether the prisoners act collaboratively (do not betray each other) or individualistically (betray each other).

Though von Neumann proved his first game theoretic principle in a 1928 paper ("Theorie"), and *Theory of Games and Economic Behavior* was published in 1944, it was in the context of the nuclear threat, when anxieties about what Arendt describes as the magnified dangers of human action were amplified, that game theory became influential by capturing the "spirit" of the times and addressing such anxieties through its calculated, risk-averse models of operation. As Amadae observes, after the publication of game theory pioneer Thomas Schelling's paper "The Reciprocal Fear of Surprise Attack" (1958), "defense analysts routinely viewed the nuclear arms race as a Prisoner's Dilemma"; indeed, Amadae goes as far as to suggest that this debate rendered game theory so influential that its strategies came to shape "all purposive [behavior]," both "during and beyond the Cold War era" (79, 20). As we saw, the key characteristic of this "beyond"—that is, the post–Cold War, neoliberal era—for Amadae is the glorification of the individualistic pursuit of one's interests despite others; and the Prisoner's Dilemma, schematized in figure 1, serves to demonstrate how game theory's preemptive logic promotes such pursuits.[4]

The Prisoner's Dilemma matrix outlines the four possible outcomes emerging from a situation in which two people are being questioned separately about a joint law violation. As the table of payoffs shows, the ideal outcome would be to not admit to the violation (upper left corner): if each person trusts their partner to do the same, then the police will not obtain the confession needed to press charges, and so neither of the two will lose anything. Though ideal, this option entails the danger of being betrayed by one's partner, who, to avoid risking a full sentence, might decide to confess (upper left and lower right corners). From this perspective, pursuit of the ideal outcome is deemed irrational, just as, in the question of nuclear proliferation that rendered The Prisoner's Dilemma so influential, the mutually beneficial outcome of bilateral disarmament is ruled out because the emphasis is on avoiding the risk of unilateral defection. In short, The Prisoner's Dilemma in its different guises dictates that to behave rationally is to behave individualistically

---

[4]   Figure 1 is derived from the first matrix appearing in a note by A. W. Tucker—the very note that ultimately led to this scenario's becoming known as The Prisoner's Dilemma.

Stevens Kenton	Kenton acts	Kenton does not act
Stevens acts	+1 +1	−2 −2
Stevens does not act	−2 −2	−0 −0

Figure 2.   The Stevens-Kenton Dilemma. The matrix indicates potential gains and losses for each "player" depending on whether they act/confess their feelings or they do not.

(lower right corner). Although doing so means "bring[ing] about a collectively self-defeating outcome" (Heap and Varoufakis 37–38), the biggest risk (of receiving a full sentence) is at least averted.

The stakes are of course much higher in the case of risks like long prison sentences or indeed a nuclear war compared to the apparently "catastrophic possibilit[ies]" that Stevens tries to avert in *The Remains of the Day*. While the two are clearly not equivalent, and the novel is evidently not a meditation on the implications of game theory, the logic of calculated risk aversion is very much detectable in Stevens's behavior too. He does, after all, repeatedly tell us of his methods for averting various risks throughout: when, for instance, he endeavors to avoid a potentially disruptive discussion about a misplaced ornament (60–61); or when he strives to think of ways of minimizing the embarrassment before an awkward conversation with Mr. Cardinal (92–94); or when he tries to calculate where to stand during a special occasion so as to allow the guests enough privacy while being sufficiently present to serve them (75–76). On all such occasions Stevens seeks to identify all potential risks in advance, takes us through his different options, weighs their merits against their drawbacks, and arrives at "the best strategy" in each case (60). Most importantly, though, the logic of risk aversion is discernible in Stevens's approach to what matters to him more than any of the above-mentioned incidents: his relationship with Miss Kenton. Indeed, we can go as far as to say that what we might think of as the Stevens-Kenton Dilemma (fig. 2) presents us with a scenario that is structurally comparable to the Prisoner's Dilemma.

This "dilemma" concerns the question of why neither Stevens nor Kenton acts on the feelings they evidently have for each other. Though the option of acting enables the ideal outcome in which Stevens and Kenton end up happy together (upper left corner), it also entails risks. Stevens might act, for instance, but Kenton might not reciprocate, and vice versa; in this case, the former would end up being unhappy while the latter would have to deal with the awkwardness of it all (upper right and lower left corners). Avoiding these risks means ruling out the route to the only mutually beneficial outcome in favor of a suboptimal one: if neither Stevens nor Kenton acts on their feelings, then neither gains anything, but at least neither risks losing, either (lower right corner).

Stevens's and Kenton's reluctance to act points to an outlook such as that emerging from figure 1, which places risk avoidance at the heart of rational behavior. This affinity suggests that Stevens's preoccupation with avoiding what he imagines to be "catastrophic possibilit[ies]," combined with his tendency to magnify the importance of even the most minor actions, can be read as part of a broader intellectual constellation in which human action features as particularly dangerous and in which game theoretic models of behavior emerge as the antidote—these being models that, according to Arendt, preclude proper decision making and, as such, amount to models of nonaction. At the same time, we can see that the Stevens-Kenton dilemma presents us with a situation in which this legacy of nonaction assumes both more literal and more expansive dimensions. Indeed, at no point does Stevens appear to debate whether to act on his feelings for Kenton; his nonaction features less as something he properly decides on and more as something of a quasi-mechanical default. The logic of risk aversion here, moreover, emerges in the realm of romantic love—a realm that serves to bring to the forefront the fact that Stevens cannot be said, in any meaningful sense, to be pursuing his best interests.

Telling in this regard are Ishiguro's thoughts on a new novel in which, as he puts it, the characters would be "the casualties" of a "world-view" that encourages them to follow, rather than restrain, their various desires and that therefore ends up leaving them with the feeling that they are always "missing out" on something (Shaffer 14). Although Ishiguro has yet to publish such a novel, one populated with characters who pursue action on all fronts, his observation inevitably redirects attention to his existing, nonacting characters. If, as his comment suggests, the protagonists of his still-to-come novel would essentially conform to the neoliberal vision of subjects-as-individual-actors who relentlessly pursue their interests and urges, then *The Remains of the Day* presents us with a different—and differently damaging—aspect of the contemporary moment. Here, action is seen as always potentially dangerous—and as we have seen, this is so not in the realm of military strategies or prison sentencing calculations but in the realm of the private and of romantic love—while nonaction emerges as the preferable alternative, even when this is against one's best interests. The novel, then, serves to alert us to an overlooked aspect of the calculating, individualistic behaviors that, as Amadae has it, become established as the rational modus operandi in the post–Cold War, neoliberal era (xvi). Through Stevens and his preoccupation with risk aversion we can see how rather than being prompted unendingly to pursue self-serving action, one might be prompted to slip into the sphere of nonaction instead.

Averting the Crisis; or, Carrying On

A logic at the heart of which is risk aversion and the spirit of nonaction is also detectable in *The Unconsoled*, which transports us to an unnamed European city that is "close to crisis" (99). To prevent the eruption of this crisis, a plan—or "schedule"—outlining the course of action to be taken is produced, and Mr. Ryder, a famous pianist, is tasked with carrying it out. It soon transpires, though, that Ryder is not aware of the exact contents of this schedule; it is as if he has been put into the impossible position of an actor who is to perform in accordance with a script to which he does not have access. Ryder, then, does not understand his role properly, but this is not to say that he is like those "lesser butlers" who, as Stevens puts it in *The Remains of the Day*, fail to "inhabit" their role "to the utmost" (43). For such individuals, Stevens says, the execution of their duties is "like playing some pantomime role" or like putting up a "façade" underneath which there is an "actor" (ibid.)—an agential subject who remains distinct from the role that is being performed. Unlike these "lesser butlers," Ryder cannot be described as an agential actor—and neither can anyone else in this narrative. Agency and action are split, with the figure of the agent, on one hand, being embodied in the absent yet somehow all-pervading schedule or "script" that dictates Ryder's performance, and the figure of the actor, on the other, being embodied in the character of Ryder himself.

The fact that the narrative is structured either around episodes in which Ryder becomes aware of things that he is expected to do or around episodes in which he is doing things that he does not seem to know he is doing until he catches himself in their midst indicates that he operates in a nonagential and mechanical-like fashion. On the other hand, the fact that these episodes culminate in moments of realization suggests that Ryder's behavior is unlike the seamlessly mechanical mode of operation that Stevens strives for in *The Remains of the Day*. The fact that Ryder keeps catching himself doing things means that the mechanical quality of his behavior is momentarily interrupted. Much scholarship on the novel concentrates on Ryder's evident memory failures and trauma-induced emotional repression as a way of explaining these moments of sudden awareness (Quarrie 143), but what is more striking is that even such instances of lucidity fail to instigate agential action. This failure is rendered all the more conspicuous by the peculiar mode of narration employed in the novel, which suggests that Ryder is hovering between two oppositional states of being: he features as a first-person narrator who, on one hand, is largely unaware of what is going on with and around him while on the other exhibiting signs of remarkable omniscience. He is, for example, time and again seen to access the personal experiences and opinions of other characters, in this way revealing an extraordinary capacity that puts him in a position to behave like an incredibly informed agential actor, but that, instead, he channels to the end of nonaction. When, for instance, he accesses an apparently private conversation and learns that a journalist—who describes him, among other things, as "a difficult shit" (166)—plans to trick him into getting photographed in front of a controversial monument, he goes along with this plan without so much as hesitating.

Ryder's modus operandi, in short, seems to consist not in acting but in just carrying on. As he says to Boris at one point, "I have to keep going on these trips" because "you can never tell when it's going to come along. I mean the very . . . important trip, the one that's very important, not just for me but for everyone, everyone in the whole world" (239). As far as Ryder is concerned, change will come about when it comes about; he does not consider whether direct agential action would be necessary to bring it forth. This, indeed, is a narrative in which action is throughout synonymized with nonaction. The inhabitants' strategy for dealing with the crisis, for instance, is meant to culminate with a final event in the form of a concert, but this ends up being a nonevent in which Ryder does not perform his much-anticipated piece—the very piece we assume is expected somehow to change things. And yet the reaction to this outcome is not one of intense disappointment, and it does not indicate frustrated expectations either; the townspeople have, after all, stuck to the same plan for some time, periodically replacing one musician with another instead of trying a different tactic, as though meaningful change is not really what they are after. Their underlying conviction, it seems, is that the averting of crises is paradoxically achieved not through change but through maintaining the status quo.

This sense of a paradox emerges on a formal level, too, through the lack of distinction between the past that Ryder's narrative relates and the present in which the relating occurs. As Matthew Mead observes, the present *as* present is effectively absent from Ryder's narrative, the present tense appearing only in "remembered speech" (507). The very fact, of course, that this present (now past) *is* remembered necessarily implies the passage of time, but this is a passage that suggests stasis rather than movement or progression from the past. This paradoxically static movement, moreover, assumes spatial dimensions throughout the novel, whenever Ryder travels, often for miles, from one building in the city to another only to find out that the buildings he enters upon his arrival are somehow adjacent to, or contained within, the buildings that he has left behind, as though no distance has been covered despite all the traveling. Even in the final scene, when Ryder sets off for a new journey, his train in fact goes around the city in an endless loop. Just as Ryder is here on the move but goes nowhere, and just as the narrative suggests that time passes but in a passage that signals an entrapment in the past, so too the townspeople's strategy for dealing with the crisis effectively amounts to the continuation of the status quo, in what appears to be a plan of action that in fact amounts to nonaction.

This strategy is underpinned by a rationale akin to that promoted by Albert Wohlstetter in response to a different crisis: that concerning the "delicate balance of terror." Indeed, the much-talked-about crisis in *The Unconsoled* remains abstract throughout, in this way shifting the attention away from the specific content of the crisis to something that clearly matters more—namely, the logic with which it is approached. Just as Wohlstetter argues that the key to deterrence of a nuclear war lies in a "sustained effort" to *maintain* (rather than abolish) the "balance of terror" (8), so too the sustained efforts of the townspeople in the novel are directed not at change, which would be disruptive, but at the preservation of the status quo. So it is that the crisis always remains imminent but the risk of full eruption does not materialize—and, notably, this is so not just in the novel's peculiar city but also around the world. As Ryder says, "The fact is, people need me. I arrive in a place and more often than not find terrible problems. Deep-seated, seemingly intractable problems, and people are so grateful that I have come" (37). Ryder has apparently been ascribed, both locally and globally, the role of a "great man" capable of performing "great deeds," but the achievement of this mock-Aristotelian figure, it seems, is ultimately to keep the situation at a standstill; the "greatness" of Ryder's actions consists precisely in that they amount to nonactions.

Crucially, though, the affinity between the seemingly global strategy employed in *The Unconsoled* and Wohlstetter's own global crisis-aversion strategy does not suggest that the novel simply points toward the persistence of a logic such as that underpinning the latter: a logic according to which the preservation of stability, however "delicate" this may be, is preferable to the dangers of action and its promise of change. Rather, the novel also hints at the mutation of this legacy of nonaction. As we saw, Arendt objects to the game theoretic strategies that rise to prominence from the mid-twentieth century onward because they preclude proper decision making and in so doing effectively paint the human subject-as-agential-actor out of the picture. What *The Unconsoled* presents us with, by contrast, is the reemergence of this previously vanishing subject. As though in conformity with the neoliberal glorification of the individual as an agential subject capable of, and responsible for, bringing about prosperity, at center stage in Ishiguro's novel is a character who features as a glorified savior figure—a great actor who is believed to be capable of singlehandedly dealing with the widespread crisis that plagues the city. At the same time, though, this ideal of the capable individual actor is severely compromised by the fact that Ryder's behavior is, as we have seen, largely deter-mined by a "script" to which he does not have access but which he is nevertheless compelled to follow in a mechanical-like, nonagential fashion. *The Unconsoled* thus uncovers a paradox in post–Cold War ways of thinking subjectivity. On one hand, the subject as the site of agential action seems to have once again reared its head through the neoliberal glorification of the individual. On the other hand, we remain within the nexus of a predetermined, algorithmic pattern of nonaction that gained prominence during the Cold War and that has exploded in the era of the digital and of computer networks—an era in which, as Alexander R. Galloway and Eugene Thacker put it, to be an individual is to exist "inseparably from a set of [determined] possibilities and parameters," always functioning "within a topology of control" (40). In centralizing a character who occupies the paradoxical role of the nonacting actor, *The Unconsoled* captures and brings to the fore this fundamental paradox that defines our own era, imbuing the figure of the nonactor with a thoroughly con-temporary significance.

The Impossibility of Action

In *Never Let Me Go* we are introduced to yet another world in which the status quo is maintained, this time in a narrative in which the future is either already the past at the time the story is being told or appears to be always already mapped out—a narrative, then, in which action as a route to change seems to have been "impossibilized." Here, Kathy H. gradually reveals that she is a cloned woman whose organs will be "donated" to noncloned individuals one by one until she "completes," but she nevertheless keeps calm and goes along with this. Unlike Ryder, though, who betrays a belief that change could come about—when the "very important trip" comes along—Kathy tells a story in which the possibility of change is virtually nonexistent.

The episode that gives the novel its title, in which Kathy shares her memory of dancing, with a pillow in her arms, to her favorite song—"Baby, baby, never let me go . . ."—suggests as much (70). Indeed, it contradicts those who, in addressing the key question of Kathy's nonaction, have either accused her of being complicit (Cooper 106–17), or excused her for being the victim of a mechanism that keeps her compliant by leading her to "misapprehend social injustice as privilege" (Currie 161). In both cases, the implication is that Kathy *could* have acted had she not been complicit, or "duped." The dancing scene, though, serves to undermine any such suggestion. Like the imagined woman in the song, Kathy has been given to understand that she cannot have babies but in misinterpreting the song's refrain, she reluctantly allows herself to imagine that this could potentially be proved wrong (70). The outcome of this anticipation, of course, is by this time already known; the future that Kathy "remembers envisaging" in this narrative of recollected or retrospective anticipation, as Mark Currie notes, is now the past (Currie 155). Crucially, Kathy says that she had realized "even at the time" that her interpretation of the refrain "didn't fit with the rest of the lyrics," and by extension, that any anticipations for an alternative future that this interpretation gave rise to would not become reality (*Never Let Me Go* 70). The importance of Kathy's retrospection, then, lies in something more than merely knowing what "did and did not" happen in the end (Currie 155); Kathy also knows what *could* or *could not have* happened. As a cloned being produced solely to make organ donations, her biological makeup does not include the reproductive function, and so any action that she might have taken could not have changed this. We are once again confronted with a turn toward nonaction that offers a different vision to the neoliberal orthodoxy of the individual as a credible agent of change. While we might will Kathy to act, this is a situation in which the possibility of alternatives—even in the form of hypothetical "could haves"—is foreclosed.

This is consolidated and accentuated at the end of the novel, when Kathy and Tommy learn that Hailsham, the school they attended, was in fact an experiment designed to prove that cloned beings have "souls" and that the harvesting of their organs should stop (255). As Miss Emily reveals, though, people were not willing to go "back to the dark days" of "their own children, their spouses, their parents . . . [dying] from cancer," from "motor neurone disease," from "heart disease" (257–58). Hailsham fails; and what makes this failure all the more resounding is that it is not confined to the past. It is not just that Hailsham is testimony to the fact that an alternative "could have" for Kathy and the other clones has already been attempted and rejected but that this rejection dooms to failure any alternative imaginable "could be" for the next generation of clones also. Project Hailsham, in other words, has shown that people view the benefits of the system as outweighing its "uncomfortable" costs and that they see no reason to "reverse" the process (257).

The system does appear to secure a "net gain." With each clone making an average of three organ donations, the sacrifice of one individual enables the prolonged life of approximately three others. Clearly, however, this net gain does not point to "Adam Smith scenarios" such as those that Halpern explores in *Eclipse of Action*. While Smith's liberal capitalist system allegedly benefits (even if unevenly) the entirety of a given population, this is a situation where the gains of noncloned individuals explicitly and directly translate as the cloned individuals' losses. What we have here is a clear conflict-of-interest scenario that exhibits key affinities with a game theoretic brand of rationality; this type of calculation of payoffs is, indeed, in line with the infamous logic that military strategist and game theorist Herman Kahn outlines in *On Thermonuclear War* (1960). Here, Kahn departs from the key

Prisoner's Dilemma principle of opting for a mutually suboptimal outcome that averts risks. Instead, he notoriously argues for the launch of a nuclear attack on the USSR despite the "awful" losses that the United States would suffer as a result of the ensuing retaliation; there are, he claims by way of defending this position, "degrees of awfulness" (say, tens of millions of dead rather than hundreds of millions) that are manageable (19–20). In advancing this argument, Kahn shifts the emphasis away from the interests of the individual subject in favor of an ultrarational system within which overall benefits are seen as outweighing overall costs.

Such a logic is traceable in *Never Let Me Go*. Just as causing the death of a sizeable part of the population is, for Kahn, an acceptable cost for a victory that would be enjoyed by others, so for the people referred to by Miss Emily, the procedural murder of the clones through the harvesting of their organs is the "less awful" option. While partially set in the Cold War period, then, *Never Let Me Go* enables us to witness this brutal logic as it operates not in the context of military strategizing but in the workings of an otherwise peaceful society. In this context, the novel explores a situation in which the individual's interests are trampled by a system based on ultrarational calculations, and in so doing it presents us with a vision that helps illuminate the condition of the human subject in our own era—an era that claims to place the individual center stage. In *Never Let Me Go*, the individual is literally expendable and left without the capacity to act and effect structural change, just as, in societies based on a mixture of unfettered market forces and algorithmic control, individuals are seemingly reduced to numbers or pieces of data and stripped of individual and collective agency.[5] It is this dramatization of individuals in the throes of a brutal but ultrarational system that makes *Never Let Me Go* resonate at once with the contemporary world and its foundations.

Change here is not only undesirable for those who benefit from the system but unimaginable for those who do not. As the rumor about the "deferrals" suggests, the only imaginable alternative for the clones is not one of a real escape but merely one of temporary relief, and this, as it turns out, is only a myth. Most importantly, however, even were Kathy (either as an individual or as part of a group) to act—say, to escape—the outcome of the action could not be envisaged as a change in the system itself. As the failure of Project Hailsham suggests, the novel dramatizes a conflict-of-interest situation in which, as in a game theoretic scenario, the opposing "player"—the noncloned population—would respond in such a way as to minimize its losses: namely, by producing more clones for organ harvesting. In this sense, Kathy's narrative is not just a narrative of *recollected* or *retrospective anticipation*, whereby past alternatives (or "could haves") have been closed off, but also, as Currie suggests, a narrative of *anticipated retrospection* (161) whereby a future (or a "could be") in the narrative present can be looked at *as if* in retrospect, *as though* it has occurred. Although Currie argues that this renders visible a paradox that is latent in "any novel"—"the paradox of a future which already exists" by virtue of the novel having already been written (162)—*Never Let Me Go* is a novel of

---

[5]   For a similar point on the link between market forces, algorithmic control, and a lack of agency or "the power to act," see Paul Mason, *Clear Bright Future: A Radical Defence of the Human Being* (xii, 186–89).

anticipated retrospection in another sense too: namely, in that it forecloses speculation not just on what could happen differently in the narrative future that has already been written but on possible alternatives in an entirely hypothetical future. As we saw, in the speculative event of future action whereby Kathy and the other clones escape, the plausible outcome would be the reestablishment of the same system via the production of more clones to replace the escapees. As in a game theoretic universe, then, we are here able to extrapolate, and outline in advance, the outcomes of such alternative scenarios as though they have already occurred. Although nonaction is clearly against Kathy's best interests as an individual, the capacity to act and bring forth structural change is radically devalued—both in the past and present and in a hypothetical future. This is a narrative in which the only "rational" option seems to be to keep calm and carry on: the option, that is, of nonaction.

"The Likes of You and Me"

Though *The Remains of the Day*, *The Unconsoled*, and *Never Let Me Go* all centralize nonaction, each also features instances in which action surfaces—not as a capacity to which everybody can lay claim but as one that only a certain category of people ought to exercise. In *The Unconsoled*, for instance, it is only characters like Ryder—and not the townspeople—who are seen as capable of occupying the role of the actor (however paradoxical this role turns out to be). This divide between actors and nonactors is also present, and articulated as such, in *The Remains of the Day*; addressing a "you" whom he presumes to be a butler too, Stevens here says that "the great affairs of the nation" are "beyond the understanding of those such as you and me" and should therefore be left to "those great gentlemen at the hub of this world" who can be trusted to carry out the actions that matter (209, 257). Rather than reviving the Aristotelian model of the "great men" of action, however, this divide serves further to undermine the worthiness of the capacity to act as such. This is perhaps most obvious in *Never Let Me Go*, where Miss Emily and Madame not only fail to achieve change but, as we have seen, condemn to failure future acts of resistance in advance, effectively making redundant the very figure of the actor. As for *The Remains of the Day*, gentlemen like Darlington, who can supposedly be trusted to perform the right actions, in fact get it very wrong.

Significant in this regard is Stevens's argument that Darlington could not have known that his actions would, "with the passage of time," "tur[n] out" to be "misguided" (211). All actions, Stevens implies, can have unpredictable consequences outside the control of the actors who perform them, and so he refrains not only from condemning Darlington but also from praising Reginald Cardinal, who, in opposing Darlington, finds himself on the right side of history. The implication, in other words, is that not even those who are "at the hub of this world" can grasp the ramifications of their actions—an implication that contradicts Stevens's own assertion that "the great gentlemen" know better than "the likes of you and me" (257, 211). This, however, is not to be mistaken for a democratic demolition of hierarchies such as those identified by Rancière. What emerges from Stevens's analysis is not the idea that ordinary people are as well-placed to perform the right actions as the aristocracy but rather that nobody is fit to do so.

It is precisely this point that Mr. Lewis's crucial toast, "To professionalism," hammers home (107). Lewis, the American delegate at one of Darlington's dinner parties, describes the host and his guests as "gentlemen amateurs" who are "well-meaning" but have "no idea what sort of place the world is becoming" (106). While, in one of the novel's most poignant scenes, these gentlemen discredit the notion of democratic action by "proving" that ordinary people like Stevens are unfit to participate in decisions of global economic and military significance, Lewis says that they themselves are not fit for such a task either. "The days when you could act out of your noble instincts," he tells them, "are over," and he asks them to stop meddling "in matters they don't understand" (107). If at the heart of the matter is the ability to "understand"—which in this instance refers to the ability to determine accurately the best course of action in a given situation—then Lewis is anticipating one of his country's most influential contributions to world affairs in the twentieth century. "You here in Europe need professionals to run your affairs," he asserts (107), and indeed it is the strategies of just such intellectual professionals—the game theorists—that the US government came to fund, employ, and promote in the following decades, effectively enabling them to run world affairs. In looking ahead to the "sort of place the world is becoming," Lewis anticipates the technocratic tendencies that these professionals helped establish during the Cold War—tendencies that, by the time *The Remains of the Day* was published, were not confined to nuclear strategies and foreign affairs but were extended to the realm of economics and to politics at large.[6] This episode thus provides a kind of concretization of the intellectual legacy of nonaction, which filters down into the era of neoliberalism: the system of technocracy par excellence.[7] In the technocratic societies that Lewis heralds, acting on one's emotions, "noble instincts," or indeed principles is deemed to be inappropriate and is replaced by risk-minimizing strategies devised by experts. Agential action, in this sense, is radically devalued—and professionally so—regardless of whether the agent is a "great gentleman" or one of Stevens's "likes."

Conclusion: The Irrational Rationality of Nonaction

In this reading of Ishiguro I have suggested that the key issue of nonaction in his work can be seen as part of a broader turn against action, which, in much of the literary imagination of the mid-twentieth century onward, manifests itself through the centralization of the figure of the nonactor. In Ishiguro's work, this figure serves to offer a glimpse into the ways in which the question of action illuminates the condition of the individual in the contemporary world. This preoccupation with the capacity to act, as we have seen, goes beyond the literary realm, pointing to a wider intellectual constellation in which nonaction features as a rational imperative. In forming part of such a constellation, the mechanical-like, nonagential, risk-averse, and change-thwarting behaviors of Ishiguro's protagonists, as I have sought to

[6]   Amadae's *Prisoners of Reason* (2015) constitutes a full-length study on this.

[7]   As David Harvey points out, "Neoliberals . . . tend to favour governance by experts and elites" (66). On this point see also Arthur MacEwan, 172.

demonstrate, point to a legacy of nonaction that becomes consolidated with the rise of game theory in the mid-twentieth century and that persists, in different guises, in our own era. In fact, the complex temporalities that define these novels flag up the importance of the past, prompting us to look back to it in our effort to understand these apparently peculiar characters. Ryder's perpetually past present in *The Unconsoled* (whereby the present tense in his narrative is consigned to the past), as well as his perpetually present past (whereby his past literally appears within his present), constitutes an example of this. As for *Never Let Me Go*, while the device of the frame narrative does distinguish the present from the past, it does so without giving a sense of a clean break from it. Rather, as both a narrative of anticipated retrospection and a narrative of retrospective anticipation, this novel poignantly suggests that any visions Kathy may have, or may have had, of an open future—and therefore a future that can potentially turn out to be different from the one that has already been mapped out in the past—are illusory. Complex temporalities are also at work in *The Remains of the Day*, where Stevens remembers, in the present of his narrative, incidents like Lewis's toast to professionalism, which anticipates a technocratic Cold War future that is already materializing when Stevens tells his story in the 1950s and that is firmly established, in a much more widespread mutation, by the time the novel is published. In amalgamating the past with the present, such temporalities support the tracing of affinities between these post–Cold War narratives and wider tendencies that begin rising to prominence from the mid-twentieth century. In so doing, they prevent us from treating the behaviors of Ishiguro's protagonists as mere peculiarities or idiosyncrasies, enabling us instead to understand them as mutations of a logic that, as we saw with Arendt, posits human action as dangerously unpredictable and that, as the rise of game theory shows, promotes models of behavior that amount to nonaction. In this way, Ishiguro's nonactors serve to foreground aspects of the contemporary condition of the subject that are often obscured by the orthodoxy of the individual as an agent of action and change.

It is, after all, toward the existence of a broader condition or wider system of values that Ishiguro's narrators point by explicitly or implicitly addressing themselves to individuals whom they assume to be their "likes." Such an assumption serves partly to "de-strange" or "de-other" these characters by implying that their outlook, including their attitudes toward action, is aligned with values that are shared by others: at the very least, by the "you" that they address. That the role of this "you" comes to be occupied by us of course complicates matters, since we are unlikely to be their "likes": butlers, clones, or famous musicians/saviors. And yet, had we not failed to "inhabit," as Stevens might say, the role of the "you" that they ascribe to us, full identification would still have been thwarted. Ishiguro's narrators are often at pains to distinguish themselves from the communities with which they otherwise identify. Like many other clones, for instance, Kathy is a "carer," but she is keen to say from the beginning that she has reason to believe that she is an exceptionally good one. Similarly, Ryder—who is aware that his role as a musician/savior has also been ascribed to others—lets it be known that his own services (unlike, say, Brodsky's) are required not just in the novel's city but around the world too. In the same vein, while Stevens sees himself as part of a community of butlers, he repeatedly seeks to establish that he is not of the "lesser" variety. Therefore, when these characters assume that we, their addressees, are to be included among their "likes," this inclusion is also an exclusion that keeps us at a distance from them. Thus the process of *de*-othering that characterizes all three of these novels is complemented by a simultaneous process of *re*-othering. Indeed, we are forced to understand Kathy's nonaction on the grounds that the system under which she operates rules out the possibility of its abolition and, in doing so, diminishes the worthiness of individual action as means to achieving lasting change. But if Kathy's attitude of keeping calm and carrying on is, in this sense, rational, its irrational element does not escape us either: though she could not have abolished the system in its entirety, she could have at least pursued her own best interests by attempting to escape with Tommy. Likewise, although we can recognize the rationality of risk aversion in Stevens's failure to act on his feelings for Miss Kenton, we are nevertheless distanced enough from him to discern that his theoretically rational behavior is in practice an irrational and avoidable prohibition on, as Ishiguro puts it, "be[ing] loved by . . . the one woman he cares for" (*My Twentieth Century* 19). Similarly, the townspeople's strange strategy in *The Unconsoled* is on one hand "de-stranged" by the fact that it ultimately meets its objective of preventing a catastrophic eruption of "the crisis"; but if this success renders the strategy rational, at its core lies an irrationality that serves to "re-strange" it. Success here amounts not to resolving the crisis but to keeping the situation at a standstill by preserving the possibility of the very outcome whose actualization it aims to prevent.

It is this oscillation between *de*-othering or *de*-stranging and *re*-othering or *re*-stranging that enables us to engage properly with Ishiguro's nonactors, prompting us both to understand and to assess critically their attitudes. In being distanced from them, we are in a position from which we can recognize that the values by which they have lived their lives—to echo Ishiguro's Nobel lecture—are the wrong ones. On the other hand, in being prevented from treating them as radically "other" and in viewing the figure of the nonactor as part of a wider intellectual legacy that evidently continues in different mutations and inflections in our own era, we are left to wonder whether in fact we have more in common with them than we might like to think.

*   *   *

MARIA CHRISTOU is a Presidential Fellow in Modern and Contemporary Literature at the University of Manchester, UK. Her first book is titled *Eating Otherwise: The Philosophy of Food in Twentieth-Century Literature* (2017). She is currently researching a second monograph on what she terms "the turn to the potential."

Works Cited

Amadae, S. M. *Prisoners of Reason: Game Theory and Neoliberal Political Economy.* New York: Cambridge UP, 2015.

Appiah, Kwame Antony. "Liberalism, Individuality, and Identity." *Critical Inquiry* 27.2 (2001): 305–32.

Arendt, Hannah. *Between Past and Future: Eight Exercises in Political Thought*. New York: Penguin, 2006.

Arendt, Hannah. *The Human Condition*. Chicago: U of Chicago P, 1998.

Arendt, Hannah. *On Violence*. London: Lane, 1970.

Aristotelis [Aristotle]. *De Arte Poetica Liber*. Oxford: Oxford UP, 1965.

Aristotle. *Poetics*. Trans. Ingram Bywater. *The Complete Works of Aristotle: The Revised Oxford Translation*. Ed. Jonathan Barnes. Vol. 2. Princeton: Princeton UP, 1995.

Armstrong, Nancy. "The Affective Turn in Contemporary Fiction." *Contemporary Literature* 55.3 (2014): 441–65.

Barth, John. *The Floating Opera and The End of the Road*. New York: Anchor, 1988.

Beckett, Samuel. *Watt*. London: Faber and Faber, 2009.

Cooper, Lydia R. "Novelistic Practice and Ethical Philosophy in Kazuo Ishiguro's *The Remains of the Day* and *Never Let Me Go*." *Kazuo Ishiguro: New Critical Visions of the Novels*. Ed. Sebastian Groes and Barry Lewis. Houndmills: Palgrave Macmillan, 2011. 106–17.

Currie, Mark. *The Unexpected: Narrative Temporality and the Philosophy of Surprise*. Edinburgh: Edinburgh UP, 2013.

Galloway, Alexander R., and Eugene Thacker. *The Exploit: Theory of Networks*. Minneapolis: U of Minnesota P, 2007.

Halpern, Richard. *Eclipse of Action: Tragedy and Political Economy*. Chicago: U of Chicago P, 2017.

Harvey, David. *A Brief History of Neoliberalism*. Oxford: Oxford UP, 2005.

Heap, Shaun P. Hargreaves, and Yanis Varoufakis. *Game Theory: A Critical Text*. 2nd ed. London: Routledge, 2004.

Ishiguro, Kazuo. *An Artist of the Floating World*. London: Faber and Faber, 2001.

Ishiguro, Kazuo. *Never Let Me Go*. London: Faber and Faber, 2006.

Ishiguro, Kazuo. *A Pale View of Hills*. London: Faber and Faber, 1991.

Ishiguro, Kazuo. *The Remains of the Day*. London: Faber and Faber, 2005.

Ishiguro, Kazuo. *My Twentieth Century Evening and Other Small Breakthroughs: The Nobel Lecture*. London: Faber and Faber, 2017.

Ishiguro, Kazuo. *The Unconsoled*. London: Faber and Faber, 2005.

Ishiguro, Kazuo. *When We Were Orphans*. London: Faber and Faber, 2012.

Kahn, Herman. *On Thermonuclear War*. Princeton: Princeton UP, 1960.

Lukács, Georg. *The Meaning of Contemporary Realism*. Trans. John Mander and Necke Mander. London: Merlin, 1963.

MacEwan, Arthur. "Neoliberalism and Democracy: Market Power versus Democratic Power." *Neoliberalism: A Critical Reader*. London: Pluto, 2005. 170–76.

Marcus, Ben. *Notable American Women: A Novel*. New York: Vintage, 2002.

Mason, Paul. *Clear Bright Future: A Radical Defence of the Human Being*. London: Lane, 2019.

Matthews, Sean, and Kazuo Ishiguro. "'I'm Sorry I Can't Say More': An Interview with Kazuo Ishiguro." *Kazuo Ishiguro: Contemporary Critical Perspectives*. Ed. Sean Matthews and Sebastian Groes. London: Continuum, 2009. 114–25.

Mead, Matthew. "Caressing the Wound: Modalities of Trauma in Kazuo Ishiguro's *The Unconsoled*." *Textual Practice* 28.3 (2014): 501–20.

Poundstone, William. *The Prisoner's Dilemma: John von Neumann, Game Theory, and the Puzzle of the Bomb*. New York: Anchor, 1993.

Quarrie, Cynthia. "Impossible Inheritance: Filiation and Patrimony in Kazuo Ishiguro's *The Unconsoled*." *Critique* 55 (2014): 138–51.

Rancière, Jacques. *The Lost Thread: The Democracy of Modern Fiction*. Trans. Steve Corcoran. London: Bloomsbury, 2017.

Rancière, Jacques. *The Politics of Literature*. Trans. Julie Rose. Cambridge: Polity, 2011.

Schelling, Thomas C. "The Reciprocal Fear of Surprise Attack." Rand Corporation Papers, 16 April 1958 <https://www.rand.org/content/dam/rand/pubs/papers/2007/P1342.pdf>.

Shaffer, Brian W. "An Interview with Kazuo Ishiguro." *Contemporary Literature* 42.1 (2001): 1–14.

Tucker, A. W. "The Mathematics of Tucker: A Sampler." *Two-Year College Mathematics Journal* 14.3 (1983): 228–32.

von Neumann, John. "Zur Theorie der Gesellschaftsspiele." *Mathematische Annalen* 100.1 (1928): 295–320.

von Neumann, John, and Oskar Morgenstern. *Theory of Games and Economic Behavior*. Princeton: Princeton UP, 1944.

Wagner, Valeria. *Bound to Act: Models of Action, Dramas of Inaction*. Stanford: Stanford UP, 1999.

Walkowitz, Rebecca L. "Unimaginable Largeness: Kazuo Ishiguro, Translation, and the New World Literature." *Ishiguro's Unknown Communities*. Ed. Lisa Fluet. Spec. issue of *Novel* 40.3 (2007): 216–39.

Wohlstetter, Albert. "The Delicate Balance of Terror." *Survival* 1.1 (1959): 8–17.

Letters and the Contemporary Novel: Materiality and Metaphor in Ian McEwan's The Children Act

KATE WILKINSON

Daily communication today is predominantly digital, but novels continue to be interested in paper letters. Letters appear frequently in twenty-first-century fiction, in contemporary storyworlds as well as in historical settings, and the reasons for this continuing interest deserve investigation. What do letters, written on paper, offer to the novel in the twenty-first century? One answer, which I explore here, is that the material letter has a contemporary value as metaphor. In this case study I use Jean-François Lyotard's idea of the *differend* to read Ian McEwan's *The Children Act* (2014), and I consider the significance of letters in this narrative of a legal decision and its aftermath. Lyotard's framework in *The Differend* provides an analysis of the kind of dispute that *The Children Act* dramatizes: a dispute that is unresolvable because the process for regulating it is unable to register the wrong that one side suffers. McEwan explores an intractable contemporary conflict between religious belief and the secular law, which the secular law must regulate in an actual courtroom: the novel is situated in the context of recent legal-medical disputes about the best interests of children who are terminally ill.[1] Lyotard develops the processes of a courtroom as a kind of metaphor for a wider conception of the unresolvable dispute. In their different modes, these two texts consider intractable conflict and the ethics of its regulation, the workings of which can be analyzed through the suggestive correspondences between the dynamics of the differend and those of material letters. These correspondences derive, I argue, from the letter's material properties, which underlie its ability to function as metaphor. The letter's temporal structure of delay and the silences and instability that delay produces, in particular, have productive affinities with the workings of the differend, and these are significant in McEwan's novel. These correspondences help to delineate the conflicts of *The Children Act* and to reveal the value of the letter as metaphor more generally. This case study presents an example of the letter as a metaphorical resource—here illuminating the dynamics of an unharmonizable dispute and hinting at a way forward—whose flexibility and nuance can help to account for contemporary novels' continued interest in the possibilities of the letter.

While the practice of letter writing has declined with the shift of daily correspondence to the Internet, the letter persists in the contemporary novel in multiple

---

[1] The case of Charlie Gard in 2017, for example, was widely reported in the United Kingdom. Charlie Gard, eleven months old, had a severe, progressive disease for which no treatment existed (and to date does not exist). His parents wanted to pursue an untried therapy; the treating hospital's view was that it was in the child's best interests to withdraw life support and provide palliative care. The hospital applied for a ruling that it was lawful and in the best interests of their patient to do so (see "Great Ormond Street Hospital v. Yates and Gard").

Novel: A Forum on Fiction 53:3 DOI 10.1215/00295132-8624570   © 2020 by Novel, Inc.

forms. Critical work has pointed, for example, to a resurgence in the use of epistolary narrative techniques in recent fiction, which has embraced digital textual communications as well as paper letters. Rachel Bower describes a growing interest in epistolary conventions at the end of the twentieth century and the beginning of the twenty-first. Bower analyzes what these conventions offer to novelists in a global literary market and their efforts to create transnational dialogue. Maria Löschnigg and Rebekka Schuh's 2018 edited collection *The Epistolary Renaissance* focuses primarily on the narrative characteristics of epistolary fiction and how these produce new meanings in contemporary contexts. Essays highlight the suitability of epistolary techniques for handling multiple perspectives, representing communication networks, and exploring how characters position their public and private selves through social media platforms. Janet Gurkin Altman's foundational study of epistolary form, although it predates the widespread use of digital technologies, is helpful for considering the growing contemporary interest in epistolary narrative. Altman's working definition of epistolarity is "the use of the letter's formal properties to create meaning" (4). Working primarily with eighteenth-century texts, she considers, for example, how the letter mediates between presence and absence, the letter's ability to occupy both public and private realms, and its ability to make both writer and reader visible. These aspects of her study indicate that epistolary narrative techniques have considerable resources to offer to fictions that engage with digital communication platforms, their often public or staged nature, and the subjectivities they mediate. Letters in contemporary fiction take further new forms in speculative worlds. The delays and crossings that belong to epistolary discourse shape an imagined interplanetary communications technology in Michel Faber's *The Book of Strange New Things* (2014), for example, and focus the novel's exploration of our human experience of time. Letters also structure Amal El-Mohtar and Max Gladstone's fantasy novel *This Is How You Lose the Time War* (2019), spanning multiple worlds and millennia. Two time-traveling agents from warring empires write to each other, using paper at first and then increasingly ingenious media—the growth rings of trees, even the flight patterns of insects—in order to keep their illicit correspondence safe from surveillance.

While epistolary narrative techniques are enjoying a resurgence, the material letter itself, I suggest, has also become a focus of renewed attention in twenty-first-century fiction. By material letter I mean a unique object that is directly accessible to human touch; it is distinct from a letter in digital form such as an email or image file, which is a conceptual object produced by computational processes.[2] We can understand the letter's particular materiality as a compound characteristic, with

---

[2]   In his study of new media and materiality, Matthew G. Kirschenbaum draws on Kenneth Thibodeau's model for defining digital objects. We can understand the physical digital object as signs inscribed on a medium, such as the tiny depressions burned on the surface of a CD-ROM; the logical digital object as data recognized and interpreted by processes; and the conceptual digital object as the object we deal with in the real world, such as a digital photograph on a screen. As Kirschenbaum describes, the materiality of digital media is a rich field of critical and theoretical study. Approaches to materiality consider its emergence through the multiple interactions between readers, electronic texts, and media devices; materiality consists in readers' bodily and interpretive encounters with digital texts and technologies (Kirschenbaum 2–11).

attributes that affect the experiences of both writer and reader. Perhaps the most obvious of these is that a material letter's writer touches it to produce it, whether by handwriting, typing, or simply feeding paper into a printer. One visual record of this individual touch is handwriting, though typed letters too can include traces of the process of their composition, such as crossings out and insertions, which are not visible in the same way in a text or an email. Edward Allen identifies these traces in Ernest Hemingway's idiosyncratic use of his Corona typewriter, for example, and finds them significant for close readings of Hemingway's letters (Allen 193). A second attribute of the material letter is that the reading experience is multisensory: touch, hearing, and smell come into play as well as sight. A reader opens or tears an envelope and unfolds sheets of paper, which have a specific texture, weight, and scent. Readers of texts or emails instead handle a mass-produced device (a phone, tablet, or computer) that has many other functions and through which no physical trace of a human sender arrives. Third, a letter today is sent in an envelope: the content is hidden when the letter is received. The reader must open the envelope to read the letter and, in some cases, to establish who has sent it. This sense of sealed content is far less evident in digital communication. A social media post identifies a writer, for example, and before a reader opens an email a sender's name is already visible, often with the opening lines of the message. A fourth significant attribute of a letter's materiality is that delays are inherent in any exchange. Digital transmission may occasionally be subject to delay, as a result of a human error in addressing a message or a technical failure. But when it works as intended, we perceive it as virtually instantaneous, whereas delay is an essential attribute of the material letter, which derives from its physical form.

In our present context of instant messaging and digital objects, there is evident interest in recent fiction in the gaps and glitches of physical letter writing and in tangible documents, and writers are turning to the properties and possibilities of material letters to explore a range of contemporary issues. In Rupert Thomson's *Katherine Carlyle* (2015), for example, a young woman is trying to come to terms with the loss of her mother, her difficult relationship with her father, and her knowledge that she was conceived by in vitro fertilization. As Kit embarks on a solo journey of self-discovery through Europe, she disposes of her smartphone and laptop. She communicates only with her father, sending two letters that she cannot be certain he receives and to which she ensures he cannot reply, as she keeps him unaware of her location. These letters structure Kit's sense of absence in the novel and at the same time create a narrative space in which she fantasizes about being sought and found. The uncertainty of the letters' delivery gives metaphoric expression, too, to Kit's unease about the technological circumstances of her own conception: "The idea that the letter might lie unopened until such a time as someone decides to dispose of it isn't easy to bear, or even think about" (Thomson 186). Material letters are significant in a number of recent novels concerned with memory and its workings (for example, Barnes; Taylor; Hall), while in others found archives of family letters prompt revisions of family relationships (Fuller; Constantine),

Eva Illouz and Esther Milne, for example, explore these interactions in relation to Internet dating sites and emails, respectively.

including a son's struggle to understand and accept the transition of his beloved parent, whom he remembers as the mother who abandoned him decades earlier (Mootoo). A more explicit focus on the materiality of the letter is clear in a corpus of novels whose narratives and typographical design celebrate the technology of print—the kind of novels that Jessica Pressman has identified as having a "bookish" aesthetic. She characterizes this aesthetic as a literary strategy for our cultural moment, arguing that "the threat posed to books by digital technologies becomes a source of artistic inspiration and formal experimentation in the pages of twenty-first-century literature" (465). Recent and elaborately formatted examples of this bookishness experiment with the material letter as part of this strategy: J. J. Abrams and Doug Dorst's *S.* (2013) and Zachary Thomas Dodson's *Bats of The Republic* (2015) both include loose-leaf reproductions of the letters that are significant in their stories.

Without taking facsimile form and without being visible as narrative, material letters are eloquent in recent novels' engagements with histories and historiography. A poet's letters suggest an unknown queer history in Alan Hollinghurst's *The Stranger's Child* (2011), for example: letters glimpsed at different points in the novel's ninety-year time span but never shown to the reader. The poet Cecil Valance writes to his male lovers before and during the First World War, and the novel tracks the shifting significance of his letters, first for his friends and family members and then, later, to academics. The letters point to events that are out of our reach as readers, their biographical significance as clear as the narrative's refusal to offer biographical completeness. We see only fragments and the envelopes of Cecil's letters, which in their fleeting appearances and uncertain fates offer a metaphor for our inability fully to know or reconstruct the past—even as they embody that possibility. The unread letters in Ivan Vladislavić's novel *Double Negative* ([2010] 2013) take the form of "dead" letters; that is, letters that have been neither delivered nor yet destroyed. Saved by the widow of a postal worker who had brought them home decades earlier, these letters hold potential testimonies from apartheid-era South Africa. In one magical scene, the letters come to life as the widow unfolds the shivering forms of men, women, and children who begin, wordlessly, to bear witness, "until the air was so thick with stories it couldn't be breathed" (Vladislavić 161). In this doubly metaphorical transfer, the letters open into soft, breathing bodies, and the bodies are stories that we cannot hear. The dead letters attest to a need for remembrance, but the possibility falters as the paper bodies are refolded and returned to their envelopes, their future uncertain.

As these examples indicate, material letters offer a range of possibilities to the novel that digital communications do not, and these possibilities inform my reading of *The Children Act*. In the discussion that follows, I consider the significance of letters in McEwan's exploration of a legal and ethical conflict, as an illustration of fiction's renewed interest in letters' narrative and metaphorical resources. The letters in *The Children Act* are written by seventeen-year-old Adam Henry, a Jehovah's Witness, to a High Court judge who rules on his case. Fiona Maye must decide whether Adam, who is still legally a child, has the capacity and the right to refuse a lifesaving blood transfusion. While these letters are unusual—how many seventeen-year-old boys today write letters?—they are significant in the novel rather than an incidental curiosity. Here the properties of the material letter, I argue, suggest a metaphor for the differend, which illuminates the dynamics of the novel's conflicts and begins to suggest how a move beyond them may be possible. A novel might "begin to investigate an encounter between love and belief, between the secular spirit of the law and sincerely held faith," McEwan has said ("Ian McEwan: The Law versus Religious Belief"), and readings of *The Children Act* have attended in different ways to this encounter. Ronald Soetaert and Kris A. F. Rutten see the novel as a companion piece to McEwan's earlier *Saturday* (2005) because of its focus on the relation between cultures, "science (again represented by medicine), art, and religion (confronted with the secular law)" (Soetaert and Rutten 80). They identify McEwan as part of the "Third Culture Club," aligned with the New Atheist movement and New Humanism. Tammy Amiel Houser also observes this alignment, noting that reviews of the novel have seen it as a peak in the expression of a conflict between rationalism and religion. Her reading of the novel as a Hegelian tragedy brings complex relations between them into view. *The Children Act*, she writes, "focuses on the dangers that arise when modern rationality refuses to recognize its own limitations and its complex entanglement with religious faith" (57). In this reading, I turn to the difficulties that inhere in the regulation of this encounter. Adam's faith is at odds with the secular law, yet it is the secular law that provides the process for regulating the conflict—a situation that Jean-François Lyotard posits in his concept of the differend:

> *As distinguished from a litigation, a differend* [différend] *would be a case of conflict, between (at least) two parties, that cannot be equitably resolved for lack of a rule of judgment applicable to both arguments. One side's legitimacy does not imply the other's lack of legitimacy. However, applying a single rule of judgment to both in order to settle their differend as though it were merely a litigation would wrong (at least) one of them (and both of them if neither side admits this rule).* (Lyotard xi)

In *The Differend*, Lyotard describes a type of conflict and at the same time aims to diagnose why it presents as irresolvable. "A case of differend between two parties takes place," he explains, "when the 'regulation' of the conflict that opposes them is done in the idiom of one of the parties while the wrong suffered by the other is not signified in that idiom" (9). For example: social and economic laws, which regulate relationships between employers and workers, require that workers' labor is conceptualized as a form of capital that they own, otherwise labor cannot signify in the terms of those laws (10). Disputes about land rights have also been cited as instances of the differend: Aboriginal peoples of Australia have an understanding of their relationship to the land on which they live, for example, and this cannot be acknowledged in any system based on property rights (see Readings 87–88). Given the absence of a universal genre in which the regulation of disputes can take place, the differend suggests that there is a tension inherent in the regulation of any conflict. The regulation in *The Children Act* takes place in a courtroom, the setting that also supplies the terms of the differend. Lyotard's chosen metaphor for elaborating the dynamics and ethics of the differend is that of a judicial process, and he calls on an extensive terminology of litigation and plaintiffs, of testimony and tribunals. While the overarching metaphor here is judicial, his detailed analysis attends to language: it is conducted in terms of phrases, genre, and idiom, each with its specific meaning in the framework he sets out. A differend is the product of "phrases in dispute," of a structural incompatibility between the different "phrase regimens" that belong to a "genre" of discourse (Lyotard 28–29). *The Children Act*, too, is occupied with genres, particularly of writing: the status writing confers, its performative power, and its potential to disrupt or resolve. Adam's letters to Fiona and her responses to them, I suggest, also stage an encounter between two "genres" of discourse that prove to be unharmonizable. This second encounter comments on and complicates the first, extending its terms from the legal regulation of a conflict into the personal realm. In this staging the material and metaphorical properties of letters are significant, in particular the metaphor of the letter as the body and the letter's temporal structure of delay. Fiona's delayed responses to Adam's letters produce crucial silences in the novel, and the differend offers a way to read them that complicates a sense of silence as failure.

The Children Act signals its concern with the reaches of the law and with writing in its opening invocation of Charles Dickens's *Bleak House* (1853). "London. Trinity term one week old. Implacable June weather. Fiona Maye, a High Court judge, at home on Sunday evening, supine on a chaise longue" (*Children Act* 1). The reference develops: Fiona Maye in her Gray's Inn flat works alone among her artworks and bookshelves, like Dickens's lawyer Tulkinghorn in his Lincoln's Inn apartment. Her "Bokhara rug" is an echo of his "Turkey-carpet," while his "silver candlesticks" are replaced by her "silver-framed family photos." Tulkinghorn "has some manuscript near him but is not referring to it"; Fiona has, on the floor, "by the chaise longue, within her reach, the draft of a judgment" (Dickens 119; *Children Act* 1). Critics have explored how the plots of *Bleak House* emphasize the uncertainties of deciphering and writing as they play out against the background of the impenetrable legal processes of the Court of Chancery (Beer 24–25; Saggini 150–58). In public and in private, writing in *Bleak House* means problems. Legal documents are opaque and letter-writing campaigns ineffectual (Dickens 27, 41); even the practices of reading and writing themselves can be suspect (181). And as Lady Dedlock and Tulkinghorn are both aware, letters can be particularly disruptive. There is evidence of her affair with Captain Hawdon in the form of his letters; if they are found, his handwriting will reveal the secret (148–50, 337–38, 357). Fiona Maye of Gray's Inn is neither a refigured Tulkinghorn nor a twenty-first-century Lady Dedlock, but the opening allusions position her in a narrative that will be concerned with the law, with writing, and with letters.

Fiona's own writing in its regulatory context is careful, considered, and precise—a characterization that also extends to her person.

> *Among fellow judges, Fiona Maye was praised, even in her absence, for crisp prose, almost ironic, almost warm, and for the compact terms in which she laid out a dispute. The Lord Chief Justice himself was heard to observe of her in a murmured aside at lunch, "Godly distance, devilish understanding, still beautiful." Her own view was that with each passing year she inclined a little more to an exactitude some might have called pedantry, to the unassailable definition that might pass one day into frequent citation.* (*Children Act* 13)

The Lord Chief Justice's praise applies as much to Fiona's professional abilities as it does to her prose style; her writing *is* her character. Fiona's own assessment also ties her writing and herself together, her style—and the hoped-for citations—a reflection of her ageing. In the legal profession, writing confers status and secures recognition, and Fiona is comfortable here. The rituals of writing and of the court proceedings are intimately connected, for example, as she starts the hearing of Adam's case. "At her elbow was a slim pile of creamy white paper beside which she laid down her pen. It was only then, at the sight of these clean sheets, that the last traces, the stain, of her own situation vanished completely. She no longer had a private life, she was ready to be absorbed" (62). As she prepares to write, there is an echo of her near-godly authority in the image of the blank page: the figure of the divine as a scribe whose writing marks the passage from potentiality to actuality (Agamben 246–47). McEwan finds the authoritative distance of written legal judgments reminiscent of a novelist's omniscience, he has said. He admires the "precise, delicious" prose of judgments, with "the background to some dispute or dilemma crisply summarised, characters drawn with quick strokes" ("Ian McEwan"). His narrative voices often suggest an authorial pleasure in adopting such expert professional registers: we might think of the neurosurgeon Henry Perowne in *Saturday*, for example, or Wenn and Camia, authors of the fictitious psychiatric case review appended to *Enduring Love* (1997). The narration of *The Children Act* seems to relish its crisp legal phrases as it walks us through Fiona's thought processes. "First the facts," it informs us, and directs our attention to the developing stages of an argument: "Regarding the all-important matter of intent" (8, 28).

In the form of legal judgments, Fiona's writing is absolutely performative: her wording determines the course of people's lives and the circumstances of their deaths. She has recently ruled on a case of conjoined twins, whose parents were opposed on religious grounds to a surgical separation that would save one but kill the other. Without the surgery, both children would die. Though the "legal and moral space was tight," Fiona found a "novel formulation" with which to make the case for one twin's survival. "In this dire contest there was only one desirable or less undesirable outcome, but a lawful route to it was not easy. Under pressure of time, with a noisy world waiting, she found, in just under a week and thirteen thousand words, a plausible way" (27). The regulation of this terrible situation appears to lie in the act of writing itself rather than in a process of deliberation. The legal decision is equated with the task of written argument, the "route" of thirteen thousand words. Fiona's colleagues tell her that her judgment is "elegant and correct"—correctness of expression and decision are conflated here—and their reassurance arrives on paper too, in "the kind of letters worth saving in a special folder" (28). Fiona's personal unease about the conjoined twins' case appears also to become a matter of wording. She "was awake at night for long hours, turning over the details, rephrasing certain passages, taking another tack" (29), as if reworking the prose might smooth out the ethical difficulties of the decision. Her writing seems as much the instrument of the twins' separation as the surgeons' tools: "She was the one who had dispatched a child from the world, argued him out of existence in thirty-four elegant pages" (31).

While Fiona's judgments acknowledge religious beliefs, they do so only in the secular law's terms—the "idiom" in which the regulation of the conflict is conducted, to put this in Lyotard's terms. In a case of two Jewish girls, for example, whose parents do not agree about their religious schooling, Fiona's "judgment paid respect to the Chareidi community, the continuity of its venerable traditions and obser-vances," and adds "that the court took no view of its particular beliefs beyond noting that they were sincerely held" (37). If her phrasing must be closely worked, the narrative makes clear, it is not in order to win a debate or to mediate between the parties but to close down the possibility of legal challenge. She has given her ruling verbally in court, but now "the prose needed to be smoothed, as did the respect owed to piety in order to be proof against an appeal" (8). The function of her argu-ments is not to weigh the respective merits of conflicting positions but to apply the relevant legal principles: that which was irresolvable in a dispute may still stand.

The frequent references to writing in the opening scene of *The Children Act* focus attention on a judgment that Fiona is finalizing, and she appears in command. We read that she sets out definitions, cites appropriate authorities, and anticipates the reactions of parties in the case. This is the work of crafting secure and ideally "unassailable" phrases, and it demands rigor and precision. The narrative repeat-edly directs our attention to her writing but in fact includes no examples of it; we have to rely on summary and report. In relation to Adam, it is Fiona's verbal ruling that follows the two presentations of his case, the first made by counsel with a full dramatis personae present in court (62–89) and the second by Adam himself during Fiona's visit to his bedside (99–118). The account of Fiona's verbal ruling includes the final section as direct speech (121–24), but her writing is only ever described or paraphrased. We are put at a distance, as we cannot read it directly—but we do read Adam's letters, as if over Fiona's shoulder.

His first letter arrives in Fiona's chambers a few weeks after her ruling. In her world of precise and regulatory writing, it is clearly out of place. "At the sight of an undersized pale blue envelope resting on top, she almost called her clerk back to open it. She was in no mood to read for herself one more outpouring of illiterate abuse or a threat of violence. She turned back to her work, but couldn't concentrate. The impractical envelope, loopy hand, absent post code, the postage stamp slightly awry—she'd seen too much of it" (136). Impractical, loopy and awry: Fiona reads these as signs of looseness and lack of focus, expecting "loopy" content as well as handwriting. The letter's color is unsettling, like the "pastel-coloured envelopes" that brought her the "venomous letters of the devout" after her judgment in the case of the conjoined twins (29), and it seems to bring Adam directly into Fiona's chambers. When Fiona and Adam meet at the hospital before her ruling, she is struck by his pallor, his frailty, and the purplish tinge of his features. "It was a long thin face, ghoulishly pale, but beautiful, with crescents of bruised purple fading delicately to white under the eyes, and full lips that appeared purplish too in the intense light. The eyes themselves looked violet and were huge." She notices too that his "build was frail, his arms protruded like poles from the hospital gown" (99). The undersized letter now recalls its writer and his sickly color, and the metonymic "hand," as a metaphor for the envelope's written script, brings Adam's body, his frail arms, again into view. The letter stands in for bodily presence. This metaphorical transference mobilizes a long history of associations between letters and bodies, particularly associations with women's bodies, intimacy, and sexuality.

Amanda Gilroy and W. M. Verhoeven trace the origins of critical traditions that have construed the letter as a specifically feminine form, a fiction based on a notion that both women and letters have a certain transparency. "Though readers from Fielding on have questioned such epistolary innocence," they observe, "the dominant critical tradition equates letters and love, women's writing and the writing of the heart" (3). The boundaries between eighteenth-century conduct writing for women and the novel were porous, and epistolary novels including Samuel Richardson's *Pamela* (1740) and *Clarissa* (1748) took up their places in an existing "cultural correspondence" in which plots of seduction and betrayal were already circulating (Gilroy and Verhoeven 2).

Adam's handwritten letter to Fiona describes his experience of the blood transfusion and his subsequent recovery, but the long-standing metaphor of the letter as the body, from epistolary narratives of seduction, is seeping into his account. "They thought they were going to have to hold me down. But I was too feeble for that and even though I was furious, I knew what you wanted me to do. So I held out my arm and they got started. The thought of someone else's blood going into mine was so disgusting that I was sick right across the bed" (137). Restraint, submission, blood, and a bed: this is the language of a first, coerced sexual experience. While histories that equate the epistolary genre with the romantic or erotic almost always suggest a female figure at the center of a male-authored text (Gilroy and Verhoeven 4), Adam's letter implicitly reverses these gender roles. His youth and this medical violation contribute to the unsettling character of his letter. Terry Eagleton has suggested that the letter in epistolary novels has the potential to unsettle because it can exist on a "troubled frontier between private and public worlds, symbol at once of the self and of its violent appropriation" (54). It is the combination of its intimacy and its sealed form that disturbs boundaries. "Nothing could be at once more intimate and more alienable, flushed with the desire of the subject yet always ripe for distortion and dishonour" (54), he claims. A confusion of intimacy, desire, and feelings of violation is certainly at play in Adam's letter. He is turning to Fiona, the person whom he holds responsible for his transfusion, as he questions his religious faith. "I feel you've brought me close to something else, something really beautiful and deep, but I don't really know what it is," he writes. "I wrote you lots of stupid letters and I think about you all the time and really want to see you and talk again. I daydream about us, impossible wonderful fantasies, like we go on a journey together round the world in a ship and we have cabins next door to each other and we walk up and down on the deck talking all day" (139). His fantasy sounds like a honeymoon, a dream of time spent in the exclusive company of "My Lady"—and outside the context of the courtroom, the honorific address takes on a mischievously romantic tone. (We could see a nod to Dickens's "my Lady Dedlock" here; another careful life threatened by unruly letters.) Adam's stated appeal to Fiona's professional qualities, to her public self—"I need to hear your calm voice and have your clear mind discuss this with me" (139)—is undermined by the effusive intimacy of his writing. Fiona herself acknowledges none of the letter's connotations, noting only "innocence and warmth" (140), and she sends him no reply; her response is silence.

Lyotard suggests in *The Differend* that we attend to silences as forms of negation, which can alert us to what cannot yet be expressed. The framework he elaborates begins with "the phrase": this is what there always is, the only object that is "indubitable" (xi). From this starting point, he explores the operating structures of language and their relationship to justice. A phrase always belongs to a "regimen" or set of rules, such as describing, or showing, or questioning. A phrase from a particular regimen can be linked onto one from another, according to the "genre of discourse" that supplies the rules and defines the goal to be attained; this may be to teach, to be just, to seduce, and so on. And as there is no universal genre to regulate these linkages across different regimens, questions of "thought, cognition, ethics, politics, history or being, depending on the case" are therefore always at stake when they are made (xii). A phrase suggests a set of related structures and positions rather than a transmissible message, and these positions constitute the phrase's "universe": "It should be said that addressor and addressee are instances, either marked or unmarked, presented by a phrase. The latter is not a message passing from an addressor to an addressee both of whom are independent of it," Lyotard emphasizes. "They are situated in the universe the phrase presents, as are its referent and its sense" (11). These four instances or elements—addressor, addressee, referent, and sense—structure the place of silence in the differend. Silence is also a phrase, and it suggests a denial of one or more of these instances, as Lyotard explains with reference to the testimonies of Holocaust survivors and the warped reasoning of a Holocaust denier:

> *The survivors remain silent, and it can be understood 1) that the situation in question (the case) is not the addressee's business (he or she lacks the competence, or he or she is not worthy of being spoken to about it, etc.); or 2) that it never took place (this is what Faurisson understands); or 3) that there is nothing to say about it (the situation is senseless, inexpressible); or 4) that it is not the survivors' business to be talking about it (they are not worthy, etc.). Or, several of these negations together.* (14)

A silence does not itself indicate what kind of negation is taking place in particular circumstances but alerts us to an occurrence. Its further significance is that it can indicate the need for new phrases and linkages, necessary to express a differend and address its wrong:

> *The differend is the unstable state and instant of language wherein something which must be able to be put into phrases cannot yet be. This state includes silence, which is a negative phrase, but it also calls upon phrases which are in principle possible. The state is signaled by what one ordinarily calls a feeling: "One cannot find the words," etc. A lot of searching must be done to find new rules for forming and linking phrases that are able to express the differend disclosed by the feeling, unless one wants this differend to be smothered right away in a litigation and for the alarm sounded by the feeling to have been useless.* (13)

This introduces both a temporal dimension and a sense of possibility to the differend's dynamics. Something "cannot yet" be put into phrases, and at the same time, "cannot yet" allows a future in which it might be. There is a sense here of an ethical imperative that attaches to silence, of an obligation to search for new modes of expression.

This instability and sense of "not yet" find expression in the novel in the material properties of Adam's letters. A received letter, not yet answered, is not yet unanswered either. The material form of letters unavoidably connects them with delay. Whether it lasts for seconds or for years, there must always be a delay between sending a letter and its receipt, and a delay between receipt and reply. In these delays there are silences and also possibilities: the possibility that a response will arrive, that a response will be sent, that a response will be written and not sent. There may yet be a linking phrase; the linking phrase may also be silence. Fiona's silence, in the terms of the differend, is itself a phrase. "Better to send nothing at all than cast him down," she decides, sending no reply to Adam's first letter. "If she changed her mind, she could write later" (140). The second part of her rationalization seeks to position her decision as a delay, so that Adam's letter is "not yet" answered—but her silence rather suggests the wrong of a differend. The note she tries to write is a failure; she is unable to operate outside the judicial idiom. We cannot read her attempt, reliant once again on a report, but we can read her silence in its "phrase universe": it points to a negation of Fiona's position as addressor. Adam's request is not my business, her silence suggests; this matter is outside my competence. She has already clearly delineated its boundaries in Adam's case: "It was not her business or mission to save him, but to decide what was reasonable and lawful" (35). In Lyotard's framework, negation does not necessarily imply an intention to negate or a withholding. The wrong of silence is diagnosed rather in structural and operational terms: "In the differend, something 'asks' to be put into phrases, and suffers from the wrong of not being able to be put into phrases right away" (Lyotard 13). Both the genre of Adam's letter and its narrative ask for a connection that cannot be understood or answered by crisp judicial prose. Fiona does not or cannot acknowledge the letter's connotations, even to herself, but her silence does not close the matter. The "not yet" of the letter form—like the "cannot yet" of the differend—leaves open this asymmetrical encounter.

Adam's second letter repeats the request he makes in the first, returning to his theme of the transfusion as a violation. "Sometimes the idea of having a stranger's blood inside me makes me sick, like drinking someone's saliva. Or worse," writes Adam (*Children Act* 142), and the unspecified "worse" again foregrounds the sexual body. Adam is "jealous" of the people involved in the cases Fiona has heard since his own, insistent, worried that "you might not recognize me." You don't have to reply, he tells her, "which means I wish you would" (142). His implicit plea is again for the recognition of a connection between "My Lady" and himself, and Fiona again sends him no answer. To Adam this is another silence, but readers can again see what he cannot, which is that Fiona is resetting the terms of their encounter. She reinterprets his letter as a prompt to professional action and she does write, but not to him: she emails Adam's social worker to ask for a report on his progress, which she swiftly receives. In this idiom, she is safely back within the limits of her competence.

Fiona is already in difficulty with Adam's letters, and when he delivers himself instead of a third letter, to ask if he can come and live with her, she is thrown by the unexpected dialogue. She attempts to shift its terms back to safer ground, "grave in her manner" (164) and succumbing to "her habit of summarizing the views of others" (165). But Fiona's conduct of this face-to-face meeting is again troubled by another register, which recalls that of his letters. "She watched him as he spoke, taking in the transformation. No longer thin, but still slender. New strength about the shoulders and arms. Same long delicately structured face, the brown cheekbone mole nearly invisible against a complexion darkened by young health. Mere traces of the purple pouches under his eyes. Lips full and moist, eyes in this light too black for colour" (157). Fiona's gaze lingers on Adam's body and face. His arms and his coloring—no longer undersized and pale—recall by the comparisons his appearance when they first met in the hospital. Moments later, Fiona dwells again on "the contours of his cheekbones and lips" under the ceiling light; it was "a beautiful face" (160). As if trying to prevent a lover's declaration, she arranges without discussion for Adam to leave her and travel to a relative's house. And when he does ask, in spite of her efforts, it is significant that his first letter comes to her mind. "He had stalked her through the country, through the streets, walked through a storm to ask her. It was a logical extension of his fantasy of a long sea voyage with her, of their talking all day as they paced the rolling deck. Logical and insane. And innocent" (167). She avoids the word "honeymoon," however much his fantasy sounds like one, but implicitly acknowledges it in her insistence upon its innocence. Adam also moves to dismiss the meaning of "living with" that is clearly present for both of them. "I wouldn't get in the way, I mean, with you and your husband," he tells her (167). Their uncertain meeting hangs between registers, disturbed by unspoken associations. This is the case too with Fiona's kiss goodbye, "more than the idea of a kiss, more than a mother might give her grown-up son" (169), but at the same time oddly chaste. The kiss is problematic in many ways yet also strangely undramatic, unsurprising—an extension for the reader, perhaps, of the metaphors of the body and of epistolary seduction that have persistently hovered over Adam's letters.

Adam's own metaphors are far more direct in the final words he writes to Fiona. "The Ballad of Adam Henry" arrives on her desk in a familiar blue envelope, a poem in rhyming couplets. It tells the allegorical story of a young man who drowns his heavy cross in a river, persuaded by a treacherous dancing fish who kisses him and dives out of sight, later revealed to be "the voice of Satan" (180). (Adam is only eighteen, Fiona reminds herself.) Fiona reads the poem but opts out of the effort of deciphering its heavily edited last line. "The last words of the final verse were lost to a skein of spidery lines that looped around second thoughts, to words deleted and reinstated and to other variants with question marks. Rather than attempt to decipher the mess, she read the poem again, then lay back with eyes closed. She minded that he was angry with her" (181). This description of the line is far longer than the line itself could be, its phrasing more tangled and troubled than Fiona's usual crisp style. She begins "to daydream a letter to him, knowing that she would never post it or even write it" (181); this time she acknowledges that her nonreply is silence. Fiona keeps the poem, but without having read the last line she does not fully understand it—or at least she cannot yet understand it. The poem itself, neither unread nor yet fully read, is in an unstable state in the narrative. Fiona finally makes out the last line six weeks later, after she learns that Adam, who at eighteen is now legally an adult, has refused a second blood transfusion and has died. "The Son of God had delivered a curse," she realizes, finally seeing the words: "May he who drowns my cross by his own hand be slain" (204). Fiona's delay in deciphering the words transforms them. Seen in retrospect, they are no longer a curse or a warning but a suicide note (210).

Fiona accepts that she has failed Adam. She does not respond to his letters; she kisses him and sends him away; she gives him nothing to replace the security that his religion and the community of Jehovah's Witnesses had represented. "There, in court, with the authority and dignity of her position, she offered him, instead of death, all of life and love that lay ahead of him. And protection against his religion. Without faith, how open and beautiful and terrifying the world must have seemed to him" (212). Whether it is an act of religious belief or suicide, Adam has died. Dominic Head, in his study of McEwan's work up to and including *Saturday* (2005), suggests that a "refusal of consolation" is a defining and even exaggerated element in McEwan's fiction: "Even the positive resolution of novels like *Enduring Love* and *The Child in Time* still leaves us deeply unsettled" (Head 12). The most dramatic of these refusals, he suggests, occurs at the end of *Atonement* (2001), when we learn that the reuniting of lovers Cecilia and Robbie is in fact Briony Tallis's invention, "a consoling feature of her latest draft, but not of McEwan's novel" (12). The ending of *The Children Act* lets Fiona's failure stand: in the final words she tells her husband "of her shame, of the sweet boy's passion for life, and her part in his death" (213). There is no positive resolution here, but in Fiona's admission there is also, I suggest, something other than an absolute refusal of consolation.

Fiona has not been able to find the words to answer Adam's letters; it is only after the terrible news of his death that she attempts for the first time to articulate this. To recognize the feeling of a differend that "cannot yet" be put into phrases is also to recognize its ethical imperative, Lyotard explains. When one cannot find the words, "searching must be done" to find new expression for what that feeling discloses; the situation "must" be able to be put into new phrases (Lyotard 13). Here, perhaps, Fiona's search begins: "Adam came looking for her and she offered nothing in religion's place, no protection, even though the Act was clear, her paramount consideration was his welfare. How many pages in judgments had she devoted to that term? Welfare, well-being, was social. No child is an island. She thought her responsibilities ended at the courtroom walls. But how could they?" (212–13). Fiona invokes the precise wording and "the clear injunction of the Children Act of 1989" (122), to which she has referred during her hearing of Adam's case; they are imprinted in her thinking.[3] But even as she holds in mind the Act's wording and

---

[3]   Section 1 of the Act begins: "Welfare of the Child. (1) When a court determines any question with respect to—(a) the upbringing of a child; or (b) the administration of a child's property or the application of any income arising from it, the child's welfare shall be the court's paramount consideration" (Children Act 1989).

familiar terms, it is possible to read the beginnings of a move beyond them as she asks in what sense they can truly mark the limits of her responsibility. The question is not, now, whether her ruling has been correct, as she has operated correctly within the terms of the law, but whether there could be other terms in which to operate. A differend may arise in legal judgments where values or beliefs are in conflict, but the wrong can only be articulated in another, new idiom.

> *In the differend, something "asks" to be put into phrases, and suffers from the wrong of not being able to be put into phrases right away. This is when human beings who thought they could use language as an instrument of communication learn through the feeling of pain which accompanies silence . . . that they are summoned by language, not to augment to their profit the quantity of information communicable through existing idioms, but to recognize that what remains to be phrased exceeds what they can presently phrase, and that they must be allowed to institute idioms that do not yet exist.* (Lyotard 13)

The ending of *The Children Act* suggests Fiona's belated recognition of that which exceeds what she can presently phrase. The feeling of pain comes too late for her to be able to give Adam an answer, yet she begins to understand that it is only by moving outside the courtroom walls that she might find an idiom in which she could acknowledge and address Adam's unspoken question: without religious faith, how is he to live?

"What is at stake in a literature, in a philosophy, in a politics perhaps, is to bear witness to differends by finding idioms for them" (Lyotard 13). The encounter between Adam and Fiona, after her ruling—between his plea for connection and her judicial professionalism—is shaped in the narrative by Adam's letters. It echoes the irresolvable conflict on which Fiona must rule and at the same time complicates it, winding together the personal and regulatory realms in the novel. *The Children Act* meditates on forms of writing and mobilizes the properties of material letters as metaphor; both are critical in its staging. The novel illustrates the type of dispute that Lyotard identifies, while its letters also offer ways to examine the dynamics of the differend: they give expression to incompatible idioms, silences, and the delays of that which "cannot yet" be phrased but must be phrased. *The Children Act*'s textual and metaphorical staging, then, can begin to explore the wrong at the heart of a fictional differend. It can also begin to suggest, in ways that legal rulings never could, that new idioms are both necessary and possible.

*   *   *

KATE WILKINSON is a teaching associate at Queen Mary University of London. She researches contemporary fiction, letters, and media, and she is the author of "*The Book of Strange New Things*: Letters, Delay, and Experiences of Time," in *Michel Faber: Critical Essays*, edited by Rebecca Langworthy, Kristin Lindfield-Ott, and Jim MacPherson (2020).

Works Cited

Abrams, J. J., and Doug Dorst. *S.* Edinburgh: Canongate, 2013.

Agamben, Giorgio. *Potentialities: Collected Essays in Philosophy.* Trans. Daniel Heller-Roazen. Stanford: Stanford UP, 1999.

Allen, Edward. "Typecasting Hemingway; or, Mine's a Corona!" *Cambridge Quarterly* 42.2 (2013): 183–94.

Altman, Janet Gurkin. *Epistolarity: Approaches to a Form.* Columbus: Ohio State UP, 1982.

Barnes, Julian. *The Sense of an Ending.* London: Cape, 2011.

Beer, Gillian. *Arguing with the Past: Essays in Narrative from Woolf to Sidney.* London: Routledge, 1989.

Bower, Rachel. *Epistolarity and World Literature, 1980–2010.* Basingstoke: Palgrave Macmillan, 2017.

Children Act 1989. UK Public General Acts, 1989, c. 41 <http://www.legislation.gov.uk/ukpga/1989/41/section/1>. Accessed 2 April 2020.

Constantine, David. *The Life-Writer.* London: Comma, 2015.

Dickens, Charles. *Bleak House.* Ed. George Ford and Sylvère Monod. New York: Norton, 1977.

Dodson, Zachary Thomas. *Bats of the Republic: An Illuminated Novel.* New York: Doubleday, 2015.

Eagleton, Terry. *The Rape of Clarissa: Writing, Sexuality and Class Struggle in Samuel Richardson.* London: Blackwell, 1982.

El-Mohtar, Amal, and Max Gladstone. *This Is How You Lose the Time War.* London: Fletcher, 2019.

Faber, Michel. *The Book of Strange New Things.* Edinburgh: Canongate, 2014.

Fuller, Claire. *Swimming Lessons.* London: Penguin, 2018.

Gilroy, Amanda, and W. M. Verhoeven, eds. *Epistolary Histories: Letters, Fiction, Culture.* Charlottesville: U of Virginia P, 2000.

"Great Ormond Street Hospital v Yates and Gard." *Courts and Tribunals Judiciary,* Neutral citation no. [2017] EWHC 972 (Fam), Case no. FD17P00103, 11 Apr. 2017 <https://www.judiciary.uk/wp-content/uploads/2017/05/gosh-v-yates-and-gard-20170411-1.pdf>.

Hall, Steven. *The Raw Shark Texts.* Edinburgh: Canongate, 2007.

Head, Dominic. *Ian McEwan.* Manchester: Manchester UP, 2007.

Hollinghurst, Alan. *The Stranger's Child.* London: Picador, 2011.

Houser, Tammy Amiel. "Tragedy in Ian McEwan's *The Children Act.*" *Genre* 51.1 (2018): 53–79.

Illouz, Eva. "Romantic Webs." *Cold Intimacies: The Making of Emotional Capitalism.* Cambridge: Polity, 2007. 74–114.

Kirschenbaum, Matthew G. *Mechanisms: New Media and the Forensic Imagination.* Cambridge, MA: MIT P, 2008.

Löschnigg, Maria, and Rebekka Schuh, eds. *The Epistolary Renaissance: A Critical Approach to Contemporary Letter Narratives in Anglophone Fiction.* Berlin: De Gruyter, 2018.

Lyotard, Jean-François. *The Differend: Phrases in Dispute* Trans. Georges Van Den Abbeele. Minneapolis: U of Minnesota P, 1988.

McEwan, Ian. *Atonement.* London: Cape, 2001.

McEwan, Ian. *The Children Act.* London: Cape, 2014.

McEwan, Ian. *Enduring Love.* London: Cape, 1997.

McEwan, Ian. "Ian McEwan: The Law versus Religious Belief." *Guardian* 5 September 2014 < https://www.theguardian.com/books/2014/sep/05/ian-mcewan-law-versus-religious -belief >.

McEwan, Ian. *Saturday.* London: Cape, 2005.

Milne, Esther. *Letters, Postcards, Email: Technologies of Presence.* New York: Routledge, 2010.

Mootoo, Shani. *Moving Forward Sideways Like a Crab.* Brooklyn: Akashic, 2014.

Pressman, Jessica. "The Aesthetic of Bookishness in Twenty-First Century Literature." *Michigan Quarterly Review* 48.4 (2009): 465–82.

Readings, Bill. *Introducing Lyotard: Art and Politics.* London: Routledge, 1990.

Saggini, Francesca. "The Author's Secret. Disguises of Epistolarity in Victorian Mystery Narratives." *Letter(s): Functions and Forms of Letter-Writing in Victorian Art and Literature.* Ed. Mariaconcetta Costantini, Francesco Marroni, and Anna Enrichetta Soccio. Rome: Aracne, 2009. 147–73.

Soetaert, Ronald, and Kris A. F. Rutten. "A Rhetorical Analysis of the Two Cultures in Literary Fiction." *Perspectives on Science and Culture.* Ed. Kris Rutten, Stefaan Blancke, and Ronald Soetaert. West Lafayette: Purdue UP, 2018. 67–88.

Taylor, Sam. *The Amnesiac.* London: Faber and Faber, 2007.

Thomson, Rupert. *Katherine Carlyle.* 2015. London: Corsair, 2016.

Vladislavić, Ivan. *Double Negative.* London: And Other Stories, 2013.

Fiction Cares: J. M. Coetzee's Slow Man

BENJAMIN LEWIS ROBINSON

In 1977 Michel Foucault held lectures at the Collège de France titled *Security, Territory, Population*, in which he began to sketch a genealogy of the modern liberal welfare state—or "society of security," as he initially called it—tracing it back to the Christian notion of pastoral care (11). He went on in the final years of his life to concern himself with techniques for what he called the "care of the self." Also in 1977, Carol Gilligan published an article in the *Harvard Educational Review* that would subsequently be worked into a book, *In a Different Voice* (1982), prompting the emergence of what became known as "feminist ethics of care." She drew a contentious distinction, made more controversial by the gendered character of her findings, between a (masculine) abstract rights-based ethical orientation guided by the concept of justice and a (feminine) contextualized and relational orientation of responsiveness—or care. While Foucault's work exhibited a profound suspicion of care in its modern institutionalized forms as a principle of government and sought to recover ancient practices of care that would resist such governance, advocates of feminist care ethics sought in contrast to excavate actual but underacknowledged forms of care as essential to the texture of communal life: "*Caregiving* is the concrete (sometimes called hands-on) work of maintaining and repairing our world" (Tronto and Fisher 43). Both approaches, however, respond and attest to a contemporary crisis of care: for all the talk of care, for all the "managed care" in modern liberal societies, care in an authentic sense—that is to say, in a sense that was actually careful—was felt to be lacking.

In the same years that Foucault, in Paris and California, was exploring the history of care in its implication with modern "political rationality" and Gilligan was formulating a feminist ethics of care at Harvard, J. M. Coetzee, writing in Cape Town, published *In the Heart of the Country* (1977), *Waiting for the Barbarians* (1980), and *Life & Times of Michael K* (1983). Much can be understood about the political and ethical character of Coetzee's work and the controversies to which it has given rise, once it is situated with regard to this ongoing crisis of care. For Coetzee's writings, produced in a South African context in which urgent questions of injustice seemed rightly to trump questions of care, can be read as attentive literary investigations of the ambivalences of care.

The tension between care and justice is a persistent point of contention in feminist care ethics debates. On the one hand, attention to care facilitated the criticism of abstract and rights-based conceptions of justice; on the other, there was concern that care ethics renounced the political aspirations that had informed the feminist project to date and in fact risked reinforcing attitudes of submission and exploitation that needed—for the sake of justice—to be contested. A fundamental irreconcilability between justice and care is at the center of *Waiting for the Barbarians*, in

My thanks to the Harry Ransom Center, the University of Texas at Austin, for permission to cite from the J. M. Coetzee Papers.

which an imperial magistrate finds himself caught up in the security operations of the authorities he is supposed to represent. *Life & Times of Michael K* presents a person of color, disenfranchised and dispossessed, living through a state of emergency, who rather than join the guerrillas to fight for justice would prefer to be a gardener and to "tend" the earth (105). While in contemporary care ethics efforts have been made to reconcile justice and care (Sevenhuijsen), in Coetzee's early writings the two terms present, rather, an antinomy of modern political life.

In 2000 Deborah Stone, a public policy expert, published a cover article in *The Nation* titled "Why We Need a Care Movement," advocating the recognition of a "Right to Care." The article conflates rights-focused and care-centric attitudes and in so doing exhibits a fundamental difficulty with talking about care: in order to give concern about care the sort of positive, compelling, and ultimately political force needed to produce a "movement," the author has to resort to the discourse of rights that care ethics had shown to be problematic, if not suspect. Such efforts to assert the significance of care struggle to gain momentum. Despite the ongoing and undeniable importance of practices of care in the social reproduction of everyday life, care remains largely neglected in public discourse and is seriously considered only insofar as it has been translated into the indifferent idiom of social security. All this points to an issue that, coupled with the unsettling question of gender, persistently dogs the discourse of care: the problem of genre. In what genre, in what tone, or (reciting Gilligan) in what "voice" can one talk about care without losing the concretion and responsiveness that advocates of care want to claim for it? Care is handicapped—but it is precisely such metaphors that a real discourse of care would want to discard—by an inability to assert itself as such.

It is this problem—the genre of care—that is taken up in Coetzee's 2005 novel, *Slow Man*, in which a surprising affinity between care and fiction comes to light. In contrast to the edifying discourse of rights and duties and in contrast to grander affects and emotions, care seems always in the end to be "just care," as if it fails to live up to certain criteria of reality or authenticity in much the same way that one says something is "just fiction." Care, like fiction, appears to be constitutively accompanied by the reproach of *frivolity*—a troubling word the significance of which *Slow Man* is devoted to unraveling. While Coetzee's South African novels were compelled to explore the tensions between justice and care, the Australian writings of Elizabeth Costello engage what I would call the "justness" of care. In *Slow Man*, the perceived shortcomings of care are no longer measured against the political criteria of justice but are felt as an immanent disappointment with care itself.

If, therefore, in a literary exploration of such earnest issues as disability, aging, intergenerationality, and migration *Slow Man* turns into a reflection on the ontology of fiction, this is not mere metafictional frivolity. An exploration of fiction belongs rather to the analysis of the justness of care. Not only does this amount to an unfolding of the ways in which care is expressed in fiction and by fiction, it also surprisingly—and dishearteningly for those of a more earnest disposition— amounts to a reflection on the role of fiction in "maintaining and repairing our world." In contrast to the austerity and earnestness that tend to define theories of justice, a theory of *justness*—if such a thing can still be called a theory and is not "just fiction"—implies a reflection on its constitutive frivolity. To be heartfelt, the discourse of care needs also to be lighthearted, even if this comes at the cost of being taken seriously. On account of these difficulties, *Slow Man* is one of Coetzee's most painstaking novels but also his most frivolous—indeed, it is "just a joke."

Is It Serious?

No one is less amused than Paul Rayment, the novel's unwilling and unlikable protagonist. In the opening of the book he is hit by a car, knocked off his bike, and has to have his leg amputated on account of the injuries sustained. Between the accident and the amputation, when owing to pain and painkillers he goes in and out of consciousness, he has a curious revelation: "Something is coming to him. A letter at a time, *clack clack clack*, a message is being typed on a rose-pink screen that trembles like water each time he blinks and is therefore quite likely his own inner eyelid. E-R-T-Y, say the letters, then F-R-I-V-O-L, then a trembling, then E, then Q-W-E-R-T-Y, on and on" (3). Only in chapter 13, when the famous Australian writer Elizabeth Costello—who in Coetzee's fictional corpus stands as a literary persona for the author—appears in the text, ringing Rayment's doorbell and reciting to him the opening lines of the book, will the reader's suspicions be confirmed. The message is not that of an "occult typewriter" (19), as Rayment in his delirium had believed, but rather a patently literary representation of the writing process by which the hapless Rayment is brought into being as a literary figure: "'What is this?' he mouths or perhaps even shouts, meaning *What is this that is being done to me?* or *What is this place where I find myself?* or even *What is this fate that has befallen me?*" (4). On one level, the level of the narrative, Rayment is trying to come to terms with an accident that will lead to the loss of a limb. On another—if these levels can really be differentiated—he is suffering a fate perhaps more traumatic: the drama of becoming a fictional character. "*Is it serious?*" (4) he wants to ask. This turns out to be his most persistent concern: is it serious, is it in earnest, is it for real? Above all, let it not be, as the typewriting or the trope of typewriting seems to suggest: *frivole*, frivolous. In order to recover himself, he considers asking as a pretext: "*Where are my clothes? Where are my clothes, and how serious is my situation?*" (4). The confusion of the frivolous and the serious is already laid bare: Rayment, whose name sounds in English like raiment, is literally just a cover, a pretense, a fiction. Only later do we learn that Rayment is of French descent; his name ought actually to be pronounced to rhyme with the French: *vraiment*—seriously?

Dogged earnestness is not, to be sure, just a peculiarity of *Slow Man*'s protagonist. The experimental presentation of a literary figure who is consumed by a concern with realness and reality belongs to Coetzee's own theoretical and practical engagement with the problem of realism in life and in literature (see Wicomb; Lamb; Mulhall; and Zimbler). This preoccupation is not to be separated in Coetzee's work from an acknowledgment of, or an anxiety about, the ostensible frivolity of fiction—above all in the face of the everyday realities of such places as South Africa, where, furthermore, the European literary tradition can with good reason be perceived as suspect. In Coetzee's Australian novels, this concern about frivolity is tackled directly—to the extent that this is possible.

Is it serious? His leg is a "bit of a mess"—the young doctor informs Rayment that it will have to be surgically amputated, they will "save what they can" (5). Although Elizabeth Costello will later insist, "Your missing leg is just a sign or symbol or symptom, I can never remember which is which, of growing old, old and uninteresting" (229), the presentation of Rayment's predicament seems rather to be part of a long-standing preoccupation in Coetzee's work with disability as something other than a literary trope (see Hall; and Neimneh and Al-Shalabi). The grim realities of life without a leg are described in uncompromising practical and administrative detail. And Rayment, subject to the good and kindly but, he feels, ultimately indifferent attentions of the hospital nurses and doctors, pictures to himself what has happened to his body in graphic terms: "*Care of my leg? . . . You anaesthetised me and hacked off my leg and dropped it in the refuse for someone to collect and toss into the fire. How can you stand there talking about care of my leg?*" (10). There seems to be an attempt to take disability seriously, so to speak, and to do so in a manner that contributes to a contemporary tendency that Tobin Siebers refers to in *Disability Theory* as the "new realism of the body" (25). Pain, a decisive parameter of Sieber's new realism, is addressed in *Slow Man* in no uncertain terms: "*Pain is nothing*, he tells himself, *just a warning signal from the body to the brain. Pain is no more the real thing than an X-ray photograph is the real thing.* But of course he is wrong. Pain is the real thing, it does not have to press hard to persuade him of that" (12). "Pain is the real thing"—reality is, first and foremost, corporeality. The seriousness of Rayment's situation is conveyed by the realist description of his disablement. One cannot avoid the suspicion, however, that the sense of seriousness is a function of the description of disablement. Reality, corporeality, is not just attended to and brought into focus—it is realized by such description. The reality of corporal debilitation thus figures for the reality of reality, exemplary of what Siebers himself diagnoses as "the temptation to view disability and pain as more real than their opposites," adding:

> *The perception already exists that broken bodies and things are more real than anything else. The discourse of literary realism began in the nineteenth century to privilege representations of trash, fragments, and imperfect bodies, while modern art turned to the representation of human difference and defect, changing the sense of aesthetic beauty to a rawer conception. These discourses soon penetrated society at large. Somehow, today, a photograph of a daisy in a garden seems less real than a photograph of garbage blowing down a dirty alley.* (67)

As it happens, Rayment is a collector of early Australian photographs. He is captivated by the reality of analogue photography—both by what his fellow "realist" Roland Barthes refers to as the "that-has-been" (77) of the photograph, the photograph as an "emanation of *past reality*" (88), and by the historical reality of the photographs themselves in their singular materiality. Among the prized Faucherys in his collection—photographs of the Australian gold rush of the 1850s by the French photographer Antoine Fauchery—the one that "haunts him most deeply" depicts a large, impoverished family standing outside a cabin, "frightened, frozen, like oxen at the portal of a slaughterhouse. The light hits them flat in the face, picks out every smudge on their skin and their clothes. On the hand that the smallest child brings to her mouth the light exposes what might be jam but was more likely mud. How the whole thing could have been brought off with the long exposures required in those days he cannot even guess" (52). For Rayment this photograph presents the primal scene of Australian history. If Australia lacks history in the European and Eurocentric sense—which as a matter of course discounts the history of the land's Aboriginal peoples—Rayment discerns here a different kind of "aboriginal" history that is exposed only through the photographic medium. The photograph presents the barren reality of "bare life" stripped of the narrative history of human and human-made events. "Look that is where we come from," Rayment observes, "from the cold and damp and smoke of that wretched cabin, from those women with their black helpless eyes, from that poverty and that grinding labour on hollow stomachs" (52).

Rayment's fascination with photography owes to its capacity to capture this ostensibly nondiscursive aspect of reality, presenting realities that cannot—at least not with the same effect of reality—be spoken, named, or narrated. For this reason, despite the artificialness of the scenario betrayed by the technical necessity of long exposure, he finds the realness of the image in no way diminished. It is the disclosure of abjection—the wretchedness, the poverty, the hunger—in the photograph that conveys its haunting reality. Ironically, Rayment's preoccupation with reality turns out itself to be the product of the project of realism. The problem of reality in *Slow Man*, which in turn produces an interrogation of the frivolity of fiction, is the outcome of "the representation of reality in western literature" (Auerbach 23). As his particular interest in photography shows, Rayment is a literary character who expects a realness that can be found nowhere in reality but only in, and according to, the aesthetic criteria of certain forms of realism.

Just Care

The Apostle Paul was converted when he, as tradition has it, fell from his horse upon hearing the word of the lord and was blinded by a flash of light. In the biblical account, having benefited from the insight afforded by this blindness, Paul's sight is restored by the Christian, Ananias. He is immediately baptized. The cure consummates his conversion. Paul Rayment is knocked off his bicycle and left disabled. It is not a flash of light that takes his sight so that he may see a greater truth, but a revelation of the flesh. There is no promise of recovery, only rehabilitation, "no cure, just care" (63). Paul's conversion is to the truth of life as a life of the flesh—a post-theological biological-literary conversion. His Croatian nurse pronounces "flash" as "flesh," a slippage marked and remarked on throughout *Slow Man*: "Flash. A flash of lightning," Paul corrects her, "Flesh is what we are made of, flesh and bone" (54). It is this harsh reality of the flesh with which Paul, the slow man, will have to come to terms (see Vermeulen). At the beginning of the twenty-first century, the terms with which to address the old theological problem of the flesh in the ostensibly secular liberal-capitalist society of Australia are the terms of care. The disclosure of the flesh through disablement is thus also an unfolding of the contemporary discourse of care in its biopolitical, ethical, and aesthetic dimensions (see Hallemeier; and De Boever).

"Frivole" (3), Paul reads out of the mystical typescript on the rose-pink screen. The appearance of the foreign word is not quite as artificial as it seems: French is his mother tongue even if he is not altogether at home in the language. He immigrated with his mother, sister, and Dutch stepfather to Australia as a child. Now, however, divorced, childless, and on the threshold of old age, he has, as he writes on the forms in the hospital, "Family: *NONE*" (9). After the accident he feels he has "no future" (12). He is plagued with regrets that revolve, initially at least, around the script of what Lee Edelman calls "reproductive futurism" (2; see Parvulescu). It is the lack of family—and above all of a child, a son—that in the period following the accident galls him the most about what he now considers to be indeed a frivolous existence. Recalling the typed message, which he no longer takes seriously, he nonetheless reflects:

> Yet frivolous *is not a bad word to sum him up, as he was before the event and may still be. If in the course of a lifetime he has done no significant harm he has done no good either. He will leave no trace behind, not even an heir to carry on his name.* Sliding through the world: *that is how, in a bygone age, they used to designate lives like his: looking after his interests, quietly prospering, attracting no attention . . .* A wasted chance. (19)

An unreproductive life that leaves no traces and passes nothing on: this is Paul's understanding of the word *frivolous*. It refers to a careless life—squandered, inconsequential—one that is therefore not worth caring about. A life just lived. If the accident brings into focus the carelessness of his previous life, it also leaves him in a situation—aging, disabled—in which nothing remains, so to speak, but care. With the loss of his leg, Paul's life begins in earnest. He has the chance to make up for past frivolity. This would be the meaning of his "conversion." But—and this is the question that Paul gloomily works through in the rest of the book—can a life of just care constitute a real life?

The immediate practical concern is of course: *who is going to take care of him?* Paul responds: "I would prefer to take care of myself" (10). Of course the matter is not altogether in his hands. Not only is he incapacitated until he has accustomed himself to take care of his altered body, there is also a welfare apparatus in place, the task of which it is to ensure that those considered unable to take care of themselves are taken care of. The question as to how he will "cope" with his altered body and circumstances brings a social worker onto the scene (16). If he is to escape institutionalization and maintain his cherished, if ultimately spurious, sense of autonomy, he will have to engage a "care-giver," preferably a nurse with "experience of frail care" (17). If his insurance will not stretch to it, the welfare officer adds, he will have to budget for it himself.

As a result of the accident, the whole question of "care" is disclosed in its vertiginous complexity. Not least, there is the question of what the word *care* is supposed to mean. When Marijana Jokić, the Croatian nurse he employs, asks: "So who is going to take care of you?" (43), he finds himself struck by the ambivalence of the phrase:

> *The more he stares at the words* take care of, *the more inscrutable they seem. He remembers a dog they had when he was a child in Lourdes, lying in its basket in the last stages of canine distemper, whimpering without cease, its muzzle hot and dry, its limbs jerking. "Bon, je m'en occupe," his father said at a certain point, and picked the dog up, basket and all, and walked out of the house. Five minutes later, from the woods, he heard the flat report of a shotgun, and that was that, he never saw the dog again.* Je m'en occupe: *I'll take charge of it; I'll take care of it; I'll do what has to be done. That kind of caring, with a shotgun, was certainly not what Marijana had in mind. Nevertheless, it lay englobed in the phrase, waiting to leak out. If so, what of his reply:* I'll take care of myself? *What did his words mean, objectively?* (43–44)

"To take care of" in its broadest sense, in the full scope of its semantic usage, has to do with attention to finitude—with attending to and drawing attention to the precariousness of corporal existence. Care is "humane," but it is not always "tender" (237). In contrast with bigger words and more dramatic affects, *care* is the expression of a biological if not a biopolitical compromise with finitude and an aesthetic compromise with the most unattractive, abject, and also banal realities of embodied biological existence. It seems as tenuous as the bodies it attends to. And it is perhaps for this reason that there is something uneasy, suspect, disappointing, and even, as Paul senses among the young caregivers at the hospital, ultimately indifferent about care. A word that says so much seems ultimately to ring hollow. Care is a "frivolous proposition" (Derrida 123).

"What did his words mean, objectively?"—Paul finds himself worried about the reality of care, its authenticity. For the "advent" of Marijana he is thankful: she has a matter-of-fact way about her that he appreciates. As he settles into Marijana's "regimen of care" (32), he finds himself reflecting on the queer intimacy they share: "A man and a woman on a warm afternoon behind locked doors. They might as well be performing a sex act. But it is nothing like that. It is just nursing, just care" (33). Compared with the supposed authenticity of sex, whatever pleasure he enjoys at the hands of Marijana is "just nursing, just care." Paul recalls a line from the catechism—"*There shall be no more man and woman, but . . .* "—that he attributes to "St Paul his namesake, his name-saint, explaining what the afterlife will be like, when all shall love all with a pure love, as God loves, only not as fiercely, as consumingly." What this form of non-appetitive love seemingly beyond sex, beyond sexuality, beyond the impetus or imperative to reproduce, might involve is "impossible for the mortal mind to conceive" (33), as Paul (the unsaintly one) concludes.

The tension between, or the confusion of, a mode of attention and affection understood as authentic, natural, and real, called *love*, and a deficient or indifferent mode that is *just care* motivates the all-too-realistic drama of the book. Paul Rayment, the aging male patient, falls in love with his nurse, Marijana Jokić, or in any case declares what he feels for her to be love: "I love you. That is all. I love you and I want to give you something. Let me" (76). Later he will reflect on how his "labile" declaration must have seemed to Marijana: "How it must have jarred and irritated her: words of love from an object of mere nursing, mere care. Irritating but not, in the end, serious" (172). Nonetheless, he is serious—even if he realizes he is making a fool of himself. Labile he may be, but the feeling is real and for that reason deserves the "biggest of the big words" (213)—*love*. Although it is certainly not unmotivated by a carnal dimension, Paul in all earnestness—but also ridiculously—compares his love with the love of the Catholic god he had been brought up to believe in but no longer does: "[H]e loves Marijana at this moment with a pure and benevolent heart, as God must love her" (144). Would not precisely this kind of "love" be better described with the ostensibly secularized and desexualized term *care*? Why the hyperbolic inflation of his passion? Even when Paul does descend to speaking of care—of caring for Marijana and her children—he does so in escalatory terms that culminate in an expression that is, once again, nothing less than theological: "He wants to take care of them, all of them, protect them and save them" (72).

What Paul has to offer, however, what he has to give, is altogether limited, conditional. He offers to pay the private school fees of Marijana's eldest son, Drago, and of her other children as well. If Marijana interprets this as the offer of a "new life," it is Paul's turn to insist on the limitedness and delimitation of care: "I offered to take care of you. I offered to take care of the children too. But I did not offer a new life. . . . There is no such thing as a new life" (246). Although it may appear to do so, care does not promise a new life, certainly not a higher one. It remains immanent to and conditioned by life just as it is—and this "justness" is what is ultimately disappointing about care. Care is always, to cite Paul at the end of the book, "something else. Something less" (263).

When Marijana scolds Paul for calling on her in an "emergency" that, in her professional opinion, was not one, Paul resentfully responds that he thought nursing was a "vocation": "I thought that was what set it apart, what justified the long hours and the poor pay and the ingratitude and the indignities too, such as those you mentioned: that you were following a calling. Well, when a nurse is called, a proper nurse, she doesn't ask questions, she comes. Even if it is not a real emergency. Even if it is just distress, human distress" (213). To be a "proper nurse" is to respond to the most minor of human forms of distress as if to a transcendent calling—even if, as Paul pathetically adds, "it is just love" (213). Marijana, who trained in art restoration in Croatia before emigrating, states: "My job in Australia is nurse" (211). Marijana does her job well, so well that Paul can hardly believe her attentions are just nursing. And Paul is so moved by Marijana's caregiving that he cannot believe what he feels for her may in turn be just care.

In Paul's unwritten letter, he attempts to make explicit a difficult distinction, one that perhaps ultimately resolves into indifference, between just caring and caring from the heart, between "mere good nursing" and "loving care" (261), between being "humane" and being "tender" (237)—and finally, perhaps, between the word and the real thing. Throughout the book these different senses of care are mistaken for one another or taken one for the other. And precisely this slippage and interchangeability of "cares" seem to be the problem: even the most seemingly attentive modes of caring are always haunted by their indifferent counterpart: vocation by job, intimacy by institution, loving by nursing, the authentic by the counterfeit. In short, care is always potentially *just care*—inauthentic, unreal, frivolous.

Coetzee's novel unfolds an ambivalence about care that a few generations ear-lier was already at the center of Heidegger's *Being and Time* (1927). Care (*Sorge*), according to Heidegger's analysis, is what it means to exist or *to be there* (*Dasein*). In revealing that being is always already caring, however, Heidegger articulates a fundamental insecurity about the ultimate deception or disappointment of all "cares." For, according to his analysis, the caring constitutive of human existence is traversed by a thoroughgoing inauthenticity—or to use the more appropriate term that occurs to the protagonist of *Slow Man*, frivolity. No matter how well taken care of, no matter how concerned or attentive one may be, care is permeated by an anxiety about its own frivolity. If care indeed defines the meaning and the reality of finite embodied existence, it seems nonetheless—and Heidegger's analysis is altogether symptomatic in this regard—never to be quite real or meaningful enough. Surely all this, the meaning of being, cannot be *just care*? It is this anxious concern with the frivolity of care that solicits the question—as pressing for Hei-degger as for Rayment—of "authenticity."

To be sure, *Slow Man* presents a more modest "existential analysis"—that of a white European man of a certain age, disabled, to whom the care-structure of modern life has been brought into focus in a manner that can no longer be avoided "in the mode of an evasive turning away" (Heidegger 128). Paul Rayment finds himself confronted with what he takes to be the frivolity of his existence. His attempts, however, to convert to a life of authentic cares are complicated by the fact that the possibility, or consolation, of authenticity cannot be seriously considered, for he is, after all, a fictional character. Beyond all other concerns about the seri-ousness of his situation, he will have to contend with a question more worrying still: is there anything more frivolous than a fictional life—than the life of fiction? This flagrant and apparently gratuitous metafictional gesture proves in fact to be integral to the analysis of care. For, as I will argue in the sections to follow, *Slow Man* is concerned, on the one hand, with the care of fiction—the kind of care afforded by and to fiction as a cultural practice and institution—and, on the other, with the fiction of care—with the fictional as the mode of being of care itself; that is to say, of care when it is just care.

"A Serious Affair"

Until Rayment's declaration of "love" to Marijana, *Slow Man* seems to be a stren-uously realistic presentation of the realities of aging, disability, and their attendant personal and institutional cares and worries. In the background, however, one senses throughout a nagging concern: Why care about Paul Rayment? Why should we take this all-too-familiar story seriously—the story of a comfortably off, aging, lonely and largely unsympathetic male patient, disabled but not debilitated, who claims to fall in love with his young, competent, and attractive immigrant nurse, who, for her part, just wants to do her job? Does this sort of "two a penny" (82) story warrant literary attention? And does not the literary treatment of such questions ultimately deserve to be met with indifference? It is, one assumes, concerns of this sort that bring Elizabeth Costello to her character's door and into his life as an uninvited and unwelcome guest.

"Fiction, being a serious affair," Coetzee wrote in notes made in the early 1970s for a book that he never completed, "cannot accept pre-requisites like (1) a desire to write, (2) something to write about, (3) something to say. There must be a place for a fiction of apathy toward the task of writing, toward the subject, toward the means" ("Burning the Books"). This challenge of what I would call the indifference to fiction has been a lasting preoccupation of Coetzee's literary work. Much of his writing is devoted to figures who do not care, or who are unable to care, about the attentions of literature, for they live under conditions in which literature appears frivolous if not indeed morally or politically suspect.

A genealogy of this political ambivalence of fiction was sketched by Foucault at the end of "The Life of Infamous Men," published in 1977, the same year he delivered the lectures that appear in *Security, Territory, Population*. Fiction, he suggests, emerged with the institution of the modern security apparatus. Beginning in the seventeenth century, everyday life in all its multifaceted detail was turned into a matter of political-scientific investigation and regulation—into a security concern, in short. Fiction perversely radicalized this project by investigating the "quotidian beneath the quotidian"—the insignificant, the ostracized, the abject (Foucault, "Life" 174). Drawing on the etymological relation between the Latin *cura* (care) and *securitas* (security), one can say that while the security apparatus takes care of what really matters, fiction cares about what is not worth caring for—hence the ever-present charge of the frivolity of literary concerns.

"Fiction cares" might accordingly be the motto of a significant tradition of modern literature. But what it cares about most of all is—indifference. With his formula: "I would prefer to take care of myself" (10), Paul joins a line of literary characters—most famously Melville's Bartleby, but also Kafka's Odradek and Coetzee's own Michael K—who reject or frustrate or are simply indifferent to the conscientious concerns not only of the representatives of authority or security in such fictions but of the *dispositif* of fiction itself. On the basis of such figures, it is tempting to suggest that fiction is constituted out of a passionate confrontation with the indifference to fiction. While Rayment may arrive at an accommodation with the welfare apparatus—an accommodation that at least provides a modicum of the privacy and independence he desires—it is another matter to evade the solicitous attentions of his author. "Can I not persuade you," he begs Costello at one point, "to leave us alone to work out our own salvation in our own way?" (141).

Paul Rayment does not care for Elizabeth Costello. She is old, unattractive, unwell—not his type. He fundamentally mistrusts her profession—the writing of fiction—and the ambiguity of his place in her work is occasion for considerable "existential" anxiety. Reading some writing that she has left out, he finds "Something unseemly about this writing, the fat ink sprawling carelessly over the tramlines; something impious, provocative, uncovering what does not belong in the light of day" (121). It is true that Costello is invasive—not only her handwriting crosses lines—indeed she sometimes seems ubiquitous. Nonetheless she appears less an agent of the police, as suggested by Foucault's analysis, than a vagrant, a figure without a determinate place of abode, who sleeps on her character's sofa, lives out of a suitcase, and on occasion roughs it with the "hoboes" (159) in the streets and parks of Adelaide. In short, Costello, representative of the disparaged institution of literature, appears as someone who could do with some care. While Coetzee's South African novels were occupied with the complicities of literature in the security apparatus of the state or other colonial, patriarchal, or paternalistic institutions, his Australian Costello writings, in contrast, seem devoted to excavating modalities of care that evade the logic of security altogether, as if this were indeed the "serious affair" of fiction.

Why does Costello so tenaciously persevere with a character who, as she tells him, "occurred to me—a man with a bad leg and no future and an unsuitable passion" (85)? Costello enters into his story struggling with what she, not without irony, calls her "affection" for Paul: "What do we call it when someone knows the worst about us, the worst and most wounding, and does not come out with it but on the contrary suppresses it and continues to smile on us and make little jokes? We call it affection. Where else in the world, at this late stage, are you going to find affection, you ugly old man?" (235–36). Costello does not want to give up on Paul, neglect his uninteresting story, and expunge his tenuous existence. She perseveres with him out of the affection—and for the sake of the affection—that her fiction affords. But is she herself convinced? Are the smile and the little jokes enough to rescue the unloved and the unlovely from oblivion and to offer them a worthwhile existence—an existence worth writing about? Or is this ideal of the attentions of fiction itself a fiction? A surprising subtext emerges, a subtext insofar as *Slow Man* is narrated largely from the point of view of Paul, of a failed love story between Elizabeth and Paul. Costello too is in search of "loving care" and reluctant to make do with "mere good nursing" (261). She entertains a fiction of living with her character as a kind of (late) life companion. Rayment, however, refuses such a frivolous arrangement. The book ends with Costello asking: "Is this love, Paul? Have we found love at last?" He responds: "No, . . . this is not love. This is something else. Something less" (263). The fiction has to be abandoned. No more love in fiction, no more love of fiction either—just affection, just care.

Costello's fiction cannot get off the ground because Rayment is too "gloomy" to make for a compelling literary character—"my knight of the doleful countenance" (256), she quips. Unlike his illustrious literary forbear, however, Rayment is completely devoid of the quixotic facility to invest his suffering with enchantment. If in Cervantes's *Don Quixote* Sancho Panza soberly observes, "[I]t's my opinion, simpleton and sinner though I am, that it isn't an enchantment at all, but real bruises and real misery" (part 1, chapter 37), then in the figure of Mr. Rayment, who is resolved never to ride again, a radical reduction is attempted so as to exclude anything other than "real bruises and real misery" as mere fiction. "Gloom" in *Slow Man* presents the zero degree of fictionality, the greatest possible literalism with regard to reality. But is this gloomy attitude really realistic? Or is Rayment ultimately as ridiculous, as positively comic on account of his denial of reality, as Quixote? This conundrum is thematized at the close of the book, where it emerges that the word *gloomy*, used in English to describe Paul's dogged earnestness and despondency with regard to reality, turns out in another language to mean pretense, unreality, even frivolousness. *Gloomy* is a "funny word," as Marijana remarks to Paul. "In Croatia we say *ovaj glumi*, doesn't mean he is gloomy, no, means he is pretending, he is not real. But you not pretending, eh?" (251). Marijana is of course joking—and on another level the whole thing is a joke, much like the one Paul remarks upon as he wanders around the sleeping Costello in his apartment: "The scribbler sleeps, the character prowls around looking for things to occupy himself with. A joke, but for the fact that there is no one around to catch it" (238).

Surprisingly to many readers of Coetzee, *Slow Man* turns out to be a witty book that affectionately pokes fun at its serious character. Indeed, it turns out to be the most "jocoserious" of Coetzee's novels, the Joycean term that Patrick Hayes draws on to describe a comic strain that is legible in Coetzee's fiction from the start. For the novel also makes light of the seriousness with which Coetzee has gone about his entire literary undertaking. It is striking that an author whose writing so uncompromisingly interrogates its own presuppositions—not least those of literature—should at the very beginning of his career, on the first page of his notes for a book he would not complete, have departed from a most questionable presupposition: "Fiction, being a serious affair . . . " In *Slow Man*, Coetzee seems finally to have circled round to question this assumption of the seriousness of literature. If the Australian Costello writings are devoted, as I have suggested, to excavating certain kinds of care of the sort that fiction can offer, this ethical and literary experiment culminates in the acknowledgment that, if it is to be really convincing in conveying such concerns, it cannot take itself too seriously. The frivolity of fiction needs to be acknowledged not only as an accompaniment but as integral to the "serious affair" of fiction. Serious fiction has to come to terms with the fact that it is always also just a joke.

Just a Joke

Published in 2005, *Slow Man* can be read as Coetzee's "Paul book." As such, it presents a contribution to a millennial fascination with the apostle Paul attested to by a spate of books and articles by contemporary philosophers and theologians. In his reading of Paul's Letter to the Romans in *The Time That Remains*, a seminar published in English in 2005, Giorgio Agamben addresses, albeit briefly, the "centrality of fiction to modern culture" (35) in his discussion of the Pauline concept of vocation (*klētos*). The particular character of the Christian calling is, according to Agamben, definitively captured in a passage in 1 Corinthians 7:29–32, where Paul exhorts the faithful to assume a form of life on the model of the "as not" (*hōs mē*): "But this I say, brethren, time contracted itself, the rest is, that even those having wives may be as not [*hōs mē*] having, and those weeping as not weeping, and those rejoicing as not rejoicing, and those buying as not possessing, and those using the world as not using it up" (qtd. in Agamben 23). In one of the excurses in the chapter, Agamben suggests that it was in Heidegger's engagement with Paul in his early *Phenomenology of Religious Life* (1921) that he first developed the structure of what would become the dialectic of authenticity and inauthenticity in *Being and Time* (1927). Turning to Heidegger's reading of Paul in those lectures, it is further striking that Heidegger presents the Christian calling, or the conversion to a Christian form of life, as an "existential" assault on reality: "[T]he reality of worldly life is targeted" (84). It is not, however, that worldly reality is disputed; it is just not decisive for the facticity of Christian life. This consists, Heidegger claims, in the carrying out (*Vollzug*) of real life in the Pauline mode, which he translates with *as if not*: "The indeed existing [*daseienden*] significances of real life are lived *hōs mē*, as if not [*als ob nicht*]" (84). In short: "something remains unchanged and yet is radically changed" (85). In a similar way, Heidegger's subsequent presentation of authenticity in *Being and Time* does not involve assuming another or a different order of higher or more significant cares from those that constitute one's everyday existence. As Agamben insists: "The authentic does not have any other content than the inauthentic" (34). It is rather a matter of finding an "appropriate" comportment to fallen, factical existence and the cares of everyday life.

Taking the Pauline *as if not* seriously, Heidegger sought to recuperate authentic reality as a "proper" mode of being. To do so, however, risks disparaging everyday reality as mere fiction (*as if not*) for the sake of an authentic mode of existence that, faced with the reality of its own finitude, suspends its entanglement in worldly concerns in order to resolutely decide on what really matters. Heidegger's austere appropriation of the calling of early Christianity in terms of authenticity does not allow for a frivolous alternative. It fails to consider the possibility of an attitude of *as not*, understood as a radicalization of the inauthenticity and impropriety of real life. To move in this direction would be to explore the reality of fiction, to which Coetzee's Paul book is devoted.

This leads back to the tortured question of the relation between reality and (literary) realism at the center of *Slow Man*. Along with Don Quixote, Madame Bovary is the main point of reference for Costello's attempts to prod her character into life: "*We only live once*, says Alonso, says Emma, *so let's give it a whirl!* Give it a whirl, Paul." In short, Costello wants a bit more bovarism from Paul—"Be a main character," she urges (229). In Agamben's passing but illuminating remarks on fiction, he praises Jules de Gaultier's *Le Bovarysme* for restoring the problem of fiction "to the level of the ontological" (Agamben 35). Gaultier's initial analysis of the "pathological" bovarism displayed by certain figures in Flaubert's realism—that is to say, an excessive attachment to an impossible fiction of their own lives—leads into a more general reflection on "an essential bovarism" not only in literature but in real life. Essential bovarism consists in the necessity for each of us to conceive of ourselves as other than we are—"*se concevoir autre*" (Gaultier 11). To exist, to really exist, is to fictionalize (see Gaultier 307). As Agamben writes: "Because he is not anything himself, man can only be if he acts as if he were different from what he is (or what he is not)" (37).

In Gaultier's reading, Flaubert's realism consists in an analysis of those instances in which the fictionalizing of the self that is constitutive of reality becomes pathological because it is ultimately unrealistic—too fictional, too novel-like for the banality of everyday reality. In *Slow Man*, Coetzee's realism seems to be devoted to addressing a different pathology—call it *Raymentism* or perhaps, to keep an element of the Frenchness as well as of incredulity: *vraimentism*. If bovarism is an all-too-earnest, and therefore ultimately frivolous, devotion to an unrealistic fiction of the self, vraimentism consists in the refusal of fiction as *just* fiction, as mere frivolity. It is paradigmatically exemplified in the dogged insistence on reality by a fictional figure in a manner that ultimately disrupts the fiction, which is to say, the reality-effect of the narrative.

Having been knocked off his bike, Paul Rayment looks back on his frivolous life and wants to really live. Failing that, he wants at least to live authentically. The time is short. What he has no time for, and absolutely refuses, is to live *as if*—hence his rejection of a prosthesis: "I don't want to look natural . . . I prefer to feel natural" (59). But is *as if* fiction's only mode of being? With the *as not*, the apostle Paul presents an alternative—one that is not without consequence for *Slow Man*. In his commentary, Agamben explicitly contrasts the Pauline ethic with Hans Vaihinger's still influential *The Philosophy of "As If."* For Vaihinger, following Friedrich Karl Forberg, the ethical consists in acting *as if* there were a god or some higher ideal or task, in a "secular" fiction that compensates for the finitude of human existence: "Enough that your heart bids you to act *as if* it were so" (322). In contrast, the form of life according to the "as not" involves excavating an all but indiscernible fictional space inside reality. According to Agamben, the Christian calling paradoxically— or ironically—insists on the irreparable finitude of everyday reality that is abso- lutely without transcendence: "The *as not* is by no means a fiction in the sense intended by Vaihinger or Forberg. It has nothing to do with an ideal. The assimi- lation to what has been lost and forgotten is absolute: 'We are made as the filth of the world, the offscouring of all things' (I Cor. 4:13)" (41). In Agamben's messianic reading, the Pauline calling—at least as it might be taken up today at the beginning of the third millennium—discloses a mode of existence abandoned to a finitude devoid of the consoling, and therefore suspect, fictions of the *as if*. And the finitude thereby disclosed is not first of all one's own but that of the world: "He knows that in messianic time the saved world coincides with the world that is irretrievably lost, and that, to use Bonhoeffer's words, he must now really live in a world without God" (42). For Agamben reading Paul, salvation consists in saving what is irrep- arably broken or lost *in its irreparability*. It consists, one might say, in a kind of care freed from the telos of cure and of security.

In Coetzee's Paul book, "Australia" is the site in which the defunct and uprooted European literary and political-theological traditions are explored for what may be saved (see Brian Macaskill's extraordinary prelude to reading *Slow Man*, "I Am Not Me"). Of the many words with a lingering theological resonance—*love, charity, vocation, blessing*—the Australian meaning of which seems to be under investiga- tion in *Slow Man*, *save* is one of the most ambiguous. Early on, the young doctor says that they will try to save his leg: "We are going to have to amputate, but we will save what we can" (5). Later Paul wants to "take care of" Marijana and her children, to "protect them and save them" (72). And later still, after falling in the shower, he calls Marijana for help, while what he is really doing is appealing for salvation: "*Come, save me!* he called across the South Australian space" (212). In *Slow Man*, the tension between saving in the mundane or medical sense—the limiting of damage, the rescuing from mortal harm, the nursing, the care—and saving in the eminent sense—a saving that would heal all wounds and lift all cares once and for all— remains unresolved.

It is Paul's attempt to "save history," as Marijana puts it (48), that brings his fixation on reality into a confrontation with the other fundamental attitude pre- sented in the book—that of the Jokić family. Paul thinks of his collection of early Australian photography as a means to save historical reality "out of fidelity to their subjects, the men and women and children who offered their bodies up to the stranger's lens," but also "out of fidelity to the photographs themselves, the photographic prints, most of them last survivors, unique" (65). Drago Jokić, Marijana's son, has a distinctly different take on them. Regarding the disproportionate amount of time Drago spends with the photographs while staying at Paul's apartment, Paul tells Costello: "He must be feeling his way into what it is like to have an Australian past, an Australian descent, Australian forebears of the mystical variety. Instead of being just a refugee kid with a joke name" (191–92). It may in fact be the case that Drago is engaging with the question of his history, or he may just be playing a joke on his all-too-earnest host. In any case, Paul discovers that one of his authentic Faucherys has been replaced with a forgery. He tells Marijana: "A copy has been substituted for the original, a copy which has been doctored, for what purpose I can't say" (245). The "doctoring" in question involves the montage of the face of Drago's Croatian grandfather into a photograph of "Cornish and Irish miners of a bygone age." Paul is incensed by such "desecration," while Costello tries to placate him insisting that it is, "Just a joke, an unthinking, juvenile joke" (218–20).

The none-too-subtle play on the "joke" in Jokić is insisted upon throughout the book. It was Marijana's matter-of-fact attitude to the reality of his situation that first appealed to Paul. But this Jokićian matter-of-factness seems in fact to be part of a very different attitude, or perhaps a different taste for reality. In Croatia, Marijana's husband Miroslav had earned a brief fame for reassembling a two-hundred-year-old mechanical duck; their second daughter gets into trouble for shoplifting "a silver chain, a chain that is not even real silver" (167); and when Paul visits the Jokić residence to confront Marijana regarding the forgery and the missing photograph, Costello, who accompanies him, enthuses: "So real!" "So authentic!" upon seeing the "colonial-style house with green lawn around an austere little rectangular Japanese garden: a slab of black marble with water trickling down its face, rushes, grey pebbles" (242). The Jokićs, as Costello remarks, "have a lifestyle to support" (243), a lifestyle that, precisely on account of its artificiality, seems to Paul to be altogether inauthentic.

Marijana shows him Drago's room, which has more digitally altered images from Paul's collection blown up as posters on the wall. There is a reproduction of the photograph of the hungry immigrant family that has been montaged to include Marijana's youngest daughter Ljuba, whom her mother often brought with her to work. Paul examines Ljuba's face, which has been imperfectly mounted onto the shoulders of the girl with the muddy hands, "her dark eyes boring into him" (249). Convinced by the reality, or rather the realism, of the original, Paul had asserted: "Look that is where we come from" (52). Should the doctored image be taken seriously to present an alternative genealogy, an alternative take on the question of origins and of origination—or is it all just a joke?

Like Costello, Marijana, as Paul will later remark, thinks that "the whole forgery business is just a joke" (259). But that is not exactly what she had said: "Just playing . . . Is not serious thing. Is just—how you say it?—slips." Paul corrects her: "Shapes. Images." "Is just images . . . " (249). That Marijana says "slips" instead of "images" suggests that there may indeed be more to them than meets the eye—a slippage between the justness and the justice of these images, perhaps. The doctored image is a dialectical one. It might therefore be called a "prosthese," which is how Marijana pronounces *prosthesis*: "*Prosthese*: she pronounces it as if it were a German word. Thesis, antithesis, then prosthesis" (62). While Paul insists on preserving what he takes to be the unadulterated photograph of a reality "that-has-been" (Barthes), Drago, whose thoughts on this matter we never get to hear, attends instead to what has not been. In a way that resonates with Agamben's messianic reading of Paul, Drago's images can be seen to "save history" in a different way, by taking care of what has been irreparably broken and lost. His doctored images present a prosthetic reality. Such images are by no means idealizations or imaginations of another world on the model of the *as if*. On the contrary, making light of the Pauline *as not*, the "joke" consists in producing realistic presentations that transfigure reality in inconspicuous and apparently insignificant ways. It corresponds to what Marijana describes when talking about Paul's (to her mind) wrongheaded resistance to getting a prosthesis: "Maybe you think, you walk in street, everybody look at you. *That Mr Rayment, he got only one leg!* Isn't true. Isn't true. Nobody look at you. You wear prosthese, nobody look at you. Nobody know. Nobody care" (62). A *prosthese* is real insofar as it is *as not*. Drago's images thus present a distinct kind of realism, one that arguably provides the model of the realism of Coetzee's novel.

Or is it just a joke? Paul remarks dourly to Costello that jokes have a "relation to the unconscious," to which Costello replies: "sometimes a joke is just a joke" (259). Costello's use of the word intends a thoroughgoing frivolity—a joke and nothing more. But Drago's doctoring can also be seen to do justice to the *just* that has disparagingly modified all ostensibly inauthentic modes of caring throughout the book: just nursing, just love, just care. The trouble is—and this is the trouble around which the book revolves—there is no telling *just* from *just*. Whether Drago's attentions are historical or photographic or simply thoughtless and juvenile, the joke, on account of the ambivalence regarding its just character, accomplishes an exposition of the justness of reality. The butt of this particular joke, Paul Rayment— "The man who can't take a joke" (259)—is affectionately shown how unrealistic his realist attitude really is. The just joke discloses, in other words, a frivolity inherent to reality—above all, to Paul's reality—that he doggedly refuses to acknowledge. The joke is a therapy for his vraimentism. In symptomatically exaggerated style, he will later reflect: "[P]erhaps, in a larger perspective, that is exactly what the Jokićs mean to teach him: that he should give up his solemn airs and become what he rightly is, a figure of fun . . . " (256). But humor, like taste—in which he so fundamentally differs from Marijana—is notoriously difficult to translate. Can he get the humor of the Jokićs?

Before leaving the Jokić residence after his vain attempt to recover the original Fauchery, he is shown the bike that Drago, with help from the whole family, has been making for him as a surprise gift. Paul is really ashamed: "He can feel a blush creeping over him, a blush of shame, starting at his ears and creeping forward over his face. He has no wish to stop it. It is what he deserves" (254). The bike is a recumbent: "[H]e dislikes recumbents instinctively, as he dislikes prostheses, as he dislikes all fakes" (255). Nonetheless, he does what he is expected to do and takes it for a spin. He knows he will never use it; it will just gather dust in his basement: "All the time and trouble the Jokićs have put into it will be for nothing" (256). But the Jokićs know this too—certainly Marijana does. Hence the significance of the theater when Paul, going through the motions of showing gratitude that he really does feel, turns to her and asks whether he should take to cycling again:

> *"Yeah," says Marijana slowly. "It suits you. I think you should give it a whirl."*
> *With her left hand Marijana holds her chin; with her right hand she props up her left elbow. It is the classic posture of thought, of mature reflection.* (257)

The scene, which furthermore recites Costello's appeal for a bit more bovarism ("give it a whirl"), is clearly just theater, just fiction. Nonetheless, Paul is genuinely moved. The gift into which the Jokićs have with such "munificence" put their time and energy, the gift which, as Paul repeats to himself, is "much more than I deserve," is at the same time altogether frivolous (254). Everyone knows it will never really be used. The gift is just a gift, exhausted in the gesture of giving—a joke of a gift, a Jokić gift. It exhibits a frivolous generosity that gives without substantively changing anything, that just gives just care.

Although it is ultimately indistinguishable from a mere lifestyle, the Jokićing mode of nursing broken bodies and doctoring the damaged figures of the world presents the image of a just form of life. Rather than worrying about authenticity, the Jokićs care for, and take care of, the justness of reality. In so doing, they exhibit an attitude in which frivolity and matter-of-factness can no longer be told apart. Ljuba, who has silently witnessed the unfolding of Paul's relationship with her mother, speaks for the first time. Remarking on the phrase *PR Express* painted on the tube of the tricycle, she observes: "You aren't Rocket Man, you're Slow Man!" (258). The—for the child, hilarious—satisfaction of finding *le mot juste*, of passing a judgment that is at the same time a joke, presents in abbreviated form the realism to which the novel aspires. *Slow Man* has been the arduous unpacking of Ljuba's punchline.

Fiction Cares

Coetzee's previous Costello writings are earnest and heartfelt pleas for the care of fiction. They present a series of attempts to think through, and even to perform, the neglected kind of care that fiction offers. In this regard, Costello can be read as a writer of a feminist ethics of care. Because they are just fiction, such modes of attention and pleas for attention tend to be disparaged, discounted, or ignored. Costello's writings are thus always also apologies for fiction, attempts, feeble because fictional, to make the case for fiction. Dark, self-deprecating, ironic, none of these texts are at all funny; they cannot be accused of making light of the serious concerns—"the lives of animals," "the problem of evil"—they address. It is with *Slow Man*, which appears to be the last of the Costello writings, that in reflecting on the frivolity of all serious fiction, Coetzee turns to a mode that can be called humorous.

In *Slow Man*, care is shown to be structurally implicated with fiction in ways that are profoundly unsettling for those who want to seriously talk about care. But it is illuminating with regard to the difficulties of convincingly advocating an ethics of care. Care, when it is just care, cannot be asserted in the form of a thesis but only expressed in the ambiguous "fictional" mode of a *prosthese*. Does the idea that something as vital as care should express itself in such an essentially frivolous way make a mockery of the whole ethical and political project? Although *Slow Man* presents the case for acknowledging a constitutive frivolity that goes into the concrete "work of maintaining and repairing our world" (Tronto and Fisher 43), it is clear that it is not going to convince anyone who does not "get" the joke or who finds it to be in poor taste or even trivializing. This aporia presented by the sense of humor insofar as it informs one's attitude to the world is thematized in the figure of slow man himself, who refuses to be what he is—a figure of fun.

Approaching from the other direction, what are the ethical implications of the rejection of fiction? Although it is difficult for readers to identify with the gloomy figure of Paul, the phenomenon of what I have called vraimentism is remarkably widespread. After all: what really matters cannot be just fiction. This trivialization of fiction on account of its frivolity has far-reaching consequences for the status and understanding of what Coetzee once called "serious" fiction. When at the end of the book Costello invites Paul to be her companion in the hope of living a fictional existence in "loving care," Paul declines. What she can offer, what they share, he feels, is "something else. Something less" (263). It is another joke, of course—a melancholy one, especially for those of us attached to fiction. If attention to fiction is an ethical question, as the Costello writings have been preoccupied with demonstrating, the irony is that fiction cannot convincingly communicate this—not without giving up on the fiction. There can be no more pathetic (yet also comical) way of conveying the abandonment and unloveliness of literature than having one's own character, disappointed by his fictionality, kindly but without tenderness refuse to go along with it and take his leave.

*   *   *

BENJAMIN LEWIS ROBINSON is university assistant in the Department of German at the University of Vienna. He is the author of *Bureaucratic Fanatics: Modern Literature and the Passions of Rationalization* (2019) and is currently engaged in a project on literature and biopolitics titled *States of Need / States of Emergency*. He is also preparing a book on J. M. Coetzee's fiction. His essay "Passions for Justice: Kleist's *Michael Kohlhaas* and Coetzee's *Michael K*" appeared in *Comparative Literature* (2018).

Works Cited

Agamben, Giorgio. *The Time That Remains: A Commentary on the Letter to the Romans.* Trans. Patricia Dailey. Stanford: Stanford UP, 2005.

Auerbach, Erich. *Mimesis: The Representation of Reality in Western Literature.* Trans. Willard Trask. Princeton: Princeton UP, 2013.

Barthes, Roland. *Camera Lucida: Reflections on Photography.* Trans. Richard Howard. New York: Hill and Wang, 1981.

Bradshaw, Graham, and Michael Neill, eds. *J. M. Coetzee's Austerities.* Burlington: Ashgate, 2010.

Cervantes Saavedra, Miguel de. *Don Quixote.* Trans. John Rutherford. New York: Penguin, 2000.

Coetzee, J. M. "Burning the Books." 19 October 1973. Manuscript Collection MS-0842, Container 33.1, handwritten notes and unfinished draft, 19 October 1973–4 July 1974. J. M. Coetzee Papers, Harry Ransom Center, University of Texas at Austin.

Coetzee, J. M. *In the Heart of the Country.* London: Secker and Warburg, 1977.

Coetzee, J. M. *Life & Times of Michael K.* New York: Vintage, 1998.

Coetzee, J. M. *Slow Man.* New York: Knopf, 2005.

Coetzee, J. M. *Waiting for the Barbarians.* London: Secker and Warburg, 1980.

De Boever, Arne. *Narrative Care: Biopolitics and the Novel.* London: Bloomsbury, 2013.

Derrida, Jacques. *The Archeology of the Frivolous: Reading Condillac.* Trans. John P. Leavey Jr. Pittsburgh: Duquesne UP, 1980.

Edelman, Lee. *No Future: Queer Theory and the Death Drive.* Durham, NC: Duke UP, 2004.

Foucault, Michel. "The Life of Infamous Men." *Power.* Ed. James D. Faubion. Vol. 3 of *Essential Works of Foucault, 1954–1984.* New York: New Press, 2000. 157–75.

Foucault, Michel. *Security, Territory, Population: Lectures at the Collège de France, 1977–78.* Ed. François Ewald, Alessandro Fontana, and Michel Senellart. Trans. Graham Burchell. New York: Palgrave Macmillan, 2007.

Gaultier, Jules de. *Le Bovarysme.* Paris: Mercure de France, 1921.

Gilligan, Carol. *In a Different Voice.* Cambridge, MA: Harvard UP, 1982.

Hall, Alice. "Autre-biography: Disability and Life Writing in Coetzee's Later Works." *Journal of Literary and Cultural Disability Studies* 6.1 (2012): 53–67.

Hallemeier, Katherine. "J. M. Coetzee's Literature of Hospice." *Modern Fiction Studies* 62.3 (2016): 481–98.

Hayes, Patrick. *J. M. Coetzee and the Novel: Writing and Politics after Beckett.* Oxford: Oxford UP, 2010.

Heidegger, Martin. *Being and Time.* 1927. Trans. J. Stambaugh. Albany: SUNY P, 1996.

Heidegger, Martin. *Phenomenology of Religious Life.* Trans. Matthias Fritsch and Jennifer Gosetti-Ferencei. Bloomington: Indiana UP, 2004.

Lamb, Jonathan. "'The True Words at Last from the Mind in Ruins': J. M. Coetzee and Realism." *J. M. Coetzee's Austerities*. Ed. Graham Bradshaw and Michael Neill. Burlington: Ashgate, 2010. 177–90.

Macaskill, Brian. "I Am Not Me, the Horse Is Not Mine, William Kentridge & J. M. Coetzee; or: Machines, Death, and Performance as Prelude to Reading *Slow Man*." *Texas Studies in Literature and Language* 58.4 (2016): 392–421.

Mulhall, Stephen. *The Wounded Animal: J. M. Coetzee and the Difficulty of Reality in Literature and Philosophy*. Princeton: Princeton UP, 2009.

Neimneh, Shadi, and Nazmi Al-Shalabi. "Disability and the Ethics of Care in J. M. Coetzee's *Slow Man*." *Cross-Cultural Communication* 7.3 (2011): 35–40.

Parvulescu, Anca. "Reproduction and Queer Theory: Between Lee Edelman's *No Future* and J. M. Coetzee's *Slow Man*." *PMLA* 132.1 (2017): 86–100.

Sevenhuijsen, Selma. *Citizenship and the Ethics of Care: Feminist Considerations on Justice, Morality, and Politics*. Trans. Liz Savage. London: Routledge, 1998.

Siebers, Tobin. *Disability Theory*. Ann Arbor: U of Michigan P, 2011.

Stone, Deborah. "Why We Need a Care Movement." *Nation* 13 March 2000: 13–15.

Tronto, Joan C., and Berenice Fisher. "Toward a Feminist Theory of Caring." *Circles of Care*. Ed. Emily K. Abel and Margaret K. Nelson. Albany: SUNY P, 1990. 36–54.

Vaihinger, Hans. *The Philosophy of "As If": A System of Theoretical, Practical, and Religious Fictions of Mankind*. 2nd ed. Trans. C. K. Ogden. London: Routledge and Kegan Paul, 1965.

Vermeulen, Pieter. "Abandoned Creatures: Creaturely Life and the Novel Form in J. M. Coetzee's *Slow Man*." *Studies in the Novel* 45.4 (2013): 655–74.

Wicomb, Zoë. "*Slow Man* and the Real: A Lesson in Reading and Writing." *J. M. Coetzee's Austerities*. Ed. Graham Bradshaw and Michael Neill. Burlington: Ashgate, 2010. 215–30.

Zimbler, Jarad. *J. M. Coetzee and the Politics of Style*. Cambridge: Cambridge UP, 2014.

Growing Up Against Allegory: The Late Works of J. M. Coetzee

BENJAMIN R. DAVIES

"There is no such thing as a llave universal. *If we had a* llave universal *all our troubles would be over."*

—Ana, *The Childhood of Jesus*

Against Allegory, Against the Novel Form

In 2004, Derek Attridge's essay "Against Allegory" set the tone for a generation of Coetzee scholars, introducing an alternative way of reading the works of the South African–born, Australia-dwelling Nobel laureate. In the essay, Attridge reacts against the practice of reading Coetzee's works as allegories. He argues that Coetzee studies should produce more literal readings. For Attridge, a "literal reading" is one where reading is an "event" comprising "an individual reader in a specific time and place, conditioned by a specific history" (39). In allegorical readings, however, "the meanings of the words solidify into the customary ingredients of such writing—characters, places, relationships, plot complications and resolutions"—and the reader "can deploy reading techniques that will lessen or annul" the presence of "strangeness" or "alterity" (40). Because of developments in Coetzee's fiction since 2004, however, our understanding of Coetzee and allegory requires updating. The Australian fiction and the *Jesus* books have in some ways exceeded Attridge's postulate. In this essay I address not only the struggles of allegory in reading but also the struggles of allegory in writing.

The critical tradition to which Attridge's essay (informally) belongs helps us understand why Coetzee's texts are responsive to this discussion. It may be called a metasuspicious tradition, since it is wary of what is labeled (such as by Keane and Lawn 126–27) the "hermeneutics of suspicion."[1] The metasuspicious is a broad critical family stretching from Susan Sontag's 1964 essay "Against Interpretation"—which Attridge's title echoes—to Stephen Best and Sharon Marcus's "Surface Reading: An Introduction" (2009). Rita Felski's *The Limits of Critique* (2015) provides a more recent approach. Broadly speaking, these critics are against the notion that a text necessarily has a meaning "hidden, repressed, deep, and in need of detection and disclosure" (Best and Marcus 1).[2]

Many of Coetzee's works, such as *Waiting for the Barbarians* (1980) or *Foe* (1986), deploy frustrated or futile interpretative quests to dramatize exactly this

---

[1]   A clear chapter on the messy history of this term can be found in Alison Scott-Baumann 59–77.

[2]   Those in favor of detection and disclosure include Fredric Jameson in *The Political Unconscious* (60) and Louis Althusser and Étienne Balibar in *Reading Capital* (86).

Novel: A Forum on Fiction 53:3   DOI 10.1215/00295132-8624606   © 2020 by Novel, Inc.

hermeneutical position. Readers have, however, been undeterred in labeling the books "allegories." We begin with Nadine Gordimer's confident assertion in 1984 that Coetzee "chose allegory for his first few novels" and continue with Lois Parkinson Zamora's 1986 appraisal that "allegory [as] a prominent literary vehicle for political dissent . . . can be illustrated especially in J. M. Coetzee's novels" (1), through to the publication of Teresa Dovey's *The Novels of J. M. Coetzee: Lacanian Allegories* (1988). In the nineties this attitude seeped into general literary wisdom among reviewers: Coetzee had, according to Charles van Onselen, a "mastery of allegory" (1998); his style, according to Elizabeth Lowry, was "sometimes parodic, sometimes allegorical" (1999). By 2009 Dominic Head, in *The Cambridge Introduction to J. M. Coetzee*, was referring to the allegorical potential of Coetzee's books as "a staple point of debate in Coetzee studies" (95).

Any history of the term recognizes that allegory is complex and demonstrates that working definitions are the only prudent ones (see Tambling; and Copeland and Struck). These histories also show the importance of distinguishing between reading allegory and writing it. Many definitions of allegory might seem hermeneutically presumptuous: the online *Oxford English Dictionary* defines it as "[t]he use of symbols in a story, picture, etc., to convey a hidden or ulterior meaning." Other definitions—such as that in Ian Buchanan's *Oxford Dictionary of Critical Theory* ("outward appearance is contrived to suggest a hidden meaning" [11]) and Chris Baldrick's *Oxford Dictionary of Literary Terms* ("a second distinct meaning partially hidden behind . . . literal or visible meaning" [8])—tend only to cover reading. In the following analysis of writing allegory, I adopt a different definition, that of Rita Copeland and Peter T. Struck, who describe "compositional" allegory as that which "seeks to express imagistically what is otherwise abstract or invisible" (Copeland and Struck 6). The virtues of this definition include that it does not assume that an author intends thereby to achieve a perfect textual correspondence. In my analysis of Coetzee's relationship with the novel form I set this understanding of allegory alongside that provided by Attridge.

Elements of Coetzee's writing seem to make his works especially amenable to discussions of allegory. But these elements point to another literary debate entirely. The recurrence of events, as well as metatextual and intellectual references, can all be read as components of allegory. These include returning to specific books (*Don Quixote* or *Robinson Crusoe*), authors (Kafka or Dostoevsky), images (carrying heavy loads on the back), and typological characters (misfits or dissenters). However, in Coetzee's larger ongoing project, they participate in a subversion of the very form his writing explores most intimately. Rather than forming neat allegories, these elements allow Coetzee to reflect on the process of writing a novel. It is most appropriate, therefore, to situate allegory not outside but within Coetzee's ideas about the novel form.

Coetzee's career has been characterized by almost unvaried use of novel forms, accompanied by a productive unease about what it means to be writing a "novel." Tension seems to arise from his varying claims about what novels are: are they neutral forms defined solely by length, or are they ideals with historical and cultural baggage? Coetzee has described them as "ultimately nothing but prose fiction[s] of a certain length" (Scott 87), but he has also suggested that they are specifically European forms. The novel outside Europe is as a result "transplanted" (Coetzee, *White Writing* 161). Thus there is some occupational dysphoria on the author's part. He has called himself both "a novelist" ("Novel Today" 2) and, more cautiously, "a writer working in the medium of the novel" (qtd. in Hayes 1). Not only, therefore, is Coetzee's work skeptical about its own status, but this doubt is redoubled by his self-awareness. He seems suspicious of what it might mean to write *a* novel when concepts of *the* novel are threatening to encroach on his prose.

The exemplar of novel institutionalizing is the twentieth-century critic Ian Watt.[3] Watt's influential study *The Rise of the Novel* (1957) demonstrated the profound effects of eighteenth-century conditions on the novels of Daniel Defoe, Samuel Richardson, and Henry Fielding. The realism elaborated in early English novels, Watt argued, had as its "primary criterion . . . truth to individual experience" (13); novel plots were about "particular people in particular circumstances" (15); and the individual character achieved "his own continuing identity through memory of his past thoughts and actions" (21). Such novels, moreover, were scrupulously specific about time (24–25) and place (27). In this conceptualization of the novel as verisimilar, what room for the contrivances and coincidences of Mary Shelley or Dickens? How to account for the bizarre landscapes of *Pilgrim's Progress* (1678) or H. G. Wells's *The Time Machine* (1895)? Nonetheless, Watt and other critics who attach a definite article to the word "novel" participate in institutionalizing an ideal into literary culture. For Coetzee, the problem is not how to avoid writing a novel, but how to disrupt our notion of *the* novel.

Sabotaging the novel from the inside requires bypassing Watt's simplified summation as well as writing against allegory. In a 1976 essay, Coetzee offers a reformulation of Watt. He analyses novelistic writing and finds that Watt's emphasis on the individual is overplayed. Rather, a "social and characterological typology assumed and shared among the reading public" means that "the sign 'Mr Podsnap' or 'Philip Marlow' [*sic*] in an initial sentence, empty to begin with, would in due course be filled with social and characterological details, some of them details of such fineness as to refine the typology . . . , the process of refining the typology being known as *making the character individual* just as adherence to the typology is known as *making the character representative*" (Coetzee, "First Sentence" 48). The metaphor Coetzee uses for the structure of this process is "typological lattice," a network of types into which an author can fit a character. This thereby "reciprocally reaffirm[s] the typology and therefore the sociology and psychology of the reading public" (48). Why write against this process, against a defining ideological feature of the novel? For Coetzee, the use of the typological lattice creates "a further reaffirmation of a class bond" among the reading public (48). Clearly, allegory may be an important tool for the author who wishes to slot his character into the typological lattice. Allegory, understood as "seek[ing] to express imagistically what is otherwise abstract or invisible," is an indispensable tool in character portrayal: in both "making the character representative" and "making the character individual." Part of the process of subverting the novel is, therefore, denying the allegorical processes that help support the typological lattice.

---

[3]   Coetzee agrees with Watt on many points; see Joanna Scott 97–98 and Patrick Hayes 121.

By what techniques does Coetzee subject the novel to abuse? We can begin with what grammar necessitates and what the novel takes full advantage of: tense. Why does Coetzee always write in the present tense? Roland Barthes has relevant ideas. Barthes's thoughts about the *passé simple*—a French past tense used exclusively in literary writing—are somewhat inaccurately translated in the English edition using the word *preterite*: "Obsolete in spoken French, the preterite, which is the cornerstone of Narration, always signifies the presence of Art; it is a part of a ritual of Letters. . . . Allowing as it does an ambiguity between temporality and causality, it calls for a sequence of events, that is, for an intelligible Narrative" (*Writing* 30).[4] While *passé simple* is more specific than the English *preterit*, we can reasonably import Barthes's ideas of what writing in the past does. The preterit is the perdurable mode of narration in English novels and may be said to be key in helping any novel stake a claim to membership in the novel tradition. In conversation with Arabella Kurtz, Coetzee himself makes a similar point about the past tense "fixing a piece of history" (Coetzee and Kurtz, *Good Story* 13). By using the present tense in almost all his texts, Coetzee avoids the preterit. He therefore avoids presuming to know fully "a world which is constructed, elaborated, [and] self-sufficient" (Barthes, *Writing* 30). He does not make the novel "an exercise in making the past coherent," as it is styled by Elizabeth Costello (Coetzee, *Costello* 39). While for Barthes there "lurks" behind the preterit "a demiurge, a God or a reciter" (*Writing* 30), Coetzee abdicates such a position for the present. This has the effect of making his narratives unfold continuously in a way that resists always being "intelligible." Typology clearly relies on history, a world "constructed, elaborated, self-sufficient." By writing in the present tense, Coetzee endangers the typological lattice.

Then why does he employ the preterit so pointedly in his 1983 work *Life & Times of Michael K*? What purpose could it serve to begin to work in the tense that he had disavowed and that he has since disavowed? Patrick Hayes's *J. M. Coetzee and the Novel* (2010) offers suggestions. Hayes writes that *Michael K* belies Coetzee's argument, made in an obscure 1988 lecture, that some novels act as supplements to history while others rival it. I follow this argument, although for reasons different from those of Hayes. Both narrators of *Michael K*—the anonymous observer of parts 1 and 3 and the inquisitive medical officer of part 2—employ the preterit. Both fail to grasp hold of the character of K. Speculation that is not yet the speculation of familiarity frets their voices. Coetzee uses the preterit, therefore, to show that K is of the long line of Coetzeean characters who, being "great escapees" (166), shirk the typological lattice even as its capturing mechanism of the preterit is deployed.

Genre, a form of categorization, relies on types—a problem for the author who wishes to subvert such a process. Just as Coetzee approaches the problem of the novel by writing both from within and against tradition, he achieves this with genre. Hayes argues convincingly that *Age of Iron* (1990) represents a story told through the "untenable genre" of epistolary fiction (134). Specifically, it undermines the English epistolary novel as forged by Richardson. Elizabeth Curren, writes Hayes further,

---

[4]   "Retiré du français parlé, le passé simple, pierre d'angle du Récit, signale toujours un art" (Barthes, *Le degré zéro* 27).

has a "mystified belief in the privileged status of epistolary communication as an especially direct and honest form" (138). Finally, he draws a parallel (encouraged by hints from Coetzee) between *Age of Iron* and Cervantes's *Don Quixote*. Both books present a genre as struggling to keep a purchase on the world (Hayes 136). Elsewhere in Coetzee's oeuvre, narrative norms are transgressed—by the lack of continuity and reliability in *In the Heart of the Country* (1977); by the interruption of *Slow Man* (2005) by a character who seems to wander in from the pages of a different book; and by the simultaneous presentation of three narratives in *Diary of a Bad Year* (2007). Alice Crary writes of this as a "formal restlessness" (126). That Coetzee consciously works against these older English novels is an enduring concern in my analysis. The movement in his fiction toward closer engagement with alternative origins of the novel, such as *Don Quixote*, becomes important in the later works, especially the *Jesus* books.

The stability of the typological lattice also depends, of course, on stability of character; discontinuity is bad for typology. It is a kind of stability that Coetzee habitually threatens. Watt views the use of proper names in the novel as "the verbal expression of the particular identity of each individual person," differentiated from the use in earlier media of what Aristotle identified as "characteristic" names (Watt 18–19).[5] In the first sentences of his first book, *Dusklands* (1974), Coetzee drew ironic attention to the roles of names in fiction: "My name is Eugene Dawn. I cannot help that. Here goes" (1). He has continued to play on problems of names and identity since. The situation is both at its most serious and at its most ludic when he foregrounds author figures. In the late eighteenth century and for some time thereafter, it was common for novels to be presented with what might be called minimal authorship. The author was supposedly either the main character presenting an account of indubitable detail (such as in *Robinson Crusoe*), or an editor of discovered diaries or letters (such as *Clarissa* or *Jane Eyre*). In books like *Dusklands* or *Diary*, however, the presentation of characters who are nominally Coetzee yet so clearly not him undermines the name on the dust jackets. (See also *Foe*, where Foe is and is not the historical Daniel Defoe, and *The Master of Petersburg* [1994], where the protagonist is and is not the historical Russian author Dostoevsky.) The technique reaches its ultimate order of reflexivity in the three books that critics have so much trouble categorizing: *Boyhood* (1997), *Youth* (2002), and *Summertime* (2009). We might say the author figure is not dead but that he cannot come to the phone right now. The authority of authorship that we have come to expect from the novel is unattainable.[6]

---

[5] Cora Diamond's account of the novel form gives a more recent expression of this. She writes that in thinking about the novel, we "often have in mind certain kinds of attention to reality: to detail and particularity. We are not, that is, handed too many characters who are simply given by their labels" (40). The same problem is dramatized in Sterne's *Tristram Shandy* (1759–67), where Walter Shandy expresses an idea much like the pre-novel literary conventions of naming (Sterne 43–44).

[6] For a shorter analysis of Coetzee and the novel, with a closer focus on the role of Watt, see Stephen Mulhall's chapter "Realism, Modernism, and the Novel" in his *Wounded Animal* (2009).

The Earlier Works

Moving the analysis to the narrative level is enabled by the role typology plays within texts. Typology has been considered with respect to Watt's and Coetzee's "reading public," but characters within stories also play a role in typologizing other characters. A simple example: a man dressed in armor, riding a horse. A knight, we say. Once we have heard from other characters in the story, however, we can refine the typology. People proclaim his chivalry, women engage in courtship with him: we see he is the type of a knight errant. Types are therefore caught between communities of characters and communities of readers. If we accept this, it is necessary to gain an understanding of how typology and allegory function in the real-life communities of which Coetzee's characters are (at least partially) representative.

Coetzee provides us with thoughts on these issues in his correspondence with Kurtz, published in *The Good Story* (2015). In chapters 8, 10, and 11, Coetzee and Kurtz discuss the formation and changes of groups in society. These "groups" are roughly what I above call *communities*. Coetzee and Kurtz talk about the formative nature of early life experiences and how they impact individuals' conceptions of groups. Kurtz states that "each individual member of a group will have internalised early family experiences in ways that will be brought to bear upon the external group situation" (129). Coetzee brings up the following question: "Must the field of forces into which the child emerges always be defined by the triangle of mother, father, and babe?" (116). He wants to explore how the parent-child relationship becomes compromised, often in a way that breaks the triangle. (Kurtz agrees that a child who grows up in a nontriangular family, such as with a single parent or numerous siblings, might attain an unusual "level of reflective thinking about themselves in relation to others" [125]). The compromised parent-child relationship is a persistent theme throughout Coetzee's works. It is the juncture upon which so much allegory depends and at which the transmission of allegory is vulnerable.

What follows is a survey of two relevant Coetzee works. The first book of his autobiographical trilogy, titled *Boyhood*, and his second novel, *In the Heart of the Country*, give access to a range of representations of the parent-child relationship and to his reworking of the novel. I consider these works significant waypoints along the genealogical line of Coetzee's characters who shirk the novel's mechanisms.

First it is necessary to hone an understanding of exactly how these ideas of "allegory" and "community" function in tandem and under what conditions they might break. When considered as that which "seeks to express imagistically what is otherwise abstract or invisible," allegory can be seen to be employed by communities—particularly nations—to create and sustain member identities. Material examples of such allegories include national symbols such as animals (the lion for England, the eagle for the United States), flags, and flowers; national anthems, myths, histories, and epics; official languages; religions; prominent landmarks and buildings; sports and sports teams; coins. Many are examples of what Michael Billig calls "banal nationalism," or cheap nationalism which is "[d]aily . . . indicated, or 'flagged,' in the lives of its citizenry" (11). While these seem like individual and distinct symbols, this passage from *Boyhood* shows how they can form the networks of allegory: "He [the young John] cannot understand why it is that so many people around him dislike England. England is Dunkirk and the Battle of Britain. England is doing one's duty and accepting one's fate in a quiet, unfussy way. . . . England is Sir Lancelot of the Lake and Richard the Lionheart and Robin Hood" (128). Coetzee is alive to the role these allegories have in constructing communities (here, a nation) and in provoking emotions and behaviors in response. So what might an eroded version of these allegories, correspondent with an erosion of the novel form, look like? This is what we see in Coetzee's later *Jesus* books; however, children who deviate from behaving in their communities, from buying into and perpetuating allegory, are present across his earlier works. Parent-child relationships appear as a major theme, on the "spectrum of uncertain literary parents," in twelve of Coetzee's thirteen novels (Seshagiri, "Boy of La Mancha" 652). (Only in *Diary* is there no major parent-child consideration.) In all cases, the relationships are somehow broken or compromised. We find filicide, patricide, the accidental death and/or abandonment of parents or children, and general alienation. These dominate the action of books such as *Michael K*, *Foe*, *Age of Iron*, *The Master of Petersburg*, and *Disgrace* (1999). With the varied and powerful roles that parents can play in a child's formative years (including guidance, pedagogy, and emotional education), the parent-child relationship has a strong part in indoctrinating children into community allegories. Coetzee's deviant child characters can therefore be related to his abiding experiment in fiction: aligning the broken-parent child relationship with the broken novel form.[7]

Coetzee's *Boyhood* shows how alienation in the parent-child relationship can endanger the process of instilling allegory into a child from the very beginning. The character of young John Coetzee is raised on a potentially confusing array of allegorical signs: he is made to sing the South African national anthem at school (*Boyhood* 24), but before the National Party stopped the broadcast in 1948 also hears the BBC news and pips on the radio (68). He tries to navigate his relationship with his father in tandem with what seem to be sanctioned community allegories. These interactions often involve sports, but his attempt to mimic his father's elation at the world stage victory of a South African boxer meets with shame and leads John to question the reasons for supporting national athletes (109). This is far more than just an interrogation of one particular sport. In the 1978 essay "Four Notes on Rugby," reprinted in *Doubling the Point* (1992), Coetzee writes that sport, "particularly in boys' schools," is "given an explicit ideological function ('character-building') while play remains suspect, frivolous. . . . The child who submits to the code and plays the game is therefore reenacting a profoundly important moment of culture: the moment at which the Oedipal compromise is made, the moment at which the knee is bent to government." Accordingly, he continues, "sports are . . . easily captured and used by political authority" (*Doubling* 125).[8] They are closely

---

[7]   I return to Mulhall's concept of "deviancy" in Coetzee below. Mulhall's use of the term is inspired by the philosophy of Wittgenstein, where it essentially means deviating from a community's expectation (Mulhall, "Health and Deviance").

[8]   The national-allegorical consequences of sport are shown elsewhere in Coetzee's analysis of the ideological functions of opening and closing ceremonies in the essay "The 1995 Rugby World Cup" (*Stranger Shores* 351–56).

associated with John's experiences of being beaten at school, where it is said that if the violation of his body "can be achieved quickly, by force, he will be able to come out on the other side a normal boy. . . . But by himself he cannot leap that barrier" (*Boyhood* 7).[9] This pseudopedagogical function of sports (designed to teach but not to enlighten) brings about "the Oedipal compromise." It demonstrates that for parents and schools which, in Coetzee's own words, are "authoritarian" and teach "obedience" (Scott 82), the common aim is to raise children within the typological lattice.[10]

Magda, the narrator of Coetzee's earlier novel *In the Heart of the Country*, demonstrates the confused results of being raised into a typological lattice. She desires desperately at times to be a self-sufficient individual (67, 89) but also struggles to comprehend a worldview outside that inherited from her father. Her patricide in one of the book's possible narratives seems, paradoxically, to cement a patriarchal influence figured through language. "I was born," she says, "into a language of hierarchy, of distance and perspective. It was my father-tongue. I do not say it is the language my heart wants to speak, I feel too much the pathos of its distances, but it is all we have" (120). This being born into a language is a recurrent theme in Coetzee, appearing in relation to the novel, the "transplanted" form of which for Coetzee is tied to English. In the latter sections of *Heart*, where Magda appears to go mad, she imagines hearing Spanish voices floating down to her from passing planes. She asserts that it is not a "local Spanish" but "a Spanish of pure meanings such as might be dreamed of by the philosophers" (156–57).

This desire to get outside her "father-tongue," to a language of "pure meanings," is a long-distance foreshadowing of the *Jesus* books, where Spanish is the only language. Magda's desire hints at the way Spanish, and especially its literary behemoth *Don Quixote*, are possible alternatives to English and the language of the novel. Nonetheless, Coetzee is habitually wary of the difficulty of transcending a language contingent on one's historical and social circumstances.[11] He therefore writes characters who struggle to escape the literary form in which they are present. I am building a picture here of the analogues in Coetzee's oeuvre between matters of allegory and community and matters of text and form. Coetzee has been shown to be perennially concerned with writing against an ideal of the novel form and consequently against allegory. This has narrative ramifications, affecting the way individuals and societies are presented in his fiction. In his *Jesus* books, examined in the next section, these analogues are shown in their most radical configuration.

---

[9]   Note the echoes of Kierkegaard's *Fear and Trembling* (*Frugt og Bæven* [1843]). There Kierkegaard talks about being unable make the "leap" necessary to perform acts of faith as strong as Abraham's. "I cannot make the movement of faith," he writes. "I cannot close my eyes and fall full of trust into the absurd, it is an impossibility for me, but I do not praise myself for it" (37; my translation). The ability or inability to make such "leaps" becomes important in the *Jesus* books.

[10]   The authority of the father is sometimes used directly as a metaphor for the authority of education, such as in *Michael K*: "[M]y father was Huis Norenius [K's school]. My father was the list of rules on the door of the dormitory" (104–5).

[11]   He expresses such doubts in *Doubling the Point* (145).

The *Jesus* Books

The parental themes of Coetzee's earlier works are present in the *Jesus* books but as part of a provocative congregation of the themes of the allegory and novel forms. They work with the understanding that parents are the nexus between the allegories of the world and their children and, furthermore, that alienation in parent-child relationships can endanger the process of instilling allegory into children. While the rest of Coetzee's oeuvre treats the broken parent-child relationship as *a* problem, the *Jesus* books treat it as *the* problem. They ceaselessly question the fundamental properties of parenthood. The intensity of focus on the erosion of parenthood, typology, and literary reference suggests that Coetzee may be making cautious overtures about moving beyond the novel. Beginning, as the books do, with the problem of parenthood, this section then moves through the allegorical and literary implications.

The first question the *Jesus* books ask is: what makes a parent? This question is difficult throughout the books because Coetzee at the outset removes the biological answer and then challenges the alternatives. The *Jesus* books are about a migrant boy, David, who loses his biological parents during a migration process. He is cared for by Simón, a man on the boat who, once they reach the shore, sets about searching for David's mother. He persuades Inés, a woman he meets seemingly at random, to take on the role. Confusingly, Simón and Inés at times claim without irony to be David's real parents (*Childhood* 125, 321) but elsewhere acknowledge that they do so "perjuriously" (*Schooldays* 5). They later deny ever having claimed this (*Schooldays* 197). A foggy picture of the prerequisites of parenthood is then complicated by the way in which the roles are gendered. The suitability of substitute parents depends on criteria that differ between the gendered roles. By questioning at every turn what it means to be a true parent, the *Jesus* books view the matter of judging what a true parent should do as precarious. Simón and Inés's position, and therefore their ability to act as nexuses for allegory, is always endangered.

The *Jesus* books therefore question how parent figures affect the children that come under their guardianship. Across his oeuvre as well as is in the *Jesus* books, Coetzee returns to the notion that parents give children some mixture of "substance" and "idea." (These concepts are not simple, but for now we can treat them as a simple opposition of the physical and the abstract.) These notions are employed in a gendered way. For example, when discussing the suitability of Inés as David's mother, Simón posits that "to the mother the child owes his substance, whereas the father merely provides the idea" (*Childhood* 124). As well as "substance" and "idea" potentially having several meanings, literal as well as metaphoric, there is an ambiguity over the question of whether these things are given at conception or birth, or both. The importance of the parental link between a child and allegories and communities is shown, in the *Jesus* books, through an understanding of "substance" and "idea" as a matter of serious debate in all parts of life.

Understanding "substance" and "idea" involves seeing how in earlier Coetzee works this metaphysics is bound up with literary meaning. As well as making up the composition of children, these things possess literary dimensions. In *Heart*, Magda says she would not be surprised if she were merely an idea her father had

had long ago and forgot (85–86). In *Foe*, Susan Barton, when she tires of Foe's fictioneering, writes: "I am not a story, Mr Foe. I may impress you as a story. . . . But my life did not begin in the waves. . . . There was a life before. . . . I choose not to tell it because to no one, not even to you, do I owe proof that I am a substantial being with a substantial history in the world" (131). This is the heart of the matter: substantiality is associated with having a history—with being, in a sense, nonrivalrous to history.[12] We are in the same territory as the "Novel Today" lecture in which Coetzee asserts that some novels "supplement" history better than others (2). However, while Susan regards substantiality as making something more real than stories, the presence of her potential daughter in the text troubles this. Susan eventually accepts that this girl is "substantial" (*Foe* 152), despite also being adamant that she derives from Foe's literary imagination. (A seed from his pen—an old euphemism.) Coetzee presents strong similarities between raising a child by instilling meaning (possibly through allegory) and the process by which authors create.

What takes the *Jesus* books beyond previous works is that, alongside a boy missing his parents and the replacements' feeling uncertain in their positions, the world of the books seems allegorically discontinuous. Allegory in Novilla and Estrella, the towns where Simón and David reside, seems to be absent or attenuated. This much has baffled critics: David L. Ulin of the *Los Angeles Times* describes *Childhood* as an "allegory [which] never extends beyond itself." Yoshiki Tajiri notes that it is "as though the allegorical mode were simply offered as a trap" (73). Roger Bellin writes that the book is "crafted to frustrate . . . forms of allegorical reading." "If you're looking for allegorical clarity," says Jason Farago, "*The Childhood of Jesus* will frustrate you at every turn." Indeed, there are few symbols of any kind of community and no indications of nationhood in the new country. There is the Spanish language, which Simón "has worked hard to master" (*Childhood* 1); a currency the value of which he must learn (18, 28); and local football teams with local supporters (28–31). Those aside, there are no anthems, few songs, almost no literature, no religion to speak of, few landmarks or specifically named buildings (the place where evening classes are held is merely "the Institute" [141]), and no national or international sporting events. (The state is manifested only through some local admin workers and law enforcement officers.) There are moments when Simón wonders at this strange lack, as when he sees that there are no courses for Ibero-Romance languages other than Spanish on offer at the Institute (143). Because of these allegorical absences, Simón feels that things in Novilla and Estrella lack "their due weight" (*Childhood* 77) and that Estrella is "a city [with] no sensation, no feelings" (*Schooldays* 66). For Simón himself, this lack presents a mild nuisance in his having to adapt to a threadbare new world. For Simón and David as a pseudo–parent-child pair, however, this presents a profound challenge in raising David. It seems to encourage his development into a supremely deviant child.

The idea of a deviant child is traced back to Wittgenstein by Stephen Mulhall in his recent essay "Health and Deviance, Irony and Incarnation" (2017). Mulhall

---

12   Substantiality as history is seen elsewhere in Coetzee. In *Boyhood* it is said that "[t]hrough the farms he [John] is rooted in the past; through the farms he has substance" (22). These are John's mother's family farms: the position that mothers give substantiality is consistent across Coetzee.

draws together four texts that influence *Childhood* (and probably *Schooldays*, although Mulhall's essay does not include that). Three of the texts are Plato's *Republic* (380 BC), Cervantes's *Don Quixote*, and the Bible. The fourth text, the presence of which, Mulhall admits, is "easier to overlook" (3), is Wittgenstein's 1953 work *Philosophical Investigations*. Parts of *Investigations* discuss a relationship between an adult teacher and a "deviant pupil," a pupil "whose responses to ordinary teaching practices diverge in a variety of ways from normality" (Mulhall, "Health and Deviance" 23). David appears to be just such a pupil, but his deviancy is not limited to being resistant to allegory: he seems unteachable in some profound respects.

David's unamenable responses to teaching involve rejecting systems that we might imagine to be beyond allegory, which is culturally contingent. He struggles with understanding money and scarcity (*Childhood* 60, 199–200), does not understand that subtracting x from x gives 0 (205), and does not buy into the system of numbers in general (*Childhood* 176–79, 268, 294–96; *Schooldays* 62, 205). He has an aversion to Spanish and expresses the desire to speak a private language (*Childhood*, 221–22). One source of much trouble in *Childhood* is the fact that at times he appears to be able to read fluently and at others not at all (264–65). (Coetzee and Kurtz discuss such "regressive behaviour," and Coetzee attributes it to being "plunged into an involuntary group" [122].) The *Jesus* books therefore present the most extreme examples of allegorical discontinuity and parental deficit, showing that they can lead to a child's shirking not only what we assume are community-specific allegories but also widely held universal truths.

Accounting for the parental and allegorical deficits described above, it is easy to see how David is affiliated with the line of Coetzeean characters whom I identified earlier as shirking the mechanisms of the novel. Incorporating the philosophical debates of the *Jesus* books into this analysis shows how metaphysics form an important part of the struggle against allegory. The lives of Novillans and Estrellans seem infused with philosophy. Becoming attuned to (or struggling against) this is part of Simón and David's experience. Although there are discussions about ethics and epistemology, the lengthiest and most central discussions are on metaphysics, particularly Platonist[13] metaphysics and nominalism. The citizens of the poleis Novilla and Estrella learn and espouse a basic form of Platonist metaphysics related to the famous Theory of the Forms. When Simón attends one of the evening classes at the Institute, he discovers that the pupils there—mostly his fellow stevedores—are engaged in a sluggish Platonist examination of furniture—of "*sillicidad*," or *chairness* (*Childhood* 145). The serious use of such a clichéd example is an instance of Coetzee's verging on parody when referring to Plato—something Mulhall observes throughout *Childhood* (Mulhall, "Health and Deviance" 20). Indeed, Simón's stevedore colleagues encounter the tangles of Platonism, such as when Eugenio rejects the existence of abstract objects despite buying into the idea of Forms.[14] Platonism is a form of metaphysical realism: it believes in the existence

---

[13]   My use of the term *Platonist* refers to the philosophies of Plato rather than to the broader tradition of philosophies associated with him.

[14]   For more information on Platonism and abstract forms, see Gideon Rosen ("Historical Remarks" section).

of universals—"something that can be instantiated by different entities" (such as whiteness)—and abstract objects, "something that is neither spatial nor temporal" (such as the game of chess) (Rodriguez-Pereyra). The concern for David, as a rebel character, is that Platonism seems in league with the allegorizing functions of the novel. The typological lattice and processes of representation depend upon universals. Examining David's philosophy, which despite being elusive nonetheless aligns roughly with some types of nominalism, can demonstrate how these positions are relevant to novels and the novel.

There are discernible and useful connections between David's nominalism and novel-resistant, metasuspicious literary attitudes. Nominalism is an antirealist stance that denies the existence of universals and/or abstract objects. (Historically, philosophers have found it possible to deny the existence of one but not the other—there are therefore many types of nominalism.)

David's approach to mathematics seems nominalist. In *Schooldays*, a local engineer called señor Robles undertakes to try to educate David in numbers but fails due to the boy's inability or unwillingness to buy into conventional mathematics. Robles tries to teach David to count with a realist mathematics: one in which particulars (such as apples and pens) take on the properties of universals (numbers) (22–32). The lesson breaks down because David does not recognize this process of particulars' participation in numbers. In the words of Simón: "Put an apple before him and what does he see? An apple: not *one* apple, just *an* apple. Put two apples before him. What does he see? An apple and an apple: not two apples, not the same apple twice, just an apple and an apple" (*Childhood* 295). The difference between David's position and that of señor Robles—in many senses the difference between nominalist and realist philosophies—is suggestively comparable to the debates I have explored so far. For example, the hermeneutics of suspicion, and such styles of reading as symptomatic reading, are dependent on texts' not falling down rabbit warrens of particularity. Allegory, which has been shown to be crucial in these readings, relies on universals (whiteness: purity, angels, the Pope) and abstract objects (the game of chess: deliberation, division, warfare) and their networks of associations. The novel as we have understood it—where characters are made individual or representative according to expediency, reinforcing class, gender, and race structures—moves between particulars and universals in calibrating its types. Through his radical philosophy, David dramatizes the resistance to this.

Why, then, treat the *Jesus* books as especially literary? Why not think of them as pieces of experimental literary criticism or perhaps as modern Socratic dialogues with plots hanging loosely from them? (Some have offered similarly unfavorable assessments.) The answer involves the role played by Cervantes's *Don Quixote*. *Don Quixote* appears in Coetzee's nonfiction as early as 1977. Reflecting on it in an interview with David Attwell, Coetzee calls *Don Quixote* "the giant on whose shoulders we pigmies of the postmodern novel stand" (*Doubling* 62). Cervantes's book appears continually as a major subject in Coetzee's nonfiction and as a more marginal but broodingly significant concern throughout his novels. (It is referenced, for instance, in *Age of Iron* and seems always to be pushing beneath the surface of *Slow Man*.) Coetzee said in a 2002 interview that he considers *Don Quixote* "the most important novel of all times" and has read it "time and again, as any serious novelist must do" (Lopez, "Miguel de Cervantes" 81). In the *Jesus* books, *Don Quixote* finally becomes the major and explicit point of reference. In fact, it is one of an exceptionally scant set of referents from our world.[15] As well as using it to teach David to read, Simón uses *Don Quixote* (an adapted children's version found in a local library) to provide instructions for life and behavior. This gestures toward the way in which the *Jesus* books are experiments in reconceptualizing the text away from the legacy of the English novel and toward alternative novel traditions.

David's warped understanding of *Don Quixote* simultaneously offers an alternative to the development of the novel, as readers in English know it, and an example of how literary forms can be captured and employed. For every character except David, the book is a strictly pedagogical tool, purely functional and used only to instruct. Simón draws endlessly on the book's allegories to encourage good behavior in David: "That is what you should be like," he says. "Like Don Quixote. . . . Protect the poor. Save the oppressed. And honour your mother" (*Childhood* 291). For Simón, literature exists only to be interpreted, for its meanings to be wrenched from beneath the surface. When they read the episode in which Don Quixote tries to fight windmills that he believes are giants, Simón criticizes David for believing, like the mad Alonso Quixano, that the buildings are monsters (180–83). Mulhall notes, however, that David's response is quite believable. Unlike Cervantes's original, in which the narrator asserts from the beginning that what are encountered are windmills, the abridged version Simón and David read merely pits the Don's view against that of his squire (Mulhall, "Health and Deviance" 28–29). Furthermore, moments after criticizing David, Simón misidentifies the author of the book as a "man named Benengeli" (*Childhood* 183). As numerous critics have pointed out, Cide Hamete Benengeli is, in our world, a character of Cervantes's, a fictional Arab historian alleged to have translated part of the story of *Don Quixote*, and thus like the diarists or editor figures to whom were attributed the texts of the early English novels. A similar peculiarity arises when David reads aloud, revealing that the first sentence of the abridged version begins: "Somewhere in La Mancha, in a place whose name I do not recall . . . " (*Childhood* 257). Compare Cervantes: "In a village of La Mancha, the name of which I purposely omit . . . " (21). The former elides the constructedness of the narrative and the deliberate and playful self-awareness of the narrating voice. The literature produced by the world of the *Jesus* books seems therefore flattened into simple surface. Simón misguidedly hopes that this copy of *Don Quixote* will show David a world of two tiers: simple surface and simple depth, where every word of literature has its allegorical referent in educational rules of behavior and community engagement. Setting this problem in an allegorically bleached world, with a pristine child as the object of the raising, Coetzee reproduces the struggle of making *a* novel into *the* novel.

---

[15] In *Childhood*, David recites a slightly incorrect version of the 1821 Schubert adaptation of Goethe's 1782 poem *Erlkönig*, which he and Simón mistakenly understand to be in English (*Childhood* 80); and when he is briefly kidnapped, David watches televised Mickey Mouse (218). There are no other cultural references.

Conclusion

It is in many of the senses described above that people have been growing up against allegory. A generation of Coetzee critics have been growing up reading against it. Coetzee has artistically grown up writing against it. David grows up resisting its claim on him. As such, David is a new version of characters Coetzee has been writing his whole career. Unlike Magda or Michael K, however, David exists without a past, without memories, without parents, and without a communal or national identity. He slips easily through the latticework even as it is being constructed around him, and the literary form in which he is contained is never certain to be the novel. The *Jesus* books therefore illustrate a version of the struggle of which Attridge speaks: the struggle of living between representation and individuation. *The Death of Jesus* (2020), the new and final book of the trilogy, takes this to a fitting end, the death of David and the struggle over interpreting his legacy: "You know how David was. He would never tell you his meaning directly. Always left it to you to puzzle things out" (155).

When allegory's role in enabling typology and the creation of the novel is acknowledged, David's struggle can be seen as the struggle with allegory. With the character of a parentless child, and with his metaphor of the author as a parent, Coetzee drills at the root of both the weakness of allegory and the weakness of the novel. If the parent-child relationship is compromised, then the proper installation of allegory into the child is endangered. Is it possible to get beyond allegory? Probably not, but it should be recognized that Coetzee's writing launches a struggle against it. From this platform he hints cautiously at forms beyond the novel.

*   *   *

BENJAMIN R. DAVIES is a Master of Arts student in Advanced Chinese Studies at the School of Oriental and African Studies, University of London. He gained his Bachelor of Arts degree in English from Brasenose College, Oxford, in 2018, with dissertation research focusing on J. M. Coetzee. He is a founding staff member and served two terms as editor of the *Oxford Review of Books*.

Works Cited

"allegory, n." *Oxford English Dictionary* < http://www.oed.com > (accessed 1 June 2020).

Althusser, Louis, and Étienne Balibar. *Reading "Capital."* Trans. Ben Brewster. London: NLB, 1970.

Attridge, Derek. "Against Allegory: *Waiting for the Barbarians* and *Life & Times of Michael K*." *J. M. Coetzee and the Ethics of Reading: Literature in the Event.* Chicago: U of Chicago P, 2004. 32–64.

Attwell, David. *J. M. Coetzee and the Life of Writing: Face-to-Face with Time.* New York: Penguin, 2016.

Baldrick, Chris, ed. *Oxford Dictionary of Literary Terms*. 4th ed. Oxford: Oxford UP, 2015.

Barthes, Roland. *Le degré zéro de l'écriture suivi de Nouveaux essais critiques*. Paris: Seuil, 1972.

Barthes, Roland. *Writing Degree Zero*. Trans. Annette Lavers and Colin Smith. London: Cape, 1967.

Bellin, Roger. "A Strange Allegory: J. M. Coetzee's *The Childhood of Jesus*." *Los Angeles Review of Books* 6 Nov. 2013 <https://lareviewofbooks.org/article/magical-child-troubled-child-on-jm-coetzees-the-childhood-of-jesus/>.

Best, Stephen, and Sharon Marcus. "Surface Reading: An Introduction." *Representations* 108.1 (2009): 1–21.

Billig, Michael. *Banal Nationalism*. London: Sage, 1995.

Buchanan, Ian, ed. *Oxford Dictionary of Critical Theory*. Oxford: Oxford UP, 2010.

Cervantes, Miguel de. *Don Quixote*. Trans. Charles Jarvis. Oxford: Oxford UP, 2008.

Coetzee, J. M. *Age of Iron*. London: Penguin, 2010.

Coetzee, J. M. *Boyhood: Scenes from Provincial Life*. London: Vintage, 1998.

Coetzee, J. M. *The Childhood of Jesus*. London: Vintage, 2014.

Coetzee, J. M. *The Death of Jesus*. London: Secker, 2020.

Coetzee, J. M. *Diary of a Bad Year*. London: Vintage, 2008.

Coetzee, J. M. *Disgrace*. London: Vintage, 2000.

Coetzee, J. M. *Doubling the Point*. Ed. David Attwell. Cambridge, MA: Harvard UP, 1992.

Coetzee, J. M. *Dusklands*. London: Vintage, 2004.

Coetzee, J. M. *Elizabeth Costello: Eight Lessons*. London: Vintage, 2004.

Coetzee, J. M. "The First Sentence of Yvonne Burgess' *The Strike*." *English in Africa* 3.1 (1976): 47–48.

Coetzee, J. M. *Foe*. London: Penguin, 2010.

Coetzee, J. M. *In the Heart of the Country*. London: Vintage, 2014.

Coetzee, J. M. *Life and Times of Michael K*. London: Vintage, 2004.

Coetzee, J. M. *The Master of Petersburg*. London: Vintage, 2004.

Coetzee, J. M. "The Novel Today." *Upstream* 6.1 (1988): 2–5.

Coetzee, J. M. *The Schooldays of Jesus*. London: Secker, 2016.

Coetzee, J. M. *Slow Man*. London: Vintage, 2006.

Coetzee, J. M. *Stranger Shores: Essays 1986–1999*. London: Vintage, 2002.

Coetzee, J. M. *Summertime*. London: Vintage, 2010.

Coetzee, J. M. *White Writing: On the Culture of Letters in South Africa*. New Haven: Yale UP, 1988.

Coetzee, J. M. *Youth*. London: Vintage, 2003.

Coetzee, J. M., and Arabella Kurtz. *The Good Story*. London: Vintage, 2016.

Copeland, Rita, and Peter T. Struck, eds. *The Cambridge Companion to Allegory*. Cambridge: Cambridge UP, 2010.

Crary, Alice. "Coetzee's Quest for Reality." *Beyond the Ancient Quarrel: Literature, Philosophy, and J. M. Coetzee*. Ed. Patrick Hayes and Jan Wilm. Oxford: Oxford UP, 2017. 125–42.

Diamond, Cora. *The Realistic Spirit: Wittgenstein, Philosophy, and the Mind*. Cambridge, MA: MIT P, 1995.

Dovey, Teresa. *The Novels of J. M. Coetzee: Lacanian Allegories*. Craighall: Ad. Donker, 1988.

Farago, Jason. "J. M. Coetzee's Stunning New Novel Shows What Happens When a Nobel Winner Gets Really Weird." *New Republic* 14 Sept. 2013 <https://newrepublic.com/article/114658/jm-coetzees-childhood-jesus-reviewed-jasonfarago>.

Felski, Rita. *The Limits of Critique*. Chicago: U of Chicago P, 2015.

Gordimer, Nadine. "The Idea of Gardening." *New York Review of Books* 2 Feb. 1984 <https://www.nybooks.com/articles/1984/02/02/the-idea-of-gardening/>.

Hayes, Patrick. *J. M. Coetzee and the Novel: Writing and Politics after Beckett*. Oxford: Oxford UP, 2010.

Head, Dominic. *The Cambridge Introduction to J. M. Coetzee*. Cambridge: Cambridge UP, 2009.

Jameson, Fredric. *The Political Unconscious: Narrative as a Socially Symbolic Act*. Ithaca: Cornell UP, 1981.

Keane, Niall, and Chris Lawn, eds. *The Blackwell Companion to Hermeneutics*. West Sussex: Wiley Blackwell, 2016.

Kierkegaard, Søren. *Frugt og bæven; Dialektisk lyrik af Johannes de Silentio*. 3rd ed. Copenhagen: Reitzelske, 1895.

Lopez, Maria J. "Miguel de Cervantes and J. M. Coetzee: An Unacknowledged Paternity." *Journal of Literary Studies* 29.4 (2013): 80–97.

Lowry, Elizabeth. "Like a Dog." *London Review of Books* 14 Oct. 1999 <https://www.lrb.co.uk/v21/n20/elizabeth-lowry/like-a-dog>.

Mulhall, Stephen. "Health and Deviance, Irony and Incarnation." *Beyond the Ancient Quarrel: Literature, Philosophy, and J. M. Coetzee*. Ed. Patrick Hayes and Jan Wilm. Oxford: Oxford UP, 2017. 17–34.

Mulhall, Stephen. *The Wounded Animal: J. M. Coetzee and the Difficulty of Reality in Literature and Philosophy*. Princeton: Princeton UP, 2009.

Plato. *The Republic*. Trans. Robin Waterfield. Oxford: Oxford UP, 2008.

Rodriguez-Pereyra, Gonzalo. "Nominalism in Metaphysics." *Stanford Encyclopedia of Philosophy*. Ed. Edward N. Zalta. 2016 <https://plato.stanford.edu/archives/win2016/entries/nominalism-metaphysics/>.

Rosen, Gideon. "Abstract Objects." *Stanford Encyclopedia of Philosophy*. Ed. Edward N. Zalta. 2017 <https://plato.stanford.edu/entries/abstract-objects/>.

Scott, Joanna. "Voice and Trajectory: An Interview with J. M. Coetzee." *Salmagundi* nos. 114/115 (1997): 82–102.

Scott-Baumann, Alison. *Ricœur and the Hermeneutics of Suspicion*. London: Continuum, 2009.

Seshagiri, Urmila. "The Boy of La Mancha: J. M. Coetzee's *The Childhood of Jesus*." *Contemporary Literature* 54.3 (2013): 643–53.

Sontag, Susan. *Against Interpretation*. New York: Vintage, 1994.

Sterne, Laurence. *The Life and Opinions of Tristram Shandy, Gentleman*. Oxford: Oxford UP, 2009.

Tajiri, Yoshiki. "Beyond the Literary Theme Park: J. M. Coetzee's Late Style in *The Childhood of Jesus*." *Journal of Modern Literature* 39.2 (2016): 72–88.

Tambling, Jeremy. *Allegory*. London: Routledge, 2010.

Ulin, David L. "J. M. Coetzee's *The Childhood of Jesus* Is a Land without Memory." *Los Angeles Times* 5 Sept. 2013 <http://articles.latimes.com/2013/sep/05/entertainment/la-ca-jc-0908-jm-coetzee-20130908>.

van Onselen, Charles. "A Childhood on the Edge of History." *London Review of Books* 5 Feb. 1998 <https://www.lrb.co.uk/v20/n03/charles-van-onselen/a-childhood-on-the-edge-of-history>.

Watt, Ian. *The Rise of the Novel*. London: Hogarth, 1987.

Zamora, Lois Parkinson. "Allegories of Power in the Fiction of J. M. Coetzee." *Journal of Literary Studies* 2.1 (1986): 1–14.

The Mob: J. G. Ballard's Turn to the Collective

JOEL EVANS

A recurrent feature of J. G. Ballard's early work is an overbearing, quasi-atavistic landscape that calls into question the agency of the coherent, upper-middle-class vision of the self; nevertheless, it remains possible to trace a preoccupation with the individual through the bulk of the author's work.[1] In other words, while landscape and space are important in Ballard's novels, they are so only to the extent that they exist in interaction with an individual agent. This interaction is summed up neatly in Ballard's self-professed interest in "inner space," crucial to which is the creation of new forms of life and dwelling brought about through unconscious drives and species of malaise.[2] All this is clear throughout the oeuvre—from Keran's abandonment of human civilization in the service of new, Triassic urges in *The Drowned World* (1962) to Maitland's twentieth-century-style Crusoeism in *Concrete Island* (1974). It is even present in a novel like *High-Rise* (1975), which deals with an indisputably cultural malaise but is ultimately concerned with a mass of atomized individuals in a kind of Hobbesian state of war. In this connection, Ben Wheatley's overt nod to Thatcherism in the recent 2015 film adaptation acquires further significance.

In Ballard's more recent fiction, however, there is a sea change: he suddenly becomes interested in the collective. Rarely do we get a glimpse of the collective or anything like a human totality in the earlier work; but particularly in his last four novels, Ballard becomes preoccupied with extending inner space to a network of subjects and trying to figure new forms of life and organization from the point of view of the ensemble rather than the individual.[3]

As we will see, this is most keenly felt in the companion works *Cocaine Nights* (1996) and *Super-Cannes* (2000), which interrogate the possibility of new, violent human collectives through the lens of the gated community (for which *Running Wild* [1988] was surely a prototype[4]). From one perspective, then, these novels explore the social and spatial logics of the phenomenon of the gated community, or what Mike Davis has called "fortress cities," appearing in the latter part of the twentieth century—urban and residential enclaves that come "complete with encompassing walls, restricted entry points with guard posts, overlapping private and public police services, and even privatized roadways" (244). The underlying factor in these novels' articulation of the gated community is the violence that is

---

[1] On the lack of agency in the face of overbearing landscapes in Ballard's work, see, for example, David Punter 9 and Andrzej Gasiorek 206.

[2] More laconically, and as Ballard himself puts it in an essay titled "Time, Memory, and Inner Space," inner space can be defined as "the internal landscape of tomorrow" (101).

[3] And so, as Philip Tew has suggested, we end up with a "malaise not individual or private, but communal" (116).

[4] *Running Wild* also marks the beginning of Ballard's preoccupation with (rewriting) the detective genre.

Novel: A Forum on Fiction 53:3   DOI 10.1215/00295132-8624624   © 2020 by Novel, Inc.

required to sustain the vision of the collective on offer. Indeed, this appeal toward violence underscores the main argument that will be made here, which comes in two parts.

First, I will contend that, despite the evidently undesirable aspects of the communities in these novels, they contain a genuinely utopian aspect. This, however, has little to do with the way the novels depict the mechanics or the content of collective human forms. Instead, the utopian element of *Cocaine Nights* and *Super-Cannes* lies in the fact that the collective form is given prominence at all, and the deep-seated reasons for this will be elaborated in due course. In addition, these formations are rendered in the absence of transcendent structures and hierarchies, a feature that intensifies the utopian element on display. In the main, this is due to the long-standing difficulties of imagining human ensembles that can somehow break free of the restraints of centralized structures without simply falling apart. As will become clear, these two elements of the utopian impulse in the novels converge with a broader matrix of cultural thought, which both signals the emergence of a preference for the collective in contemporary capitalist states and envisages the possibility of forming collectivities that are no longer reliant upon centralized structures and transcendent regimes of thought. Although Ballard's visions of the collective converge with this broader pattern, they also diverge from it in dramatic ways. Indeed, the initial analysis undertaken here, and the identification of Ballard's own way of figuring the collective, lays the groundwork for a discussion of the ultimately reactionary nature of Ballard's visions of the collective, predicated on irrationality, cruelty, and stupidity, the ultimate expression of which is violence.

Cocaine Nights and *Super-Cannes* thus appear as variants on a theme that is borne out rather less subtly in *Millennium People* (2003) and *Kingdom Come* (2006), both of which figure a version of the collective that inclines toward the irrational, violent behavior of a mob. In the first case, the point of view is that of a laughable, violence-for-violence's-sake revolution of the middle classes; in the second, the theme is explored via an explosive cocktail of consumerism and fascism. Benjamin Noys, among several similar attempts, has convincingly shown how these four novels offer different approaches to violence, whether as an endorsement of structural violence (in the classic right-wing mode), a cynical acceptance of it (in the liberal mode), or a more critical relationship toward it (396–400; see also Tew 116–17; and Matthews 131–37). However, what Noys's analysis elides is the preoccupation with violence *as such* as a universal condition of possibility in these works—a preoccupation that goes hand in hand, as we shall see, with a vision of the collective that has a distinctly reactionary tinge. In tracing both the utopian aspect of these novels and their more reactionary bent, my intention is to avoid the trap of merely assigning a critical role to Ballard's fiction vis-à-vis contemporary capitalism, and the equally questionable (albeit provocative) position of delineating nothing but the work's conceptual potency and intrigue.[5]

My analysis will take into account, rather, the complexity of the relationship of late Ballard with neoliberal societies and their potential becomings. To restate the

---

[5]   For an example of the former approach, see Eric A. Ostrowidzki. For an example of the latter approach, see Jake Huntley.

broad structure outlined above, this is achieved in three separate moves. To begin, I trace how the end point of Ballard's literary corpus takes some of the consequences of neoliberal states as a starting point for the establishment of new collectivities. Next, we will see how Ballard's depictions of the collective seem in some ways to offer an alternative to the current socioeconomic worldview. This alternative, we will see, may be situated within an emerging spirit of collectivism that is nascent within contemporary capitalist societies themselves. Last, we see that, by virtue of their ultimately reactionary nature, Ballard's late novels end up reaffirming the very system of which they initially seem so wary. In sum, the analysis here acknowledges the conceptual originality of the novels while also offering a critique of a negative attitude toward the collective that is increasingly prominent in contemporary cultural production.

The Formula

Cocaine Nights and *Super-Cannes* take as their point of departure the same formula: that to form a cohesive, functional collective its members must engage in violent acts.

Thus in *Cocaine Nights*, Bobby Crawford rejuvenates the stale, almost bankrupt noncommunity of Estrella de Mar, a resort for leisurely Europeans located somewhere on the Costa del Sol (33). He achieves this by embedding transgressive acts into the very structure of society, as he explains to Charles Prentice, the novel's protagonist: "Politics is over, Charles, it doesn't touch the public imagination any longer. Religions emerged too early in human evolution. . . . Sadly, crime is the only spur that rouses us" (245). Lurking behind all this is a kind of originary violent act, or primal scene, that the community can always refer back to and that cements all the other transgressive acts together: the fire at the Hollinger house—a brutal murder in which four people were burnt alive and the event precipitating Charles's arrival at the resort, as it is his brother Frank who has taken the rap (22–23; 317). This primal act and the other acts that follow from it make the inhabitants of Estrella de Mar "realize that they need each other, that together they're more than the sum of their parts" (260). While Charles initially sets out to investigate and expose whoever was behind the murder, he ends up embroiled in the newfound collective identity; at the novel's end he is on the verge of claiming responsibility for another, appropriately horrific act of foundational violence (329).

In *Super-Cannes* the formula is pretty much the same, albeit with a few variables. Wilder Penrose, a resident psychiatrist, cures the various (physical and mental) health complaints of the residents of Eden-Olympia by prescribing "a controlled and supervised madness" (251). These acts of supervised madness—the equivalent of the structural transgression of *Cocaine Nights*—almost invariably involve a flash mob sweeping the surrounding poorer areas, beating up the residents, and committing various other heinous acts (161–63; 220). Here, then, violence takes over from the more general forms of transgression in *Cocaine Nights*. The whole community becomes structured around daily acts of aggression, providing both meaning and cohesion through their repetition. The group-based acts of brutality are carried out because, as Penrose puts it, "the social order must hold" (255). But what was an originary act of violence in *Cocaine Nights* becomes, in *Super-Cannes*, an act of resistance. At the novel's start we are informed that David Greenwood shot and killed a series of Eden-Olympia's staff and was himself killed after doing so. The protagonist, Paul Sinclair, takes up the task of investigating this series of murders. The novel ends with Sinclair contemplating carrying out a similar act himself in an effort to put a stop to the collective malaise, as had been Greenwood's intention also.

We might offer two initial pieces of analysis of Ballard's formula here, one that is beholden to our own era of capitalism and another that reaches further back. To begin with the latter: both novels are evident repetitions of that ancient confrontation between the reason of the city, or polis, and its exuberant, irrational outside, as vividly conveyed in Euripides's *The Bacchae* (407 BCE). But whereas Euripides's play hints at the dangers of denying one's Dionysian urges, in Ballard's novels we are given a scenario whereby the polis has fully internalized these urges. In this regard, Noys's approach toward the late novels appears wholly justified, as in each case we are dealing with a different take on the obscene, violent underside of society or civilization as such. From this angle, the work of Slavoj Žižek (as Noys points out) is the perfect theoretical correlate (see, e.g., Žižek, "Plea for Ethical Violence"). Terry Eagleton has also written persuasively of the need to acknowledge and incorporate this obscene underside (1–41), a view that he too articulates through a reading of *The Bacchae*. But it is in Eagleton's description of the unaccommodated, Dionysian instinct that we can uncover a rather different link between Ancient and contemporary. "The god's bewitched camp followers," Eagleton suggests, "represent a vital collective or Dionysian democracy, but one which in disowning hierarchies is mercilessly intolerant to anyone who steps out of line" (3). This description would equally apply to Ballard's gated communities, which, while they maintain a slim facade of normative societal practices, have been displaced on the inside by a version of the collective driven by tribal violence. The Dionysian urge, then, has not undergone an incorporation into the polis in *Cocaine Nights* and *Super-Cannes* but has completely overrun it, turning it into a kind of brutal, nonhierarchical democracy of the passions.

Resonances abound here with our own immediate conjuncture, particularly the displacement of the representative-democratic ideal of government "of the people, by the people, for the people" in favor of rampant class warfare caked in xenophobia. Widening the field, however, we run into one of the key elements of the late Ballardian formula: the death of politics, as proclaimed by Bobby Crawford in *Cocaine Nights*. This is elaborated further in *Super-Cannes* via the constant reiteration of the absence of moral, transcendent structures in favor of the multinational corporation that "defines the rules that govern" all endeavors and that so alters the conditions of everyday life that "[t]here are no more moral decisions than there are on a new superhighway" (95). While it is not put forward quite so starkly, this form of economic imperative is also present in *Cocaine Nights*, where Crawford is merely the front man for Elizabeth Shand's budding empire of residential enclaves. Shand, in other words, employs Crawford for his ability to catalyze violence purely "to make the profits sing" (230). The death of politics is, by now, a staple proclamation of analyses of neoliberalism and is often seen as part of the waning of whatever fragile piece of representative democracy remains in Western states, so beholden are these to the logic of finance capital.[6] As Wendy Brown has suggested, one of the fundamental consequences of neoliberalism is that what were once representative democracies have been "hollowed out from within" by economic imperatives and regimes of thought (*Undoing the Demos* 18).

As we have seen, the proposed solution in Ballard's two novels to this bleak, postpolitical, ostensibly postdemocratic world is to form a collective based upon violent acts. But it is the postpolitical situation itself, with its hollowing out of the state and its various transcendent avatars, that makes possible these Dionysian, nonhierarchical collectives. To put it in starker terms, one can say that in these later novels, the postpolitical (analogous and correlative with neoliberal practices) acts as the determining factor for the formation of the violent, nonhierarchical collective. In this sense, the novels can be read as a critique—or at the very least, a warning against giving up on transcendent structures—particularly when viewed in the light of states that have embraced neoliberal practices. But there is also something obliquely utopian about these visions of the collective. It is this, then, that ought now to be given a proper treatment, which will itself pave the way for a critique of Ballard's apparently reactionary view of certain collective forms.

Flat Formations

The turn to the collective figured in *Cocaine Nights* and *Super-Cannes*, although seemingly made possible through the kinds of conditions neoliberalism tends to engender, is at odds with the standard neoliberal worldview based on individualism and self-determination.[7] From this point of view it is possible to approach Ballard's novels as part of a broader trend in recent cultural production in which the collective once again becomes a common thought-figure and new configurations of collectivity seem possible. This, then, is where the utopian character of the novels lies. A brief detour through cultural theory will suffice to demonstrate this broader trend within the aesthetic, political, and economic realms. The intention here is to show how Ballard's novels form part of an overall matrix of thought that has become preoccupied with collective forms in recent years rather than to suggest that the novels are representative of one particular way of figuring the collective. The distinctness of the Ballardian vision lies in a certain literary ambivalence when it comes to utopia and dystopia, a subject to which we will return in the next section.

Initially the issue can be tackled from the point of view of "spirit," which is used here in a largely Weberian sense. Žižek's notion in *Living in the End Times* (2010) that we have witnessed a new spirit of capitalism in recent years is key here. Specifically, Žižek suggests that the spirit of individualism encapsulated by the creative capitalist (as documented by Luc Boltanski and Ève Chiapello's *New Spirit of Capitalism*) has been replaced by a new collective spirit, one that contains within it the germ of communism. For Žižek this is made possible by the new raft of digital and telecommunications technologies that bring about an increasing sense

---

[6]   For the classic take on this, see David A. Harvey's *A Brief History of Neoliberalism* 76–79.

[7]   For a summary of the relation between individualism and neoliberalism, see Matthew Eagleton-Pierce 102–6.

of interrelatedness (*Living* 349). While such technologies are not a central aspect of either *Super-Cannes* or *Cocaine Nights*, we occasionally get the flavor of such phenomena, articulated in conjunction with a spirit of collectivism. In *Super-Cannes* there is a reference to the replacement of the "organization man"—that older vision of the collective-oriented capitalist—by, as Penrose describes it, the "mobil[e]," "self-motivated" individual who floats around in "a virtual hierarchy that endlessly reassembles itself" (95–96).[8]

Staying with contemporary media technologies, we might also mention Alexander R. Galloway's identification of what he sees as the paradigmatic method of thinking mediation today: that of a furious interrelation of "links and vectors," characterized by a variety of phenomena and figures of thought such as "rhizomatics, distributed networks, swarming clouds, or impersonal agents" (59, 61). For Galloway, this can largely be explained as the "network form [having] eclipsed all others as the new master signifier" in contemporary culture (62). We might add that the rise in the efficacy of these ways of picturing and actualizing mediation coincides with a rise in figuring the human collective; thus we witness a proliferation of narratives that depict the human as enmeshed in a network of relations, from films like *Babel* (2006) and *Contagion* (2011) to novels like *2666* (Bolaño 2004), *Air* (Ryman 2005) and *Generation A* (Coupland 2009). Galloway's reference to Elias Canetti's theory of crowds (61) is testament to the relevance of this theory of mediation to specifically human configurations; it would seem that Ballard's swarm-like communities can be added to the list. Indeed, the image of a kind of antihierarchy that is constantly reassembling itself in a virtual reality is particularly apt here.

Moving to political theory, we can trace a similar line of thought when it comes not only to the collective but to a version of the collective stripped of a reliance on transcendent, centralized forces such as the state, religion, patriarchy, and so on. Paolo Virno and coauthors Michael Hardt and Antonio Negri are some of the most prominent theorists of this form of the collective, which is named *multitude*. This usage is not to be confused with Thomas Hobbes's disdainful, dismissive use of the term. For Virno and for Hardt and Negri the concept of multitude becomes relevant in the contemporary era for two main reasons. The first is that, due to the apparent disappearance of absolute sovereignty in Western, neoliberal states, the concept of a unified people has given way to a series of dispersed forms of identity and lifestyles. The human collective, and potential future human collectives, are thus no longer reliant upon centralized forces when it comes to their cohesion (Virno 33–35; Hardt and Negri 105). Second, new forms of post-Fordist, affective and cognitive labor create a situation where value is created on the basis of common practices and states and is no longer contingent upon hierarchical forms of labor (Virno 61–3; Hardt and Negri 108–15). Multitude is thus also a class concept that, for Hardt and Negri, ushers in genuinely emancipatory possibilities (xvii).

These different versions of the collective figure what we might call "flat formations," whereby hierarchical structures are done away with and the possibility of genuinely democratic polities rear their head. The long history of what Jeremy

---

8   For more on the organization man, see William H. Whyte's *The Organization Man*.

Gilbert has called "meta-individualism" (70)—in which one transcendent figurehead stands in for a mass of individuals—is supplanted by a formation that is properly collective rather than having its point of reference in the individual. The correlative of this meta-individualism is, of course, the state. The notion that community is possible outside this overarching, centralized structure is certainly something the late Ballard grapples with, along with some of the theorists outlined above. Ballard's visions of the collective in *Cocaine Nights* and *Super-Cannes* thus not only form part of a broader conceptual shift in imagining a kind of flat collectivism but also, to an extent, share the utopianism inherent in such visions. This, however, is where the utopianism ends, in that we end up with a sinister, tribal democracy of the passions in Ballard's novels, the underlying principle of which is violence.

It is at this point, in other words, that the novels' utopian stance is reined in and remains a weak one. Unlike some of the theoretical frameworks outlined above, no positive vision of a collective form of life is put forward. Consequently, Ballard's literary contribution is not to be found in a straightforward utopian impulse, nor in a reworking of the detective genre, which is used as a kind of empty receptacle. Rather, Ballard's innovation is in the blend of the utopian and the dystopian, the nightmare and the dream of the collective. Writing about these two works, Jeannette Baxter coins the term "nightmare utopia" to describe how the "no place" of utopia provides an "ahistorical, apolitical and amoral" arena in which Ballard is able to conjure all sorts of "insidious forms of power and violence" (96). Nightmare utopia evokes a vision of the collective that is at once liberating and barbaric, democratic and quasi-fascistic.[9]

To think this through more thoroughly, we might turn to one of Fredric Jameson's formulations on the nature of the utopian. According to Jameson, an analysis of cultural artefacts worth its salt ought to contain both a "negative hermeneutic," which demystifies the ideological aspects of texts, and a "positive hermeneutic" that seeks to decipher "the Utopian impulses of these same still ideological cultural texts" (*Political Unconscious* 296). When it comes to Ballard's late novels—*Cocaine Nights* and *Super-Cannes* in particular—it might seem that this double hermeneutic is all too easy; the utopian impulse is constantly intermingled with a dystopian nightmare, the latter tarring the former to the extent that the novels leave themselves open to a relatively straightforward critique on ideological grounds. Here, though, it is not—as in Jameson's analysis of Balzac—that a fantasy or wish fulfillment is conjured only to be dispelled by the "unanswerable resistance of the Real" (183). Rather, wish fulfillment functions across two polarities (i.e., the utopian and the dystopian), both of which stand in some way apart from the "Real" conditions of production and yet are simultaneously, intensely molded by it. This is the problem one is faced with when it comes to the nightmare utopia. It is thus

---

[9]   Margaret Atwood's term *ustopia* would also be a good description of the Ballardian nightmare utopia. In coining this term, Atwood seeks to designate the dystopian element often found in utopian forms and vice-versa ("Dire Cartographies" 85). While it certainly fits Ballard's late novels, however, it does not capture as vividly the various dynamics involved in them as the phrase "nightmare utopia."

imperative that one isolate, as we have done, the utopian impulse in order to grapple fully with its meaning. From here it is possible not only to move on to a negative hermeneutic—which, almost by default, entails the dystopian element—but also to revisit the utopian impulse in this light, to see how it appears in the shadow cast both by its own content and by a critique based on ideological factors. It is to this task that we now turn.

The Mob

The link between fascism and the type of collective presented in *Cocaine Nights* and *Super-Cannes* inevitably reminds the reader familiar with the work of Gilles Deleuze and Félix Guattari of what they call "microfascisms," a conceptualization of the "molecular" level at which fascism occurs before being incorporated into a centralized, totalizing form of the state (236).[10] Indeed, fascism—although it remains at the molecular level—will become an overt theme in the later *Millennium People*, to which I will turn shortly.[11] Again, there are timely resonances with the present political climate in the United States and Europe, which has seen an ascendency of the far right in state and civil society and the emergence, in tandem, of something close to Deleuzo-Guattarian/Ballardian microfascism.

Stuart Hall's use of the paradoxical term "authoritarian populism" (Introduction 10; *Hard Road* 42) to describe Thatcherism is useful here, as it marks a distinction between fascism proper and the micro-level resentments fostered by the emerging neoliberal state, which have arguably increased in recent years.[12] Microfascism, then, is a key theme in Ballard's late novels as it is a key issue in the current historical conjuncture. But running through Ballard's novels is something deeper, something that both links up with the quasi-fascistic tendencies on display and transcends them: the preoccupation with violence as a condition of possibility for the existence of flat formations. When this is considered, the turn to the collective in Ballard's work begins to take on some of the qualities of a well-trodden path of disdainful attitudes toward the unaccommodated social formation. Ballard's late fiction fails to fully interrogate the transformative potential of the flat formations that it figures, and instead it invariably characterizes these as uncontrollable, irrational, and barbaric. This tendency amounts to a view of the collective that is at best conservative and at worst reactionary.

The history of such patterns of thought is long. As already mentioned, Hobbes's view of the multitude as that which "stir[s] up the *Citizens* against the *City*" (152) and that precedes the state or follows from its dissolution is a foundational thought-figure, one that we see reiterated, albeit with different inflections, in all sorts of

---

10 Huntley also makes this link (227).

11 Baxter has highlighted some of the more oblique references to actual, fully fledged fascism in *Super-Cannes*, the ominously named "Villa Grimaldi" being one example (Baxter 104–5).

12 For Hall (and as we have pointed out above in relation to neoliberal ideologies in general), Thatcherism remained a fundamentally anticollectivist project (*Hard Road* 46–48).

writers, including Gustave Le Bon, Sigmund Freud, and Edward Bernays.[13] Indeed, we have already seen a much earlier expression of this view in *The Bacchae*—although this is perhaps an even more radical enactment of the violent, "unaccommodated" formation. Nevertheless, the collective, in this case, retains its violent attributes as a key feature; and this is also the case with Ballard's novels, despite the novel configuration of the dynamics between the polis and its ostensible outside. Put differently, the traditional view of the necessity of an overarching figure of domination in *Cocaine Nights* and *Super-Cannes* is done away with, but the inherent violence of human collectives that remain outside the confines of the former remains. Cohesive human formations may be formed in the absence of hierarchical structures, but these remain fundamentally violent and irrational in the Ballardian universe. The task ahead is thus to demonstrate the broader applicability of this argument to Ballard's later work and, in turn, to demonstrate how this relates to certain contemporary ways of figuring the collective.

In *Millennium People* the focus is again on a group of people—in this case middle-class revolutionaries—whose mode of coagulation is violence. As the character Richard Gould tells the protagonist: "There's a deep need for meaningless action, the more violent the better" (249). This nonsensical need develops into a whole philosophy of the pointless act on the part of Gould, who helps provide the meaningless lives of the middle classes of Chelsea Marina with a like-cures-like solution. Meaningless acts of violence, in the view of Gould and the band of revolutionaries, are exactly what is needed to wake the middle classes out of their stupor, to "[stop] the universe in its tracks" (255). Predictably, the revolution fails, "nature" having "bred" the residents of Chelsea Marina, and the wider class of which they form a part, as "docile, virtuous and civic-minded" (292).

Despite some attempts at relating it to contemporary concepts of the multitude (see, e.g., Matthews 133), the flat formation is less well-defined in *Millennium People* than in *Cocaine Nights* and *Super-Cannes*. But what remains are the underlying principles of irrationality and violence that are attributed to a formation outside the established order. In *Millennium People* there is an extra element of ridiculousness attached to the attempts at revolution, which is compounded by the mixture of nihilism and fatalism shared by all the main characters. The deep aversion toward the collective is presented here in relation to the desire to change the political coordinates, and one cannot help but feel that this aversion is being transposed onto such desires and acts in general.

In this respect, there are some close ties between *Millennium People* and the earlier *Rushing to Paradise* (1994), which depicts radical environmentalism and feminism in a highly satirical fashion, and which, as Noys has pointed out, bears some similarities with so-called New Reactionary critiques by contemporary French novelists "of the sexual and political liberation movements of the 1960s and

---

[13]   For exemplary works, see Le Bon's *The Crowd*, Freud's *Civilization and Its Discontents*, and Bernays's *Propaganda*. Gilbert provides an insightful history of the variants (including those of Le Bon, Freud, and Bernays) of what he calls the "Leviathan logic," which brings us up to the present day and the likes of Ernesto Laclau and Chantal Mouffe (Gilbert 49–68).

1970s" (393).[14] *Kingdom Come* offers a similarly critical view, albeit not via satire but by depicting the sinister side of collective forms. Indeed, the novel's opening lines touch on many of the themes already explored: "The suburbs dream of violence. Asleep in their drowsy villas, sheltered by benevolent shopping malls, they wait patiently for the nightmares that will wake them into a more passionate world" (3). *Kingdom Come* is about what happens when the dream of violence overruns the civilized world, when violence switches from being a merely latent aspect of civilization to a manifest, predominant principle. This is expressed through a direct allusion to fascistic behavior, the main signifier of this being the Saint George's Cross, that time-honored symbol of English nationalism. The violent crowds that coalesce in the novel around the Metro-Centre shopping mall, we are informed, display "the visceral baying of a mob who had scented a nearby guillotine" (26).

The fascistic tendencies on display in *Kingdom Come* are linked to consumerism: the lives of the characters are saturated by it. The Metro-Centre is, we are told, "a cathedral of consumerism whose congregations far exceeded those of the Christian churches" (15). The description is an indication of things to come. By the end of the novel, the protagonist Richard Pearson has become involved in a wholesale occupation of the shopping mall. Adrift in the Metro-Centre, the group of occupiers develops a consumerist form of religion, which includes its own shrines and rituals made up of the various commodities to be found in the mall (244).

Whether the novel is viewed as a critique of working-class English culture or an exposé of the capacity of contemporary capitalism to incorporate outside political forces, the attitude remains the same, at least when it comes to figurations of the multitude or the collective that is set apart from the established order. The use of the word *mob* in the novel is apt here, and a good description of the way the human collective is figured through the lens of the irrational and the violent in Ballard's late novels. To be clear, what I am criticizing is not the novels' attempts to demonstrate the ways in which hollowed out political systems, rampant consumerism, and societal nihilism can lead toward fascistic and generally violent behavior. Rather, I am concerned with their view of human collectives that form outside the established order as invariably something to be feared, as uncontrollable mobs bent on doing ill. The late Ballardian conception of the collective thus appears as wholly negative; we get no real sense of what a collective can do or what it might lead to in any positive, lasting, or rational sense.

Civil War

This vision of the collective goes some way to explaining the late Ballard's obsession with gated, closed, or small-scale communities, whether located on the Mediterranean or in the suburbs of London. Where a radical critique of neoliberalism sees a potential for nonhierarchical formations, a reactionary or conservative view sees merely diffuse, degenerate microcommunities, bereft of the means of

[14]   The term *New Reactionaries* was coined in 2002 by the critic Daniel Lindenberg to characterize the work of writers such as Michel Houellebecq and Maurice G. Dantec, which Linderberg deems "hostile to liberal democracy and the liberal cultural consensus." See Noys 391–92.

rational decision making and civilized behavior. What Davis calls fortress architecture and Bryan S. Turner the "enclave society" (290) is in the work of late Ballard
largely a symbol of the collapse and fragmentation of society, in the classic reactionary mode. The argument against this reading of the Ballardian gated community would be that the novels draw our attention toward a current proliferation
"not of open borders," as China Miéville puts it, but of "mobile ones, as ferociously
exclusive as those of any other state, and more than most" (251).[15] While this might
be true, the overwhelming message of these novels, when it comes to the way in
which the collective is figured, is that of an aversion to the demos, a distaste for
formations that take place outside the established order. This casts a shadow, then,
on the utopian impulse of the texts, which, abstracted from the everyday, is mapped
onto the fortress topography that the novels take as their main setting. The gated
community, as a variant of the Ballardian collective, is a way of conceiving the
breakdown of society in relation to the synchronous utopian vision with which we
are furnished.

A literary counterpoint may be useful here. Margaret Atwood's *MaddAddam*
trilogy figures another advanced fortress topography, in which there is not only a
stark, molecular separation of rich and poor but also various enclaves within the
rich and poor areas. In *The Year of the Flood* (2009) there are both utopian enclaves
and dystopian ones, all taking place in the context of a withered state, the only
vestige of which is a corrupt, fattened private security firm. Even within the utopian, decentralized enclaves of, say, the "God's Gardeners," there are dystopian
elements, such as—as Jameson puts it in an essay on the novel—a "dystopian vision
of history" that prophesies a fall of humankind, ending in complete annihilation
(Atwood, *Year of the Flood* 15; Jameson, "Then You Are Them" 8). However, utopia
in *The Year of the Flood*, while it is constantly mixed with dystopia, is not allowed to
be overrun by the latter, as it is in Ballard's later novels—at least when it comes to
the vision of the collective. In the fortress architecture depicted in Atwood's novels
we get a broad picture of the positive and negative potentials of decentralization
and decline. Atwood is thus able to put forward various hypotheses of the ways
collectives might function, whereas in the Ballard novels under discussion the
collective is posited in a set way, with the enclave merely one of its dimensions.

The nightmare content of Ballard's novels consequently serves as a vague, cautionary call for compliance and the return to some mythical ideal in which the
potency of the multitude (or *mob*, in its thoroughly negative guise) is kept at bay. If
the logic of contemporary capitalism, then, has been ostensibly to devalue hierarchy, centralization, and normativity, this is portrayed in those of Ballard's novels
examined here as predominantly disastrous, an event that will begin and end in
violence. This would be the take-home message of the novels when it comes to

[15]   At the level of the world-system the preference for hard, *national* borders, as Wendy Brown has
shown (and as has become self-evident over the last couple of years), is a symptom of the nation
state's decline in potency. Nation states seek to display, in other words, a territorial power that
they simply no longer possess in the face of mobile capital (Brown, *Walled States, Waning
Sovereignty* 19, 24). Again, the trend toward hard borders, despite the insistence on soft ones, is
something that Ballard's novels tap into. This, however, does not take into account the attitude
toward the collective displayed in Ballard's novels.

collective forms of life. Ultimately, it is a message that places a higher value on the status quo, as the cautionary tale functions to make the existing order seem rather more appealing than its alternatives. While the novels may well appear at various points to offer a critique of the consequences of neoliberalism, the overall effect is to reaffirm this state of affairs and to reinscribe it with an air of legitimacy. As it happens, there are many contemporary avatars of the sentiment expressed here in Ballard's work. So, before making some concluding remarks, it will be useful to turn to some of these, both to further situate Ballard's turn toward the collective within an historical continuum and to draw out some last conceptual complexities.

Peter Sloterdijk's *Rage and Time* (2010) is a case in point. Sloterdijk is concerned with producing a psychopolitical rubric around rage, or *thymos* (12). The result is a kind of metaphysics of motivation, which demonstrates how rage, supposedly, can be stored up and used for political ends at the level of large-scale collectives. For example, Bolshevism (and eventually the Soviet Union) was sustained by the mechanism of the party, which articulated class consciousness and stored up rage to be used at opportune revolutionary moments (132–33). The political projects of the twentieth century heralded the era of the centrality of rage for Sloterdijk, and if we are now in an era in which the center has fallen apart, rage has followed the same course (203–6). To illustrate this prevalence of rage in the contemporary situation, Sloterdijk invokes the 2005 *banlieue* riots in Paris, which for him were not only lacking in any real purpose (other than "provocative vandalism fun") but were also wholly disowned by French political parties (206). The riots in France form part of a broader, at the very least European-wide pattern of behavior that for Sloterdijk is best summed up by what Hans Magnus Enzensberger has called "molecular civil war" (qtd. in Sloterdijk 210).

Sloterdijk's position is a strange one in which the waning of official rage is almost something to be lamented in the face of the dispersion of rage, despite the inherently destructive nature of both—at least as presented in this book. But in between the fatalistic musings of *Rage and Time* there is a glimmer of the old Hobbesian disdain for the illegitimate multitude that falls outside the political order of things. The notion of molecular civil war compounds this, and yet it adds something new to the Hobbesian scenario in that we are concerned here with a *tribal* war of all against all in which the collective is a fundamental factor that, nevertheless, remains at the size of the enclave.

Molecular civil war might well be the ultimate logic of Ballard's late novels too; indeed, we can see the germ of this idea throughout the four main works discussed here. Atwood's *The Year of the Flood*, with its various warring factions and enclaves, might be read in this light, albeit with the proviso that it lacks the distinct reactionary tinge that is present in both Sloterdijk's and Ballard's writings. Another novel that comes close to the sentiment expressed in Ballard's work and in which the idea of civil war is explored quite literally is Michel Houellebecq's *Submission* (2015). Here, another kind of molecular civil war is brought about through the representative-democratic system. When neither the newly formed Muslim Brotherhood party nor the National Front gains a majority in the presidential elections, the government allows various confrontations and acts of terrorism to take place in order to disrupt the electoral process (Houellebecq 116–17). The narrator decides it might be a good idea to leave and go to Spain, where civil war would be "slightly less imminent" (105). The implication is relatively clear: the representative-democratic system is the cause of civil war and general degeneration in both allowing extremism into power and initiating civil war as the only possible antidote. The reference to civil war in Spain implies that the connection between these things is not limited to France.

Nevertheless, France—and Paris in particular—often seems to be the locus of these millenarian visions; even Bernard Stiegler reads the 2005 riots in France as a result of having to "suffer" the deep "irrationality" of having nothing to hope for. For Stiegler, these riots signal the potential for many more of their kind. There is thus a need to "implement a new political and economic rationality in France, in Europe, and throughout the entire capitalist and industrial world" (17). All these examples display a classic reactionary sentiment: that society is degenerating and that we need in some way to restore (an often phantom) order. The reasons given are instructive. Like Ballard, all these writers suggest that the violent outbursts are a symptom of some kind of postpolitical scenario. This is so whether it is a result of an absence of places to store rage (Sloterdijk 203), a rampant case of disaffection caused by an out-of-control, affective economy (Stiegler 85–87), or a dislocation from politics itself along with a degenerative representative-democratic system (Houellebecq 39, 63).

For all their preoccupation with what amounts to a postpolitical era, such proclamations are themselves utterly political, particularly in the case of Sloterdijk and Stiegler. This can be seen, for example, in the view of the riot as something wholly removed from politics as such. Granted, the riots that took place in Paris in 2005 and London (and elsewhere in the UK) in 2011 were not driven by a political idea. Nonetheless, they were driven by political decisions and relations. At the same time, such occurrences, as Alain Badiou has pointed out, suggest the possibility of "an historical riot" which changes the parameters of the current politics, or at least "indicate[s] that the existing society . . . does not possess the means altogether to prevent the advent of an historical sign of rebellion in the desolate spaces for which it is responsible" (26).

We thus again run up against the concept of multitude, which, as we have seen, is a rather more positive concept than that of the "mobbish" descriptions outlined up until now. With this in mind, what all these apocalyptic visions of the collective suggest is a fear of an unhinged underclass that has the potential to reconfigure the status quo. Ballard's late novels certainly take part (albeit sometimes with a hint of satire) in this apocalyptic way of conceiving collectivities that fall outside of the established order. But, as we have seen, these novels also participate in a degree of utopianism and in this sense are not as clear-cut as the other writings surveyed. Furthermore, Ballard is not interested in any particular class of people. The fear of an unhinged multitude is in Ballard a general preoccupation rather than simply a form of class phobia. Finally, Ballard's versions of the collective are speculative. The late novels are tuned toward the possibilities of new collective forms and, in this capacity, they present a strange blend of reactionary and futurist worldviews, a blend that complements the "nightmare utopianism" on display.

*   *   *

JOEL EVANS is assistant professor in literature at the University of Nottingham. He is the author of *Conceptualising the Global in the Wake of the Postmodern: Literature, Culture, Theory* (2019).

Works Cited

Atwood, Margaret. "Dire Cartographies: The Roads to Ustopia." *Other Worlds: SF and the Human Imagination*. London: Virago, 2012. 66–96.

Atwood, Margaret. *The Year of the Flood*. New York: Anchor, 2010.

Babel. Dir. Alejandro González Iñárritu. Paramount Vantage, 2006.

Badiou, Alain. *The Rebirth of History: Times of Riots and Uprisings*. Trans. Gregory Elliott. London: Verso, 2012.

Ballard, J. G. *Cocaine Nights*. London: Harper Perennial, 2006.

Ballard, J. G. *Concrete Island*. London: Harper Perennial, 2008.

Ballard, J. G. *The Drowned World*. London: Fourth Estate, 2011.

Ballard, J. G. *High-Rise*. London: Fourth Estate, 2011.

Ballard, J. G. *Kingdom Come*. London: Harper Perennial, 2007.

Ballard, J. G. *Millennium People*. London: Flamingo, 2003.

Ballard, J. G. *Running Wild*. London: Flamingo, 1997.

Ballard, J. G. *Rushing to Paradise*. London: Flamingo, 1995.

Ballard, J. G. *Super-Cannes*. London: Flamingo, 2001.

Ballard, J. G. "Time, Memory, and Inner Space." *Re/Search: J. G. Ballard*. Ed. Andrea Juno and V. Vale. San Francisco: Re/Search, 1984. 100–101.

Baxter, Jeannette. "Visions of Europe in *Cocaine Nights* and *Super-Cannes*." *J. G. Ballard: Contemporary Critical Perspectives*. Ed. Jeannette Baxter. London: Continuum, 2008. 94–106.

Bernays, Edward L. *Propaganda*. Brooklyn: Ig, 2005.

Bolaño, Roberto. *2666*. Trans. Natasha Wimmer. New York: Picador, 2009.

Boltanski, Luc, and Ève Chiapello. *The New Spirit of Capitalism*. Trans. Gregory Elliott. London: Verso, 2006.

Brown, Wendy. *Undoing the Demos: Neoliberalism's Stealth Revolution*. New York: Zone, 2015.

Brown, Wendy. *Walled States, Waning Sovereignty*. New York: Zone, 2010.

Canetti, Elias. *Crowds and Power*. Trans. Carol Stewart. Harmondsworth: Penguin, 1992.

Contagion. Dir. Steven Soderbergh. Warner Bros., 2011.

Coupland, Douglas. *Generation A*. London: Windmill, 2010.

Davis, Mike. *City of Quartz: Excavating the Future in Los Angeles*. London: Verso, 2006.

Deleuze, Gilles, and Félix Guattari. *A Thousand Plateaus: Capitalism and Schizophrenia*. Trans. Brian Massumi. London: Continuum, 2004.

Eagleton, Terry. *Holy Terror*. Oxford: Oxford UP, 2005.

Eagleton-Pierce, Matthew. *Neoliberalism: The Key Concepts*. New York: Routledge, 2016.

Euripides. *The Bacchae and Other Plays*. Trans. Philip Vellacott. Harmondsworth: Penguin, 1972.

Freud, Sigmund. *Civilization and Its Discontents*. Trans. David McLintock. London: Penguin, 2002.

Galloway, Alexander R. "Love of the Middle." *Excommunication: Three Inquiries in Media and Mediation*. Chicago: U of Chicago P, 2014. 25–76.

Gasiorek, Andrzej. *J. G. Ballard*. Manchester: Manchester UP, 2005.

Gilbert, Jeremy. *Common Ground: Democracy and Collectivity in an Age of Individualism*. London: Pluto, 2014.

Hall, Stuart. *The Hard Road to Renewal: Thatcherism and the Crisis of the Left*. London: Verso, 1990.

Hall, Stuart. Introduction. *The Politics of Thatcherism*. Ed. Stuart Hall and Martin Jacques. London: Lawrence and Wishart, 1983. 9–16.

Hardt, Michael, and Antonio Negri. *Multitude: War and Democracy in the Age of Empire*. New York: Penguin, 2004.

Harvey, David. *A Brief History of Neoliberalism*. Oxford: Oxford UP, 2007.

High-Rise. Dir. Ben Wheatley. StudioCanal, 2016.

Hobbes, Thomas. *De Cive: The English Version*. Ed. Howard Warrender. Oxford: Oxford UP, 1983.

Houellebecq, Michel. *Submission*. Trans. Lorin Stein. London: Vintage, 2016.

Huntley, Jake. "The Madness of Crowds: Ballard's Experimental Communities." *J. G. Ballard: Visions and Revisions*. Ed. Jeannette Baxter and Rowland Wymer. London: Palgrave Macmillan, 2012. 215–29.

Jameson, Fredric. *The Political Unconscious: Narrative as a Socially Symbolic Act*. Ithaca: Cornell UP, 1981.

Jameson, Fredric. "Then You Are Them." *London Review of Books* 10 Sept 2009: 7–8.

Le Bon, Gustave. *The Crowd*. London: Transaction, 1997.

Matthews, Graham. "Consumerism's Endgame: Violence and Community in J. G. Ballard's Late Fiction." *Journal of Modern Literature* 36.2 (2013): 122–39.

Miéville, China. "Floating Utopias: Freedom and Unfreedom of the Seas." *Evil Paradises: Dreamworlds of Neoliberalism*. Ed. Mike Davis and Daniel Bertrand Monk. New York: New Press, 2008. 251–60.

Noys, Benjamin. *"La Libido Réactionaire?* The Recent Fiction of J. G. Ballard." *Journal of European Studies* 37.4 (2007): 391–406.

Ostrowidzki, Eric A. "Utopias of the New Right in J. G. Ballard's Fiction." *Space and Culture* 12.1 (2009): 4–24.

Punter, David. *The Hidden Script: Writing and the Unconscious*. London: Routledge and Kegan Paul, 1985.

Ryman, Geoff. *Air (or Have Not Have)*. London: Gollancz, 2006.

Sloterdijk, Peter. *Rage and Time*. Trans. Mario Wenning. New York: Columbia UP, 2012.

Stiegler, Bernard. *Disbelief and Discredit, Volume 2: Uncontrollable Societies of Disaffected Individuals*. Trans. Daniel Ross. Cambridge: Polity, 2013.

Tew, Philip. "Situating the Violence of J. G. Ballard's Postmillennial Fiction: The Possibilities of Sacrifice, the Certainties of Trauma." *J. G. Ballard: Contemporary Critical Perspectives*. Ed. Jeannette Baxter. London: Continuum, 2008. 107–19.

Turner, Bryan S. "The Enclave Society: Towards a Sociology of Immobility." *European Journal of Social Theory* 10.2 (2007): 287–303.

Virno, Paolo. *A Grammar of the Multitude: For an Analysis of Contemporary Forms of Life*. Trans. Isabella Bertoletti, James Cascaito, and Andrea Casson. Los Angeles: Semiotext(e), 2004.

Whyte, William H. *The Organization Man*. Harmondsworth: Penguin, 1960.

Žižek, Slavoj. *Living in the End Times*. London: Verso, 2011.

Žižek, Slavoj. "A Plea for Ethical Violence." *Bible and Critical Theory* 1.1 (2004): 1–15.

Ruth Ozeki's Floating World: A Tale for the Time Being's Spiritual Oceanography

ALISON GLASSIE

According to Ruth Ozeki, the Tōhoku earthquake and tsunami "broke the world."[1] The 9.0 magnitude undersea megathrust earthquake triggered a 38.8-meter tsunami that roared ashore near Sendai and caused the Fukushima Daiichi meltdown—coupling the worst nuclear disaster since Chernobyl with the biggest loss of life in Japan since the US atomic bombing of Nagasaki (Carlton et al. 1402; Parry xvii).[2] In the aftermath, Ozeki, a Japanese American filmmaker, novelist, and Zen Buddhist priest, withdrew a recently completed novel from her agent in order to "[sit] with it." "Japan was no longer the same country," she explained to me in a May 2017 phone interview; "The fictional world was completely broken [too]" (Ozeki, pers. comm.). Ozeki was left wondering how to write fiction in a world whose brokenness seemed to exceed it.[3]

Rewritten in Tōhoku's wake, what had been a suddenly "irrelevant" draft became Ozeki's Man Booker Prize–shortlisted *A Tale for the Time Being* (2013).

I am deeply grateful to Ruth Ozeki for speaking to me about her work and to Hanlon Kelley, Jeff Kelley, and Madeline Zehnder for facilitating that contact. I also thank Dr. James T. Carlton for answering my questions about his tsunami research. Incisive, generous feedback from many colleagues has shaped this manuscript at various stages. The participants of a panel at the 2017 Modern Language Association annual convention, "Ecological Catastrophe: Past and Present," commented on a preliminary version of this work. Many thanks to all.

[1]   Ozeki, pers. comm., 5 May 2017. When I discussed my preliminary research on *A Tale for the Time Being* with my friend Hanlon Kelley, she mentioned that her father Jeff Kelley knew Ozeki through the Zen Buddhist community in the Pacific Northwest. He emailed Ozeki in January 2017 to let her know of my interest in her novel's engagement with marine science and asked whether he could pass on her email address to me. In February 2017 Madeline Zehnder, a colleague at the University of Virginia, mentioned that Ozeki was Writer in Residence at Smith College and suggested I contact her there. In March 2017 I wrote to Ozeki at her Smith email address and, having received Jeff's introductory note, she responded. We arranged to speak on May 5, 2017, and I sent her my questions in advance. Over the course of the hour we spent on the phone, I asked Ozeki questions about *A Tale for the Time Being*'s engagement with washed-up objects and the post-Tōhoku meanings of marine debris; ukiyo-e prints and the Buddhist floating world; ocean gyres and garbage patches; popular marine science; environmental catastrophe; and barnacles. Henceforth, remarks made by Ozeki during this conversation will be cited as "Ozeki, pers. comm." I also had a Skype conversation with James T. Carlton (14 April 2016), which will be cited as "Carlton, pers. comm."

[2]   See Carlton et al. 1402 and Parry xvii. Richard Lloyd Parry describes the Tōhoku earthquake as "the biggest earthquake ever known to have struck Japan and the fourth most powerful in the history of seismology. It knocked the Earth ten inches off its axis; moved Japan four feet closer to America" (12). About 100 people died in the earthquake. The tsunami killed 20,000 and displaced 465,000 more; 2,700 people are still missing (Ferris and Solis; Beauregard 96).

[3]   Ozeki compared her situation with that of writers after 9/11 who "couldn't write about New York." "I was really upset," she told me. "I have relatives in Sendai" (Ozeki, pers. comm.).

According to Ozeki, the novel had always contained the story of a reader finding the diary of Naoko "Nao" (temporal pun intended) Yasutani, a sixteen-year-old girl who "wash[es] up back in Tokyo" after her father loses his Silicon Valley job (Ozeki, pers. comm.). Struggling to adjust to her family's repatriation, the despondent, suicidal Nao sets out to write down the story of her 104-year-old great-grandmother Jiko, a Zen Buddhist nun and former radical feminist writer, before she herself "drop[s] out of time" (*Tale* 7). After the tsunami, though, Ozeki changed the mechanism for the diary's discovery from a "knapsack in a library" to the "scarred plastic freezer bag, encrusted with barnacles" that washes up on a British Columbia beach several months after the tsunami (8). "It was pretty clear," she explained to me, "that things were going to start washing up" (pers. comm.). Ozeki also followed her husband Oliver's advice and inserted herself into the story as the diary's reader—a "semi-real character" named Ruth (pers. comm.).[4] In chapters that alternate with the text of Nao's diary, Ruth and her husband Oliver (also a "semi-real" character) find themselves called to respond to the story of Nao's unhappy "now," nested with a "small stack of handwritten letters; a pudgy bound book with a faded red cover; a sturdy antique wristwatch . . . the Hello Kitty lunchbox that had protected the contents from the corrosive effects of the sea," and the marine invertebrates that settled on the plastic bag containing this floating world (10).

A Tale for the Time Being's new frame story offers "scientific and imaginative testimony" to the tsunami and to the immense, multifarious raft of objects and personal effects it cast adrift—minute pieces of plastic; four polystyrene docks from the fishing port of Misawa; and the wet-well abalone boat *Saisho Maru*, which washed ashore in Washington state in 2013 with a tide pool of at least thirty living marine and coastal species in its well (Nixon 14; Carlton "Blue Brick Road"). Inviting its readers to follow along with the amateur marine science whereby Ruth and Oliver respond to Nao's diary, the heartache it contains, and the disaster that must have launched it, *A Tale for the Time Being*'s frame story dramatizes a citizen-science response to the Tōhoku tsunami, predicated on a forensic response to marine debris. The marine scientific inquiry of the novel's characters becomes both an ethical posture from which to read the evidence of "oceanic catastrophe" and a model for how to read the novel itself (Brayton 565).[5]

Borrowing the phrase "forensic unpeeling" from *A Tale for the Time Being*, Guy Beauregard argues that what animates the novel is "an extended process of imagining lives in Japan primarily but not exclusively through excerpts of Nao's diary" (97). My discussion of "forensic unpeeling" diverges from Beauregard's by foregrounding the scientific practices and perspectives that make these imaginative

---

4   I join Rocío Davis in referring to the writer as Ozeki and the character as Ruth (93). Ozeki initially rejected her husband's suggestion that in order to maintain the brokenness of the post-Tōhoku fictional world, she should enter *A Tale for the Time Being* as a character. "It just seemed," she said in a 2013 interview, "kind of metafictional and postmodern for all the wrong reasons" (Wheeler Centre).

5   During our conversation, Ozeki and I discussed her interest in citizen science, which emerged after the tsunami. "I was very interested," she said, "because in Japan, it's mothers and housewives who [were] testing and tracking exposure to radioactivity."

engagements possible. When Ozeki's readers follow along with Ruth and Oliver's marine scientific inquiry, they—like the metafictional characters—participate in what Debjani Ganguly describes as the "work of witnessing" (193). By theorizing the forensic practices of reading and marine science as forms of witnessing within and beyond *A Tale for the Time Being*, Ozeki negotiates the ethical quandary of and surrounding her novel: whether and how to use narrative to respond to layered catastrophes that wildly exceed it.

In this essay, I reveal *A Tale for the Time Being*'s narrative dependence upon marine scientific practice and the patterns of movement and agency emerging from the North Pacific subtropical gyre, the circular system of ocean currents whereby Tōhoku flotsam traveled from Japan to North America. My analysis of Ozeki's frame story, rewritten "in terms of the ocean" and around the insistent "voice of Nao," locates *A Tale for the Time Being*'s reformulation of the novel—a genre Ganguly (riffing on Bakhtin) describes as "semantically open-ended, ready to absorb . . . the indeterminacy of the present"—in its use of the ocean to sustain the rupture of the post-Tohoku fictional world (Ozeki, pers. comm.; Ganguly 3).[6] Scholarship on *A Tale for the Time Being* has, by and large, approached this novel from the perspectives of feminism, Asian American studies, and narrative theory.[7] My study, however, offers a reading informed by dynamics from physical ocean-ography, by recent findings on the species-transport implications of tsunami flot-sam, and by my conversation with Ozeki. In so doing, it offers to the "blue human-ities" and "critical ocean studies"—the environmental humanities currents that foreground the ocean and track a shift in scholarly engagement from "oceanic space" to "ontological place"—a model for reading the contemporary novel through the marine sciences (DeLoughrey, "Submarine" 32).[8]

---

[6]   Mikhail Bakhtin writes in *The Dialogic Imagination* that the novel has a "living contact with the unfinished, still-evolving, contemporary reality" (7; qtd in Ganguly 3). In *This Thing Called the World: The Contemporary Novel as Global Form*, Ganguly emphasizes the genre's open-endedness, "renew[ing] an argument for what, after Bakhtin, is popularly called the *novelization* thesis" (41). During our conversation, Ozeki described feeling the need to "drive a wedge into the fic-tional world" after the tsunami. By writing herself and Oliver into the novel and changing "the vector for the diary to wash up," Ozeki used the North Pacific itself to maintain *A Tale for the Time Being*'s contact with the broken, post-tsunami world. "The idea that the ocean connects us," she told me, "became really important." Through the interactions between Ruth and Oliver's post-tsunami present (and that of her readers) and Nao's pre-tsunami "now," which unfolds within the pages of the diary, Ozeki links the open-ended temporal qualities of "the novel" specifically to the nonlinear temporalities of ocean circulation.

[7]   See, for example, articles by Michelle N. Huang, Marlo Starr, Beauregard, and Rocío Davis.

[8]   "Blue humanities," according to Steve Mentz, "names an off-shore trajectory that places cultural history in an oceanic rather than terrestrial context" ("Blue Humanities" 69). It is a term that exhibits a general "tendency in scholarship to put the ocean at the forefront of our attentions" (Mentz, "Shakespeare and the Blue Humanities" 384). See also John Gillis. Elizabeth DeLoughrey sees "critical ocean studies" as the reflection of a recent interdisciplinary shift in scholarly attention occasioned by broader knowledge of sea level rise, which produces the "new oce-anic imaginary" to which critical ocean studies responds ("Submarine" 32–33). Geographer Philip E. Steinberg, however, observes that "oceanography"—that is, the multidisciplinary

When Ozeki's metafictional Ruth and Oliver hypothesize that Nao's plastic-bagged, barnacle-encrusted lunchbox and its contents are connected to the tsunami, they proceed to learn about ocean circulation patterns and consult with marine scientists in order to identify the marine invertebrates growing on the bag. Midway through the novel, however, the results of these efforts disprove their tsunami hypothesis. Calling *A Tale for the Time Being* an effort to "perform certain aspects of Zen philosophy" in response to the Tōhoku disasters, Ozeki cites two Buddhist concepts: impermanence and "interconnectedness, which in Buddhism is called dependent co-arising" (qtd. in Lee 28; see also Wheeler Centre). A third concept, however, is most central to my analysis. Not-knowing—that is, the pursuit of "boundless original mind"—is a practice of detaching from preconceptions, preferred outcomes, or self-identifications as "the one who knows" (Suzuki 22; Hartman). By bringing her characters' practices of citizen marine science into productive tension with not-knowing, Ozeki extends, in a literary register, a long conversation between Buddhism and the sciences.[9] In fact, *A Tale for the Time Being*'s commitments to Zen Buddhism transform its marine scientific practices into meditations on the idea that in our damaged, open-ended world, attempting to know or understand also means learning to coexist with what cannot be known, discovered, or recovered.

A Tale for the Time Being's new, fundamentally oceanographic frame story—which is also oriented by Zen Buddhist thought—enables it to explore the epistemological, spiritual, and aesthetic resources whereby we can respond to catastrophe. By examining *A Tale for the Time Being*'s metafictional structure, I will demonstrate that the approach to Nao's bundle within the novel, like the scientific study of tsunami flotsam beyond it, depends upon a revaluation of marine debris. Next, I will show that *A Tale for the Time Being* theorizes itself in terms derived from physical oceanography and the floating worlds of Buddhism and Japanese aesthetics. And in the last section of the essay, "Transpacific Time Beings," I shift to marine biology, reading the scene of barnacle identification that disproves Ruth and Oliver's tsunami hypothesis in light of Zen Buddhist not-knowing. Ultimately my study shows that the close empirical attention driving *A Tale for the Time Being*'s frame story is both a scientific and a spiritual practice, one that uncovers the deeply human—and more-than-human—stories contained in unexpected places. Even in the absence of conclusive results, the novel implies, such intimate, imperfect practices are necessary in a literal and spiritual floating world.

Forensic Unpeeling

A Tale for the Time Being's second chapter initiates the unlikely connections between amateur and professional marine science, metafiction, and Zen Buddhism that drive the novel. Nao's salutation to a hoped-for reader—"Hi! My name is Nao, and

scientific study of the global ocean—"is a discipline rarely engaged by humanities-oriented scholars" (160). The present article addresses this methodological gap.

[9]   See David L. McMahan's *Making of Buddhist Modernism* and B. Alan Wallace's edited volume *Buddhism and Science*.

I am a time being. . . . A time being is someone who lives in time, and that means you, and me, and every one of us who is, or was, or ever will be"—opens *A Tale for the Time Being* (3). In this chapter—the first of the frame story—Ruth stumbles across the bundle containing this direct address during a walk along a fitful, agential North Pacific that is "always heaving . . . up and hurling . . . back" items such as "fishing lines, floats, beer cans, plastic toys, . . . Nike sneakers . . . [even] severed feet" (8). Ozeki's frame story thus opens by foregrounding the diversity of anthropogenic marine debris; it also alludes to two separate incidents in which lost transpacific cargo traveled the world as ocean flotsam: the five shipping containers of Nike sneakers from the freighter *Hansa Carrier* (1990) and the 28,800 bath toys from the *Ever Laurel* (1992) (Ebbesmeyer and Scigliano 71–79; Hohn 10). These events changed scientific career trajectories, became subjects for popular marine science texts (including two that Ozeki cites), and excited beachcombers worldwide. They also illustrated that the movement of any object with a known time and place of release into the ocean can provide oceanographic data and that it is often possible for beachcombers and citizen scientists to participate in data collection.[10]

Nao's diary, *A Tale for the Time Being*'s other narrative strain, only finds a reader because Ruth, who "[doesn't] want to think about what might be rotting inside the bag," engages in a bit of reluctant beach-cleanup, bringing what she assumes is washed-up garbage home to throw away (8). In the exchange that ensues when Ruth's husband Oliver finds the bundle in the couple's mudroom and approaches it with curiosity, Ozeki introduces the forensic unpeeling that structures *A Tale for the Time Being*'s frame story and, by extension, the entire novel. "Do you think you could dissect your garbage out on the porch?" Ruth asks Oliver as he begins to pick apart the barnacle-encrusted plastic. "I don't think it's garbage," Oliver responds. "It's too neatly wrapped." He "continue[s] his forensic unpeeling" (9).

Here, the terms *dissect* and *forensic unpeeling* position scientific inquiry as a material, even ethical, response to bodies impacted by crime or tragedy. Oliver does not dismiss what his wife has already written off as garbage; instead, his curious, scientific approach enables Nao's story to find its readers, and *A Tale for the Time Being* to unfold as a novel. Ruth and Oliver are characters in their own right, but more importantly for Ozeki's purposes, they are readers who presume, based on the timing of Ruth's discovery and the Japanese text in Nao's diary, that the bundle is connected to the Tōhoku tsunami. "I think it's starting," Oliver tells Ruth after inspecting the bundle: "Drifters . . . [e]scaping the orbit of the Pacific Gyre. . . . All that stuff from people's homes in Japan that the tsunami washed out to sea? They've been tracking it and predicting it will wash up on our coastline" (13–14). Even as his observation of the bundle's neat wrapping might suggest other possibilities, Oliver's hypothesis, by referencing North Pacific circulation and scientists tracking tsunami flotsam, positions physical oceanography (and later, because of the barnacles growing on the bag, marine biology) as central to any effort to determine how long the bundle has been floating and whether Nao is still alive.

---

[10]   Curtis Ebbesmeyer enlisted beachcombers worldwide in data collection via the Internet; beachcombers on Oregon's Agate Beach were the first to find one of the Misawa docks (Tobias).

In *A Tale for the Time Being*'s initial forensic unpeeling scene, Ruth's preconception about the bundle limits its possibilities. Oliver, on the other hand, both unwraps Nao's story and hypothesizes its connection to the tsunami through which Ozeki introduces the Zen Buddhist concept of not-knowing. Ozeki's chief marine science interlocutor, oceanographer Curtis Ebbesmeyer, theorizes beachcombing as both a popular science and a meditative practice. "Beachcombing," he writes with Eric Scigliano, "appeals to deep-seated impulses and aspirations—to the scientist, explorer, collector, and treasure hunter in everyone. . . . It is poor man's oceanography, research as play, unconstrained . . . and open to everyone with eyes to see and feet to walk" (74). Marine science historian Helen Rozwadowski concurs. "We have historically known the ocean through work," she writes, "[y]et . . . people have [also] seriously studied the ocean through play" (166). These two theories of play as a marine scientific method emphasize attention and lack of constraint, two habits of mind that seem, at first, to oppose each other. Not-knowing brings both of these habits together.[11]

Paradoxically, Ruth's attachment to the tsunami hypothesis—an attachment that conflicts with not-knowing's emphasis on "boundless original mind"—is what makes *A Tale for the Time Being*'s marine scientific metafiction a sustained response to the Tōhoku disasters. The novel's "primary concern," according to Rocío Davis, is "the relationship between a writer and her reader, based on the notion that the act of writing might conjure a reader," but the reader's role in this process is equally important (93). Ozeki's metafictional avatar Ruth is at once Nao's primary reader, a novelist, and a beachcomber. While her preconception about the plastic-wrapped bundle as trash is what enables Nao's story to be told, both the occupation that makes Ruth an ideal reader *and* the pastime that puts her in a position to discover the diary require the unconstrained mind she often resists.

The Tōhoku tsunami is at once a catastrophe, a literary opportunity for Ozeki, and a scientific opportunity that marine ecologist and evolutionary biogeographer James T. Carlton has described as "unprecedented" ("Blue Brick Road").[12] For the first time, scientists have been able to follow the movements of a massive and diverse field of "debris from a known source and time of entry"—Northeast Japan on March 11, 2011 ("Blue Brick Road"). Objects from the tsunami began coming ashore in North America and Hawai'i in 2012. Since then, Carlton and a team of eight other marine scientists have examined the marine animal communities that traveled on 634 of these objects and documented the live arrivals from Japan of least 289 distinct invertebrate and fish species (Carlton et al. 1402). None of these species had previously been documented to have "rafted transoceanically between continents" (Carlton et al. 1402).

[11]   Zenkei Blanche Hartman describes a young child exploring a spoon, without any preconceived notions, as an illustrative example of not-knowing, also called "beginner's mind."

[12]   Carlton is a leading figure in the study of Japanese tsunami debris and a pioneer in the study of anthropogenic marine bio-invasions. He has served on the US delegations to the United Nations International Maritime Organization and the United Nations Global Invasive Species Program (*Pew Directory of Marine Fellows*).

In the past, what Carlton calls the "half-life of drifting species" would have been limited by the biodegradation of the materials and substrates on which these marine and coastal organisms hitched rides ("Blue Brick Road"). These animals, mostly invertebrates, have been able to travel longer and farther because of the durability of the anthropogenic material that finds its way into the global ocean. According to Carlton and his team, Japanese coastal animals have continued to wash up alive in North America after spending almost six years at sea—four or more years longer than previously documented cases (Carlton et al. 1402–3). The increasingly frequent storms and sea level rise associated with climate change will wash ever-greater quantities of nonbiodegradable (often plastic) material out to sea, enabling coastal species to "surmount" what Carlton and his team call "historic ocean barriers," with significant implications for evolutionary biology (1406). These findings also underscore the fact that human-produced artifacts are—for better and for worse—subject to myriad nonhuman uses.[13]

The floaters that Carlton and his team have been tracking are not GPS buoys but living creatures—"time beings," as *A Tale for the Time Being* would have it—drifting on the fragments launched by catastrophe. Carlton, who typically uses the phrase "Japanese tsunami marine debris" to specify the source of the objects he and his team study, was advised against using the word *debris* while lecturing in Japan (Carlton, pers. comm.). He recalls using the words *items* and *objects* instead, acknowledging that *debris* and its connotations are incommensurate with the tragic circumstances in which these objects and belongings were wrenched from their owners and cast adrift (pers. comm.). Tetsuya Tadano, an eleven-year-old survivor of the chaotic, largely unsuccessful evacuation of Okawa Elementary School, under-scores this incommensurability. "Our possessions," he says, "are now called gareki [rubble or debris]. Until the disaster, they were part of our life. Now, they contain our memories. I don't like to hear all those things referred to as 'rubble'" (qtd. in Parry 229). Ozeki also underscores the inadequacies of the phrase *marine debris*. "[I]n post-tsunami Japan," she told me, using the term *debris* to describe what the tsunami washed away is "disrespectful. . . . It's objects but it's also bodies. When do beloved objects become debris, and when does a body become debris?" (Ozeki, pers. comm.).

Ozeki positions the diary of the drifting, bullied teenage outcast Nao, along with other drifting characters and their stories, within a frame story in which her ideal reader initially dismisses the bundle containing half the novel as floating garbage. By using the contingent recovery and revaluation of a piece of ocean flotsam as the only point of access to these characters and their stories, Ozeki challenges *A Tale for the Time Being*'s readers to revise their understanding of "marine debris." In pre-vailing scientific usage, marine debris is implicitly plural and undifferentiated (Coe and Rogers xxi). Ozeki, by contrast, foregrounds particularity, engaging ques-tions of value and belonging through marine debris and through characters she describes as "adrift" (Ozeki, pers. comm.). For instance, Nao, struggling to adjust

---

[13]   Dolly Jorgensen argues that anthropogenic artifacts are now "part of nature" because nonhu-mans use them as habitat (138). The presence of pelagic plastics at all levels of marine food webs, including our own, troubles these categories in more malign, more somatic terms (Parker; Frangoul).

to life and school in Tokyo after her childhood in California, describes herself as a "ronin," applying the Japanese word for a masterless samurai to people who are socially, culturally, even economically adrift. "You write ronin," she writes in her diary, "with the character for wave and the character for person, which is pretty much how I feel, like a little wave person, floating around on the stormy sea of life" (*Tale* 42). Describing her metafictional avatar as similarly "adrift," Ozeki locates Ruth's "adriftness . . . in her name." Ruth, she says, translates into Japanese as "rootless" (Ozeki, pers. comm.).

Ozeki does not offer sustained treatment of the contemporary inequalities of wealth, privilege, and consumption whereby the majority of marine debris enters the global ocean.[14] Nevertheless, Nao's plastic-wrapped, sea-going Hello Kitty lunchbox signals twentieth-century and contemporary Japanese-American cultural transfer, materially encoding the transpacific histories and structures of violence (to say nothing of the petrochemicals) that enabled its production. "[T]he [plastic] material that kept Nao's diary safe from disintegration," Michelle N. Huang observes, "was produced through the same transpacific history of war that conscripted Nao's uncle Haruki #1 to his death as a kamikaze pilot in the Imperial Japanese Army and interned Ruth's relatives" (107). Through the forensic unpeeling that brings Nao's story into being, Ruth, Oliver, and *A Tale for the Time Being*'s readers learn that Haruki #1 crashed his plane into the Pacific in a secret conscientious objection to World War II; afterward, his grieving mother Jiko, Nao's great-grandmother, became a Buddhist nun. A metonym for the novel, Nao's floating lunchbox contains *A Tale for the Time Being*'s historical and thematic concerns along with her diary, her uncle's letters, and his military-issue watch. In the wake of the tsunami outside the novel, brightly colored Hello Kitty accessories—signs of more innocent cultural transfers and symbols of girlhood and playfulness on both sides of the Pacific—could be spotted among the muddy wreckage, sometimes the only material remains of their youthful owners (Parry 46).

A Tale for the Time Being's investment in the potential associations between the Tōhoku disasters and Nao's vibrant Hello Kitty lunchbox and its contents—what Jane Bennett might call a "contingent tableau"—reminds us that human histories and cultural and economic practices have always been vectors of marine and coastal species transport as well as sources of marine pollution (5).[15] By contrast, the findings of Carlton and his team challenge us to recognize that nonbiodegradable objects—the anthropogenic relics of an oceanic catastrophe—shift the propulsion of the species they carry from human histories and maritime traffic to the global ocean's surface currents and prevailing winds. Tōhoku tsunami flotsam—fish totes, vessels like the tide-pool–bearing *Saisho Maru*, even the four polystyrene and

14   Alice Te Punga Somerville critiques such transpacific historical violences and present-day consumption, privilege, and inequality. She theorizes ocean garbage patches, and marine debris more generally, as manifestations of "the disposable lives of other people," composed of "small bits of trash, discarded by those whose position is marked by what they have the luxury to throw away as much as by what they keep" (320).

15   See, for example, the introductions in North America of the European Green Crab *Carcinus maenas* (Carlton and Cohen 1809) and the Asian shore crab *Hemigrapsus sanguineus* (Richerson).

concrete docks from the fishing port of Misawa—provide substrate for the marine species they transport, while the physical forces of the ocean are the agents of transport. While it remains unclear whether the Tōhoku tsunami launched Nao's bundle, the hypothesis orienting Ruth and Oliver's forensically inflected marine science registers the efforts of professional marine scientists responding to "tsunami debris," but it foregrounds the fact that among these often-undifferentiated objects are personal items with wrenching stories.

Gyre Memory and the Floating World

A Tale for the Time Being's frame narrative operates through the dissolution, diffraction, and contingent recovery of stories circulating in an agented North Pacific Ocean. Ozeki structures *A Tale for the Time Being* around the movement of "drifters" like Nao, her family, the massive pulse of flotsam the Tōhoku tsunami launched into the Pacific, and the bag containing the improbable, heartbreaking collection of objects that includes Nao's diary. Her narrative technique thus mirrors the physical oceanographic technique of modeling the ocean's fluid dynamics via the movement of objects through time and space.[16] Ozeki explores the instabilities of narration, commemoration, and time that drive her novel through the North Pacific subtropical gyre that circulates floating objects, drifting species, and presumably Nao's diary. As a result, the ocean—which Elizabeth DeLoughrey argues "dissolves phenomenological experience . . . [and] diffracts the accumulation of narrative" ("Submarine" 33)—is actually *A Tale for the Time Being*'s most important narrative agent.

Broadly speaking, physical oceanographers distinguish between two approaches to modeling the ocean's fluid dynamics. Oceanographers working in a Eulerian vein gather data by measuring the forces that act on fixed monitoring devices and then aggregate those data to create their models (see IOOS). While Stefan Helmreich observes the importance of this modeling approach to the study of waves (271), Philip E. Steinberg reads it as "mimic[king] the terrestrial spatial ontology wherein points are fixed in space and mobile forces are external to and act on those points" (160). By contrast, the Lagrangian technique involves tracking the movements of mobile floating or drifting objects; its data come from the movement of objects through time and space rather than from the forces acting on moored infrastructure such as buoys (IOOS; Steinberg 160). Thus its models are based on movement, not on stasis.

Ozeki explains the North Pacific subtropical gyre, the literal and narrative agent that casts Nao's lunchbox and its contents ashore, in the same chapter in which she introduces Ruth and Oliver and inaugurates their forensic unpeeling. In an extemporaneous lecture on ocean circulation, Oliver explains to Ruth and to *A Tale for the Time Being*'s readers that "the Turtle Gyre goes clockwise, and the Aleut Gyre goes counterclockwise"; the motion of his hands mimics "the great arcs and spirals of the ocean's flow" (*Tale* 13). Oliver distinguishes between gyres and the surface

---

[16]   Andrew Bennett's *Lagrangian Fluid Dynamics* and Russ E. Davis's "Lagrangian Ocean Studies" offer technical discussions of ocean modeling.

currents that comprise them—for example, the Kuroshio, which runs northward along Japan's east coast—by describing gyres as "[l]ike a string of currents" or "a ring of snakes, each biting the tail of the one ahead of it" (13). "The flotsam that rides the gyres is called drift. Drift that stays in the orbit of the gyre is considered to be part of the gyre memory. The rate of escape from the gyre determines the half-life of drift . . . " (14). At the end of this description, Oliver hypothesizes the connection between Nao's floating bundle and the tsunami.

Oliver's explanation invites readers to follow along as he develops his tsunami hypothesis and presents the intertwined ideas of "gyre memory," "half-life," and "drift" undergirding it. At the same time, it distills a passage in Ozeki's most important popular marine science intertext: Ebbesmeyer and Scigliano's *Flotsametrics and the Floating World: How One Man's Obsession with Runaway Sneakers and Rubber Ducks Revolutionized Ocean Science* (2009). In *A Tale for the Time Being*'s North Pacific, the half-lives of the time beings floating around an ocean gyre "correspond," in the words of Ebbesmeyer and Scigliano, "to one revolution of a gyre." Their "rates of escape from the gyre"—and thus their half-lives—are contingent on the revolution of the gyre in which they travel (159). The half-life of a drifting Asian shore crab (*Hemigrapsus sanguineus*), for instance, depends on the composition and biodegradability of the substrate on which it travels; similarly, the half-life of Nao's story depends on the durability of its packaging. By using the term *half-life*, which Ebbesmeyer and Scigliano cannot avoid defining by use of a simile of radioactive isotopes, Ozeki gestures toward the 2011 Fukushima Daiichi nuclear disaster, the traumatic legacies of nuclear weapons testing in Polynesia and Micronesia, and the bombings of Hiroshima and Nagasaki.[17] The very term calls attention to these nuclear Pacific histories and the historical relics, remains, and contaminants of all sizes and scales contained in the Pacific Ocean.

Working from her attraction to "the poetry" she found in Ebbesmeyer and Scigliano's text, Ozeki uses "gyre memory"—that is, "the share of drifters retained in a gyre after each orbit"—to turn the circulation of the North Pacific gyre into a contingent archiving system that contains historical memory and curates the objects in its collection by, among other physical variables, windage, density, and mass (Ozeki, pers. comm.; Ebbesmeyer and Scigliano 245). "A memory of 0.5 (the global average)," Ebbesmeyer and Scigliano write, "indicates a gyre retains 50 percent of its drifters through each orbit while the other half washes up on shore, escapes to other gyres, or sinks. Half remain after the first orbit, a quarter after the second, . . . and so on, until the last drifter strands" (245). In the narrative gyre of *A Tale for the Time Being*, drifters—characters, objects, and marine invertebrates brought together by the assemblage containing Nao's diary—sink, wash up, find their way into the infamous garbage patches at the gyre's center, or continue to circulate.

---

[17]   Huang argues that "geopolitical human crisis . . . [and] natural disaster . . . must be considered together" (99). In *A Short Treatise on the Metaphysics of Tsunamis*, Jean-Pierre DuPuy quotes Günther Anders's conversation with survivors of the bombings of Hiroshima and Nagasaki. Anders reads these survivors' use of the word *tsunami* to describe the bombings as an effort "not to speak of those who were to blame, not to say that the event had been caused by human beings" (qtd. in DuPuy 50).

The title of Ebbesmeyer's scientific memoir and world history of flotsam and jetsam, *Flotsametrics and the Floating World*, unites *flotsametrics*—his term for a mode of inquiry that attends to what washes ashore—with a phrase he uses to describe the ocean as seen through the eyes of the "far flung community of beachcombers, ocean watchers, and amateur 'flotsamologists'" who are his scientific collaborators (xii). The term *floating world* explicitly—if accidentally—links physical oceanography and amateur marine science with important concepts in Buddhism and Japanese aesthetic history. Ebbesmeyer and Scigliano use the phrase to refer to the oceanic "world of beauty, order, and peril" accessible through flotsam and jetsam (2). In Japanese aesthetic terminology, the term *ukiyo-e*, or "pictures of the floating world," describes a popular genre of Edo period (1615–1868) woodblock prints (Waterhouse 33). The word *ukiyo* is a homophone that could mean either "floating world" or "sad, troublesome world" (Waterhouse 33). As "floating world," *ukiyo* connotes pleasure—specifically, the pleasures associated with popular ukiyo-e print subjects, including the kabuki theater, sumo wrestling, and beautiful women encountered while "going with the flow" in the entertainment districts of Japan's major cities (Waldman and Frazer; Waterhouse 33).[18]

At least initially, Ozeki told me, the concept of ukiyo as the floating world of pleasure was one that she "hadn't really thought about as mapping onto the novel at all." She did say, though, that Katsushika Hokusai's iconic ukiyo-e print "The Hollow of the Deep-Sea Wave off Kanagawa" was "in my mind . . . when I was writing [*A Tale for the Time Being*]. . . . The vision of Hokusai's wave was always there. . . . It was, now I'm talking about it, in the background" (Ozeki, pers. comm.; see Hokusai). This image, which is from the 1830s series *Thirty-Six Views of Mount Fuji*, features a massive wave dwarfing Mount Fuji; its perspective is of a wind-generated wave that is often mistaken for a tsunami and that originates at sea (Bryant). According to Ozeki, earlier in Japanese history, during the Heian era (794–1185), the term *ukiyo* had connotations that were closer to its Buddhist foundations of impermanence and suffering: "If we're flowing like water," she said, "there is beauty and sadness in that which is very much a part of the aesthetic of the novel" (Ozeki, pers. comm.). "Perhaps if the floating world is [in the novel]," she mused further, "it's more about [its] Buddhist underpinnings" (pers. comm.).

A Tale for the Time Being's literary meditations on Buddhist impermanence and the floating world of Japanese aesthetics rely, therefore, on the North Pacific subtropical gyre: a physical ocean system that is *"constituted by and constitutive of* movement" (Steinberg 165). Ozeki describes her use of the North Pacific gyre, both narrative agent and material metaphor, as "relate[d] to the idea of time being" (Ozeki, pers. comm.). Her most important Buddhist interlocutor, thirteenth-century Zen master Eihei Dōgen Zenji, uses "metaphors of the ocean" to describe "the fact that time is flowing in all directions" (pers. comm.). This usage, according

---

[18]   The term *floating world* also has significant literary resonance. C. Morgan Babst titled her post-Katrina fiction *The Floating World* (2017), while in *The Sea Wolf* (1904), Jack London described the "miniature floating world" of the schooner *Ghost* (26). Kazuo Ishiguro's novel of postwar Japan, *An Artist of the Floating World* (1986), uses the term in a way that tracks more closely with its usage in Japanese aesthetics.

to Ozeki, "is related to impermanence," an idea she describes as "one of the key Buddhist foundational thoughts in the book."[19] In conversation with the writings of an ancient religious master and the memoir of a contemporary oceanographer, *A Tale for the Time Being* expands the spiritual and aesthetic floating world to include the literal and the contemporary. In this floating world, the transpacific tide pool in the well of the *Saisho Maru*, the abalone boat launched by the Tōhoku tsunami, is as iconic an emblem as Hokusai's wave.

In Ruth Ozeki's floating world, the physical oceanographic concepts of gyre memory and half-life extend beyond the North Pacific subtropical gyre to topics as varied as dementia, her writing process, and the circulation of information and images from Tōhoku and its aftermath in yet another floating world, the Internet. *A Tale for the Time Being*'s orienting metaphors of the gyre and the ocean garbage patch point out, Ozeki says, "how stories break down" (Ozeki, pers. comm.). Ruth recalls the "global bandwidth . . . flooded with images and reports from Japan . . . for [a] brief period of time" before being replaced by other news (*Tale* 113). "Is the Internet a kind of temporal gyre, sucking up stories . . . ?" she wonders. "What is its gyre memory? How do we measure the half-life of its drift?" (114). Ozeki's metatextual meditation on "the half-life of information" uses images from the Tōhoku disasters—a "tidal wave observed, collaps[ing] into tiny particles, each one containing a story"—that she describes in terms of marine plastics "degrading with each orbit around the gyre" (114). "Like plastic confetti," she writes, "they're drawn into the gyre's becalmed center, the garbage patch of history and time. The gyre's memory is all the stuff that we've forgotten" (114). Here, the Internet becomes a gyre, complete with its own memory and garbage patch of microplastic-like bits. News events spawn debris pulses of images and stories which then circulate, sometimes ceaselessly, sometimes fetching up in a search or on a feed—their half-lives unknown in a virtual North Pacific.

Like texts and images, pieces of marine debris have contingent, material half-lives. Nao's bundle, Oliver reminds Ruth, could have been "[s]ucked up and becalmed, . . . [t]he plastic ground into particles for the fish and zooplankton to eat. The diary and letters disintegrating, unread" (36). These images of pelagic plastic pollution underscore the contingency of Ozeki's very novel. The "[p]ixels" comprising Tōhoku images and the typed letters of Ozeki's text "need power," usually from climate-disrupting fossil fuels; similarly, Ruth's transoceanic Internet trawling for clues about Nao's fate relies on submarine fiberoptic cables (114; and see Starosielski 1). Despite the protective plastic of the lunchbox and bags containing Nao's diary, paper—like the sea-going hack of Marcel Proust's *À la recherche du temps perdu*—"is unstable in fire and flood" (114). *A Tale for the Time Being* thus performs impermanence and contingency with the North Pacific and Internet

---

[19]   Dōgen (1200–1253) is the founder of the Soto Zen school of Buddhism and author of the *Shobogenzo* (*The Treasury of the True Dharma Eye*); this work's eleventh chapter is translated as "For the Time Being." While *A Tale for the Time Being*'s title also invites an association with Martin Heidegger's *Being and Time*, Ozeki circumscribes Heidegger's influence on her novel when Nao's father folds a page from *Being and Time* into an origami beetle.

gyres, offering a metatextual meditation on the fragility of physical and digital flotsam in the rising, acidifying seas of our contemporary floating world.[20]

Transpacific Time Beings

Like the digital material circulating in the floating world of the Internet and the *Saisho Maru*'s tide pool organisms transported across the Pacific, the plastic of Nao's bundle does not biodegrade. In order to estimate the half-life of this assemblage from the floating world, Ruth and Oliver need to determine the size, age, and species of the barnacles that have grown on its plastic wrapping. In a pivotal scene, a barnacle dissection functions as both a marine biology lesson and a forensic investigation. While the scene disproves Ruth and Oliver's hypothesis, it positions their marine scientific efforts as an intimate response to the disasters that, according to Ozeki, "broke the world."

Ruth and Oliver's neighbor Callie, a marine biologist, identifies the barnacles as "goosenecks . . . *Pollicipes polymerus*. Order Pedunculata. A gregarious pelagic species, not really native, but it's not uncommon to find them on tidewrack that's drifted in from farther out at sea" (115). With a field kit containing "a collection of forensic instruments," Callie dissects the barnacles, using specific anatomical terminology to point out "the foot, or the peduncle," and "the capitulum, or the head" (118). Based on the condition of the barnacles' calcareous plates—"pitted and dull" because of the impacts of wave action—Callie estimates that Nao's bundle has been at sea for three or four years (118). This estimate places its release into the ocean well *before* the tsunami, even though its escape from the gyre seems to coincide with the first pulses of tsunami flotsam reaching the North American mainland.

Despite the anatomical detail of the dissection, this scene presents a marine biological inconsistency that is legible to *A Tale for the Time Being*'s readers but not to its metafictional characters. This inconsistency lends force to the novel's overarching meditation on not-knowing by introducing a new element of uncertainty beyond it. Callie's identification of the barnacles as *Pollicipes polymerus*, a coastal species of gooseneck barnacle endemic to the intertidal zones of North America's west coast, is inconsistent with her description of their life cycle as pelagic, or offshore (Langstroth et al. 26). Another barnacle species, *Lepas anatifera*, lives on pieces of flotsam and grows stalks as long as fifty centimeters (123). Based on Callie's description and measurements, *Lepas anatifera* seems a better match for the barnacles on Nao's plastic bag. Callie then notes that the barnacles are "a great delicacy in Spain" (*Tale* 119). The Spanish delicacy is traditionally a third species, *Pollicipes pollicipes*, which further muddies the proverbial waters (Jacinto et al.).[21]

---

[20] For recent meditations on impermanence, textuality, and the anthropocene, see Bethany Nowviskie's 2013 talk "Resistance in the Materials," and Roy Scranton's *Learning to Die in the Anthropocene*.

[21] According to Ozeki, the ambiguity in the barnacle identification scene is unintentional. "I wish," she says, "I could say it was a red herring. I knew [barnacles] were used in forensics, but honestly I was more concerned with getting the quantum mechanics [in the novel] right . . . —tracking down astrophysicists who had expertise in Zen Buddhism" (Ozeki, pers. comm.). Strictly

When Callie identifies the barnacles for Ruth and Oliver, she invalidates the presumed connection between Nao's diary and the Tōhoku tsunami that has thus far oriented *A Tale for the Time Being*'s marine scientific metafiction. Unaware of the three-barnacle confusion that exists beyond the novel, Ruth must now confront her attachment to the disproven tsunami hypothesis: an attachment Zenkei Blanche Hartman might describe in Buddhist terms as self-identification as "the one who knows." Throughout *A Tale for the Time Being* Ozeki uses the word *narrative* to describe what is effectively a hypothesis. This is no accidental conflation. Buddhism uses "narrative as a didactic mode for illustrating ethics," but also acknowledges, according to Greta Gaard, "the limitations of narrative, even seeing narration itself as a possible form of suffering and a hindrance to insight" (297). In a similar vein, the theoretical astrophysicist Piet Hut compares the practice of not-knowing to lightly holding a "working hypothes[is]" (414). After Callie identifies the barnacles, Ruth resents them for "failing to provide the evidence she was looking for"—and for introducing evidence that disproves her hypothesis (*Tale* 119). Ruth's resentment indicates that, despite another neighbor's warning, she has "let . . . narrative preferences interfere with . . . forensic work" (33). In other words, Ruth's premature attachment to the tsunami narrative as working hypothesis obstructs the unconstrained, not-knowing mind that is central to the empiricism and Zen Buddhist practice that, together, drive her very novel.[22]

As Carlton's research illustrates, the study and identification of marine invertebrates such as barnacles has been essential in research associated with Tōhoku tsunami debris. It has also been an important forensic tool in the investigation of murders and plane crashes. In fact, barnacle forensics were used to identify wreckage from Malaysia Airlines Flight 370, missing since March 8, 2014 (see Levin). By destabilizing Callie's high-stakes conclusion about the barnacles for its readers, *A Tale for the Time Being* highlights what Ozeki calls "the unbounded nature of not knowing" (*Tale* 409). The uncertainty surrounding Nao's fate lingers for the rest of the novel; in the letter to Nao that serves as *A Tale for the Time Being*'s epilogue, Ruth confesses that she doesn't "really like uncertainty." "I'd much rather *know*," she writes, "but then again, not-knowing keeps all the possibilities open. It keeps all the worlds alive" (402).

Emphasizing the difficulty of not-knowing in relation to the fates of the thousands of people who remain missing after the Tōhoku tsunami, Beauregard writes that "Ruth's reading of Nao's diary emerges as part of an extended attempt to imagine the lives of countless others who may, or may not, have survived" (107). Beauregard, who describes not-knowing as "a Zen Buddhist notion attributed to Jiko" (107), misses the centrality of this ethical-empirical stance to the forensic

---

speaking, the ambiguity is the result of an authorial oversight. While scientific misidentifications are not the same as Buddhist not-knowing, this "mistake," to use Ozeki's term, is a fortuitous red herring that brings science and Buddhism together within and beyond the novel.

22   *A Tale for the Time Being*, Huang avers, creates affinities between the real-life Ozeki and her husband, their metafictional avatars, and the novel's readers by "invit[ing] readers to read the author and [the] character as the same" (114n5). *A Tale for the Time Being*'s readers are thus invited to believe that the metafictional Ruth wrote the novel that they are reading.

unpeeling that enables imaginative engagement with lost human lives. *A Tale for the Time Being*'s amateur marine science—flotsamology, to use Ebbesmeyer and Scigliano's term—is an imperfect but still valuable practice for encountering and interpreting the washed-up objects and assemblages, Nao's diary among them, that might otherwise be dismissed as garbage or debris. As potential clues, Ozeki's barnacles demand and receive the same forensic, ethical attention from characters and readers that Nao's very human diary does. Despite the lingering uncertainty within and beyond the novel, the unsuccessful efforts of Ozeki's metafictional characters to prove their tsunami hypothesis highlight "the inseparability of knowing, being, and doing" in broken real and fictional worlds in which the pursuit of discovery and conclusive knowledge must be a sustained practice of humble coexistence with their opposites (Barad 380).

Conclusion: Bully the Wave

On a beach in Miyagi prefecture, Nao and her great-grandmother Jiko are having a picnic. The Buddhist nun stares out at the horizon and muses: "A wave is born from deep conditions of the ocean. . . . A person is born from deep conditions of the world. A person pokes up from the world and rolls along like a wave, until it is time to sink down again. Up, down. Person, wave" (194). Jiko's seaside meditation on impermanence concludes a scene that begins when she asks Nao—a "ronin" or "wave-person" who has left school after enduring ferocious and humiliating bullying—if she has "ever bullied a wave," and then tells her to try. "Over and over," Nao writes in her diary,

> *I ran at the sea, beating it until I was so tired I could barely stand. And then the next time I fell down, I just lay there and let the waves wash over me, and I wondered what would happen if I stopped trying to get back up. Just let my body go. Would I be washed out to sea? The sharks would eat my limbs and organs. Little fish would feed on my fingertips. My beautiful white bones would fall to the bottom of the ocean, where anemones would grow upon them like flowers. Pearls would rest in my eye sockets.* (193)

Nao's hauntingly imagined incorporation of her body into a marine food web riffs on Ariel's song "Full Fathom Five" in Shakespeare's *The Tempest*. It also forecasts the revelation that Haruki #1 intentionally crashed his kamikaze plane into the Pacific. "Better to do battle with the waves, who may yet forgive me," he writes in his last letter to Jiko (328). While Ozeki wrote this chapter (which she privately refers to as "Bully the wave") prior to the tsunami, she describes it as assuming "new and tragic resonance" in the disaster's wake (Ozeki, pers. comm.). A microcosm for the oceanographically structured *Tale for the Time Being*, this chapter meditates upon life's wavelike impermanence while focusing its readers' attention on the fused human and ecological catastrophes of the Pacific itself.

A Tale for the Time Being is both transpacific and attentive *to* the Pacific; it is a "narrative of oceanic catastrophe" in which the ocean comes ashore (Brayton 565). Set against the explicit context of the Tōhoku disasters and against a thoroughgoing global environmental catastrophe that renders terrestrial discourses of sustainability increasingly untenable, *A Tale for the Time Being* offers an alternative in the floating world—not the world of pleasure and entertainment depicted in ukiyo-e prints but its older, more sorrowful Buddhist antecedent.[23] In *A Tale for the Time Being* as in physical oceanography, this floating world of the ocean—at once material reality, source of spiritual metaphor, and narrative agent—comes into focus through its movement. The novel calls attention to the assemblages of human-made objects and marine species—along with memories, images, even remains—that circulate in the gyres of the global ocean or drift aimlessly in its garbage patches; in doing so, it extends the spatiotemporal motion of ocean gyres beyond the North Pacific to the Internet and even to itself. Along with the stories they contain, vibrant floaters from the floating world "shimm[y]," in Jane Bennett's terms, "back and forth between debris and thing" (4). They choke, poison, feed, or become habitat for marine life while becoming objects of study for professional scientists and flotsamologists alike. Even as these floaters help us understand the ocean circulation patterns that provide Ozeki with an essential material and metaphoric resource and lend a significant vocabulary to literary and cultural studies, these patterns are destabilizing—with drastic implications for climate stability, nutrient cycling, and other Earth systems (Caesar et al.).[24]

Ozeki's floating world of a novel unfolds through her characters' forensically inflected reading of the stories contained in and accessible through the contents of Nao's floating bundle and the marine species that travel on it. *A Tale for the Time Being* first invites an association between Nao's floating bundle and the Tōhoku tsunami and then withholds it. As a result, the novel argues for a relationship to knowledge defined by humility, intimacy, and open-endedness: postures that will become increasingly useful given the aporetic, intensifying nature of climate and ecological catastrophe on our ocean planet. By holding scientific and spiritual practice not in tension but in tandem, Ozeki offers both as valuable but imperfect ways to coexist with what is not—or cannot be—known. The not-knowing lingering in her novel, despite the efforts of readers and metafictional characters alike, highlights the fact that, as time beings, we live in and with the contingencies of a literal and spiritual floating world.

*　　　*　　　*

ALISON GLASSIE is postdoctoral fellow in environmental humanities at the University of Virginia. Her current book project is titled "Atlantic Shapeshifters: Sea Literature's Fluid Forms." Articles drawn from her research on the influence of the ocean's ecological dynamics as well as cultural histories on the literatures of the Americas have appeared in *sx/salon: a Small Axe literary platform*, *Interdisciplinary Studies in Literature and the Environment*, and *Coriolis*. She has also published in *Blue Water Sailing*.

[23]   For a range of ecocritical critiques of sustainability discourse, see, respectively, Stacy Alaimo, Dan Brayton, and Steve Mentz (*After Sustainability*).

[24]   For literary engagements with the language of the material ocean, see DeLoughrey, *Roots and Routes*; Yaeger; and Roberts and Stephens.

Works Cited

Alaimo, Stacy. "The Anthropocene at Sea: Temporality, Paradox, Compression." *The Routledge Companion to the Environmental Humanities*. Ed. Ursula K. Heise, Jon Christensen, and Michelle Niemann. New York: Routledge, 2017. 153–62.

Babst, C. Morgan. *The Floating World*. Chapel Hill: Algonquin, 2017.

Bakhtin, Mikhail. *The Dialogic Imagination*. Trans. Caryl Emerson and Michael Holquist. Austin: U of Texas P, 1981.

Barad, Karen. *Meeting the Universe Halfway: Quantum Physics and the Entanglement of Matter and Meaning*. Durham, NC: Duke UP, 2007.

Beauregard, Guy. "On Not Knowing: *A Tale for the Time Being* and the Politics of Imagining Lives after March 11." *Canadian Literature* 227 (2015): 96–112.

Bennett, Andrew. *Lagrangian Fluid Dynamics*. Cambridge: Cambridge UP, 2006.

Bennett, Jane. *Vibrant Matter: A Political Ecology of Things*. Durham, NC: Duke UP, 2010.

Brayton, Dan. "Writ in Water: *Far Tortuga* and the Crisis of the Marine Environment." *PMLA* 127.3 (2012): 565–71.

Bryant, Edward. *Tsunami: The Underrated Hazard*. 2nd ed. New York: Springer, 2008.

Caesar, L., et al. "Observed Fingerprint of a Weakening Atlantic Ocean Overturning Circulation." *Nature* 556.7700 (2018): 191–96.

Carlton, James T. "Following the Blue Brick Road." Lecture. Williams College–Mystic Seaport Maritime Studies Program. 19 Sept. 2015.

Carlton, James T., and Andrew N. Cohen. "Episodic Global Dispersal in Shallow Water Marine Organisms: The Case History of the European Shore Crabs *Carcinus maenas* and *C. aestuarii*." *Journal of Biogeography* 30.12 (2003): 1809–20.

Carlton, James T., et al. "Tsunami-Driven Rafting: Transoceanic Species Dispersal and Implications for Marine Biogeography." *Science* 357.6358 (2017): 1402–06.

Coe, James M., and Donald Rogers. *Marine Debris: Sources, Impacts, and Solutions*. New York: Springer, 2012.

Davis, Rocío G. "Fictional Transits and Ruth Ozeki's *A Tale for the Time Being*." *Biography* 38.1 (2015): 87–103.

Davis, Russ E. "Lagrangian Ocean Studies." *Annual Review of Fluid Mechanics* 23 (1991): 43–64.

DeLoughrey, Elizabeth. *Routes and Roots: Navigating Caribbean and Pacific Island Literatures*. Honolulu: U of Hawai'i P, 2007.

DeLoughrey, Elizabeth. "Submarine Futures of the Anthropocene." *Comparative Literature* 69.1 (2017): 32–44.

Dōgen. *Shobogenzo* [*The Treasury of the True Dharma Eye*]. Trans. Gudo Wafu Nishijima and Chodo Cross. Berkeley: Numata Center for Buddhist Translation and Research, 2008.

DuPuy, Jean-Pierre. *A Short Treatise on the Metaphysics of Tsunamis.* Trans. Malcolm B. DeBevoise. East Lansing: Michigan State UP, 2015.

Ebbesmeyer, Curtis, and Eric Scigliano. *Flotsametrics and the Floating World: How One Man's Obsession with Runaway Sneakers and Rubber Ducks Revolutionized Ocean Science.* New York: Collins, 2009.

Ferris, Elizabeth, and Mireya Solís. "Earthquake, Tsunami, Meltdown—The Triple Disaster's Impact on Japan, Impact on the World." Brookings 11 Mar. 2013 <https://www.brookings.edu/blog/up-front/2013/03/11/earthquake-tsunami-meltdown-the-triple-disasters-impact-on-japan-impact-on-the-world/>.

Frangoul, Anmar. "Researchers Detect Microplastics in Human Waste." *CNBC* 23 Oct. 2018 <https://www.cnbc.com/2018/10/23/researchers-detect-microplastics-in-human-waste.html>.

Gaard, Greta. "Mindful New Materialisms: Buddhist Roots for Material Ecocriticism's Flourishing." *Material Ecocriticism.* Ed. Serenella Iovino and Serpil Oppermann. Bloomington: Indiana UP, 2014. 291–300.

Ganguly, Debjani. *This Thing Called the World: The Contemporary Novel as Global Form.* Durham, NC: Duke UP, 2016.

Gillis, John. "The Blue Humanities." *Humanities* 34.3 (2013) <https://www.neh.gov/humanities/2013/mayjune/feature/the-blue-humanities>.

Hartman, Zenkei Blanche. "The Zen of Not Knowing." *Tricycle* 21 July 2015 (republished 9 Mar. 2019) <https://tricycle.org/trikedaily/zen-not-knowing/>.

Heidegger, Martin. *Being and Time: A Translation of Sein und Zeit.* Trans. Joan Stambaugh. Albany: SUNY P, 1996.

Helmreich, Stefan. "Waves: An Anthropology of Scientific Things (The 2014 Lewis Henry Morgan Lecture)." *HAU* 4.3 (2014): 265–84.

Hohn, Donovan. *Moby-Duck: The True Story of 28,800 Bath Toys Lost at Sea and of the Beachcombers, Oceanographers, Environmentalists, and Fools, Including the Author, Who Went in Search of Them.* New York: Penguin, 2012.

Hokusai, Katsushika. "Under the Wave off Kanagawa." Woodblock Print, ca. 1831. The Met 150. Metropolitan Museum of Art <https://www.metmuseum.org/art/collection/search/45434> (accessed 13 Dec. 2018).

Huang, Michelle N. "Ecologies of Entanglement in the Great Pacific Garbage Patch." *Journal of Asian American Studies* 20.1 (2017): 95–117.

Hut, Piet. "Conclusion: Life as a Laboratory." Wallace 399–417.

IOOS (Integrated Ocean Observing System). "Lagrangian versus Eulerian Tracers." <https://secoora.org/tracers/> (accessed Nov. 23, 2018).

Ishiguro, Kazuo. *An Artist of the Floating World.* New York: Vintage International, 1989.

Jacinto, David, et al. "Stalked Barnacle (*Pollicipes pollicipes*) Harvesting in the Berlengas Nature Reserve, Portugal: Temporal Variation and Validation of Logbook Data." *ICES Journal of Marine Science* 67.1 (2010): 19–25.

Jorgensen, Dolly. "Artifacts and Habitats." *The Routledge Companion to the Environmental Humanities.* Ed. Ursula K. Heise, Jon Christensen, and Michelle Niemann. New York: Routledge, 2017. 138–43.

Langstroth, Lovell, et al. *A Living Bay: The Underwater World of Monterey Bay.* Berkeley: U of California P, 2000.

Lee, Hsiu-chuan. "Sharing Worlds through Words: Minor Cosmopolitics in Ruth Ozeki's *A Tale for the Time Being.*" *Ariel* 49.1 (2018): 27–52.

Levin, Alan. "Barnacle Forensics May Unlock Clues in Missing Malaysian Plane." *Bloomberg News* 30 July 2015 <https://www.bloomberg.com/news/articles/2015-07-31/barnacle-forensics-may-unlock-clues-in-missing-malaysian-plane>.

London, Jack. *The Sea Wolf.* New York: Signet Classics, 2013.

McMahan, David. *The Making of Buddhist Modernism.* Oxford: Oxford UP, 2008.

Mentz, Steve. "After Sustainability." *PMLA* 127.3 (2012): 586–92.

Mentz, Steve. "Blue Humanities." *Posthuman Glossary.* Ed. Rosi Braidotti and Maria Hlavajova. London: Bloomsbury, 2018. 69–72.

Mentz, Steve. "Shakespeare and the Blue Humanities." *SEL: Studies in English Literature, 1500–1900* 59.2 (2019): 383–92.

Nixon, Rob. *Slow Violence and the Environmentalism of the Poor.* Cambridge, MA: Harvard UP, 2011.

Nowviskie, Bethany. "Resistance in the Materials." *Bethany Nowviskie* (blog) 4 Jan. 2013 <http://nowviskie.org/2013/resistance-in-the-materials/>.

Ozeki, Ruth. *A Tale for the Time Being.* New York: Penguin, 2013.

Parker, Laura. "In a First, Microplastics Found in Human Poop." *National Geographic Environment: Planet or Plastics* 22 Oct. 2018 <https://www.nationalgeographic.com/environment/2018/10/news-plastics-microplastics-human-feces/>.

Parry, Richard Lloyd. *Ghosts of the Tsunami: Life and Death in Japan's Disaster Zone.* New York: Farrar, Straus, and Giroux, 2017.

Pew Directory of Marine Fellows. "James T. Carlton, Ph.D." <https://pew.org/2qREB02> (accessed 23 Nov. 2018).

Richerson, M. M. *"Hemigrapsus sanguineus* (De Haan, 1835)." US Geological Survey, Non-indigenous Aquatic Species Database, 30 Apr. 2018 <https://nas.er.usgs.gov/queries/factsheet.aspx?SpeciesID=183>.

Roberts, Brian Russell, and Michelle Ann Stevens, eds. *Archipelagic American Studies*. Durham, NC: Duke UP, 2017.

Rozwadowski, Helen M. "Playing by—and on and under—the Sea: The Importance of Play for Knowing the Ocean." *Knowing Global Environments: New Historical Perspectives on the Field Sciences*. Ed. Jeremy Vetter. New Brunswick: Rutgers UP, 2011. 162–89.

Scranton, Roy. *Learning to Die in the Anthropocene: Reflections on the End of a Civilization*. San Francisco: City Lights, 2015.

Shakespeare, William. *The Tempest*. New York: Folger Shakespeare Library, 2004.

Somerville, Alice Te Punga. "The Great Pacific Garbage Patch as Metaphor: The (American) Pacific You Can't See." *Archipelagic American Studies*. Ed. Brian Russell Roberts and Michelle Ann Stephens. Durham, NC: Duke UP, 2017. 320–40.

Starosielski, Nicole. *The Undersea Network*. Durham, NC: Duke UP, 2015.

Starr, Marlo. "Beyond Machine Dreams: Zen, Cyber-, and Transnational Feminisms in Ruth Ozeki's *A Tale for the Time Being*." *Meridians (Middletown, Conn.)* 13.2 (2016): 99–122.

Steinberg, Philip E. "Of Other Seas: Metaphors and Materialities in Maritime Regions." *Atlantic Studies* 10.2 (2013): 156–69.

Suzuki, Shunryu. *Zen Mind, Beginner's Mind*. New York: Weatherhill, 1970.

Tobias, Lori. "Japanese Tsunami Dock Came Bearing Lessons for Oregon Officials, Coastal Residents." *Oregonian* 4 June 2013 (updated 10 Jan. 2019) <https://www.oregonlive.com/pacific-northwest-news/2013/06/japanese_tsunami_dock_came_bea.html>.

Waldman, Richard, and Doug Frazer. "What Is the Floating World? The History of Ukiyo-e." *Art of Japan* 14 Aug. 2015 <https://www.theartofjapan.com/what-is-the-floating-world/>.

Wallace, B. Alan, ed. *Buddhism and Science: Breaking New Ground*. New York: Columbia UP, 2003.

Waterhouse, David. "Hishikawa Moronobu: Tracking Down an Elusive Master." *Designed for Pleasure: The World of Edo Japan in Prints and Paintings, 1680–1860*. Ed. Julia Meech and Jane Oliver. New York: Asia Society and Japanese Art Society of America in association with U of Washington P, 2008. 33–56.

Wheeler Centre. "Ruth Ozeki on Catastrophe, Thought Experiments, and Writing as Performed Philosophy." YouTube, 13 Sept. 2013. <https://www.youtube.com/watch?v=I0–yah7K7U>.

Yaeger, Patricia. "Editor's Column: Sea Trash, Dark Pools, and the Tragedy of the Commons." *PMLA* 125.3 (2010): 523–44.

Reviews

Nothing Succeeds Like Failure

WENDY ANNE LEE, *Failures of Feeling: Insensibility and the Novel* (Stanford: Stanford UP, 2018), pp. 248, cloth, $55.00.

It may seem paradoxical to assert that a book that announces itself as being about "insensibility" or "failures" of feeling has much to say about powerful emotional experience. But Wendy Anne Lee's *Failures of Feeling* demonstrates that we feel most acutely in the face of emotional detachment, neutrality, and insensibility. "Nothing," she writes, with characteristic epigrammatic verve, "incites the passions like dispassion" (1). Within the field of eighteenth-century novel studies, the striking intervention of *Failures of Feeling* is to work against the grain of what is often also called "The Age of Feeling" or "The Age of Sensibility." In contrast to the many studies that have focused on the era's seemingly unequivocal love of over-the-top displays of emotion and its emphasis on sympathy and emotional contagion, Lee argues that such a picture is incomplete. She demonstrates that focusing on the strong counter-tradition of novelistic and philosophical representations of seemingly opposite states of mind—indifference, impassivity, impersonality—is necessary to make us understand how emotion works in eighteenth-century fiction.

Lee convincingly carves out a distinct vision of a specific strain in the history of the novel, one that, while grounded in major authors and classic works (e.g., Samuel Richardson's *Clarissa*, Jane Austen's *Emma*), puts these works in a new lineage that makes both familiar novels and the less familiar seem new. She establishes a through-line of fictional works centered around protagonists who fail to feel, starting with the stock figure of the prudish woman in late seventeenth- and early eighteenth-century popular fiction (as well as her fancy French cousin, Madame de Lafayette's Princesse de Clèves), through Richardson's Clarissa Harlowe, through the persistent image of Jane Austen herself as a detached and impersonal being, through Herman Melville's Bartleby, and through all the deeply weird central characters in George Eliot's *Daniel Deronda*, with many other fictional figures making apt cameo appearances.

Clarissa Harlowe sits like a spider at the center of Lee's new account of novel history, her unbending impassivity—which scrambles the difference between intention and action, consent and nonconsent—organizing and absorbing Lee's interpretations of other novels both pre- and post-*Clarissa*. Clarissa's double relation to feelings—so unmoved herself yet moving everyone else, figures the novel's "double purpose to both construct and to eradicate the inner life" (7). Lee focuses unflinchingly on the extraordinary dilation of the novel between Clarissa's rape and her death, arguing that to be a "survivor" is to enter a zone of "shocking transparency" (67). "No depth means no violation," she comments mordantly (83), which also means, in a way, no narrative. If narratives of consummation propel the form of the novel forward, then they also require the counterweight of sublimely resistant surviving-on. From this perspective, a whole new raft of earlier and later fictions—popular "prude" narratives from seventeenth- and eighteenth-century France and England—are ready to come out of "the salvage bin of early print culture" (31) to serve as a conceptual hinge between early modern accounts of sovereignty and the development of the novel. From the perspective of Lee's reading of *Clarissa*, we discover that not only *Daniel Deronda*'s queer cast of characters (from the prudish Gwendolen to the detached Deronda and the lizard-like Grandcourt, to the most chillingly insensible of all, Deronda's unmaternal mother) but also its strange narrative irresolution place this novel in a tradition where resistant survival (as Gwendolen says, "I will try to live") moves us to some form of derangement. Each of Lee's chapters offers a similarly unfamiliar feeling across a range of novels sufficient to attract scholars of British, French, and American novels of the eighteenth and nineteenth centuries.

For me, the most significant takeaway from *Failures of Feeling* comes from Lee's claim that, in narrating tales of the insensible man or woman, novels are, in a quite literal way, narrating themselves. The novel form itself is the "ultimate insensible" (171). A large, insensate expanse of print, the novel indiscriminately absorbs everything, both resisting and enabling our emotional response. From this stems the book's contribution to conversations about the ethics of reading fiction. In its insensibility, Lee argues, the novel models an ethical capacity to confront and to tolerate the intractable otherness of other people (174).

Perhaps nowhere in *Failures of Feeling* are the paradoxes of feeling and nonfeeling so striking as in the texture of Lee's own prose. Even as she commits herself to seeing writing itself in all its neutrality and insensibility—"writing is not a relay between feeling and action but, like a prude, some third thing" (48)—Lee's writing is intensely moving. She has mastered a vivid, slap-you-in-the-face image that she finds necessary to elucidating "the blank nonstick surface of the insensible" (4). Such phrases are integral to what we could call the therapeutic dimension of critical writing. Naming and describing the affective texture of insensibility, Lee writes of Hume: "[L]ike the vacant center of a tidal wave, the insensible initiates the turbulence that surges through a population" (105). The next sentence shifts from effect to cause as it compares the insensible to "a CPR mannequin: open-mouthed, wall-eyed, its hollow torso primed for inspiration." In this way, Lee seems to position herself as a ministering angel who breathes feeling into her reader's benumbed culture, the presumption being that such criticism—like the eighteenth- and nineteenth-century works on which she focuses—offers a therapeutic, ethical practice for our time.

My interest in the current resonances of *Failures of Feeling* should not distract us from its invitation to engage political and philosophical history. Lee does not neglect to provide striking historical contexts for novelistic demonstrations of insensibility. Chapter 3, titled provocatively "The Man of No Feeling," argues that such a man underwrote a great deal of eighteenth-century literature—namely, the martyred King Charles I, whose restraint on the scaffold was memorialized in popular texts. Lee's account of how the legacy of the monarch's response to the trauma of regicide surfaces in Adam Smith's *Theory of Moral Sentiments* is especially compelling. She argues that the humiliation of such women as Clarissa, Emma, and Gwendolen Harleth actually affords them occasion to rise above the political disposition of the body and intimate the possibilities of female sovereignty, "a counterfactual commitment to a feminocentrism that is unachieved but is somehow continuously imaginable" (175). Though *Failures of Feeling* does not announce itself as feminist criticism, it nevertheless makes an important contribution to that tradition.

While Lee engages the philosophical works of Hobbes, Locke, Hume, and Adam Smith, one philosophical tradition remains curiously unelaborated in *Failures of Feeling*, and that is Stoicism. Such moral philosophers as the Earl of Shaftesbury relied heavily on the Stoics— from Epictetus to Marcus Aurelius to Seneca to Cicero—for a model of emotional restraint that could serve as the basis of civic virtue. Although we find occasional references (e.g., in

Lee's discussions of Samuel Johnson's *Rambler* essay 32 and of the gallows heroics of Charles I), I found myself expecting a more focused discussion of the relation between Lee's notion of the failure of feeling and Stoicism. Does she see these as opposed or adjacent? And what of a woman philosopher like Elizabeth Carter, who translated the Greek Stoic philosopher Epictetus? Then, too, debates over the merits of the concept and its efficacy as a basis of civic virtue were set off in response to writer and high-society fixture Frances Greville's "A Prayer for Indifference" (1759). I consider it a mark of the success of Lee's book that it left me wanting more.

Failures of Feeling is an absorbing, challenging, and profound work. Toward the end, Lee restates a version of her thesis about the relationship between feeling and the form of the novel: "[F]ailures of feeling . . . go hand in hand with narrative failure" (169). Except nothing succeeds like failure. While it may be true that the narrative trajectories of most of the novels Lee discusses flirt with tragedy and irresolution, in her hands the beauty of these works shines more brightly than ever.

ADELA PINCH, *University of Michigan*

*   *   *

ADELA PINCH is professor of English at the University of Michigan. She is author of two books, *Strange Fits of Passion: Epistemology of Emotion, Hume to Austen* (1996) and *Thinking about Other People in Nineteenth-Century British Writing* (2010). She is currently completing a monograph called "Victorian Fiction and the Location of Experience: Four Essays on Women Writers."

Spoiler Alert

VERA TOBIN, *Elements of Surprise: Our Mental Limits and the Satisfactions of Plot* (Cambridge, MA: Harvard UP, 2018), pp. 332, cloth, $35.00.

What is the audience of an interdisciplinary book? Vera Tobin's *Elements of Surprise* seems at first glance to belong to an increasingly robust field of cognitive literary studies books that use the findings and theoretical framework of cognitive psychology to explain aspects of literary form. Most previous works in this subfield, though, have been avowedly by and for literary scholars (Lisa Zunshine's *Why We Read Fiction* [2006], Alan Richardson's *The Neural Sublime* [2010], Blakey Vermeule's *Why Do We Care about Literary Characters?* [2010], Natalie Phillips's *Distraction* [2016]), offering a primer on concepts from psychology and neuroscience while taking for granted a certain familiarity with literary history and theory. *Elements of Surprise* takes none of this for granted, and the book's true audience seems to be a (lightly idealized, but one can dream) version of the general reader, one who not only consumes and enjoys fictions but is curious about *why* he or she enjoys them. Tobin does an exceptional job of writing for such a reader: her prose is clear and engaging, her reference points well distributed among the accessible (*Harry Potter and the Prisoner of Azkaban*, *The Princess Bride*) and the esoteric (*Villette*, *The Adventures of Roderick Random*).

The breadth of Tobin's appeal owes as much to her subject as to her style. Insofar as *Elements of Surprise* is a book about the way authors exploit the predictable limitations of human cognition to produce surprise effects, it represents an entry into the growing scholarly and popular literature—spanning not only psychology and neuroscience but fields like management and education—on cognitive biases. Arguably useful when we need to make quick decisions in "complex, ambiguous situations," these heuristics nonetheless make us less-than-perfect reasoners in ways that continue to fascinate experimental psychologists, who have demonstrated how poorly humans evaluate risk, probability, responsibility, and more (63–65). The term *bias*, like many of the others used in the psychological literature, has a negative valence, creating an association between cognitive heuristics and "moral weakness and failure" that Tobin is at pains to dispel (4). The reliable errors of reasoning that humans make in specific situations, in Tobin's view, are prerequisites for "the pleasures of narrative reassessment" that readers and viewers derive from well-structured fictional surprise (28–29). Well-structured surprises, in this account, steer the reader "in the direction of one set of assumptions" only to suddenly offer or demand "a new interpretation that overturns those assumptions" (35). Surprise, in other words, is a form of aesthetic pleasure that depends on having been wrong—and, as such, makes for an especially well-chosen literary object for analyses grounded in psychological research on biased thinking.

Tobin groups the cognitive phenomena that interest her most under the rubric "mental contamination effects." ("Contamination," to me, sounds not much nicer than "sin" or "bias," but it is Tobin's preferred term.) Mental contamination occurs when "information we encounter in one context seeps into our representations of other perspectives, contexts, and domains" (17)—a slippage that clearly underlines many moments of insightful and creative thinking but can also lead us to conclusions that, depending on whether they apply to real life or to literature, are either disastrously or delightfully wrong. Most of *Elements of Surprise* is devoted to explaining specific contamination effects, the textual devices by which writers can produce them, and the readerly emotions generated by their eventual correction. Take, for instance, "the curse of knowledge," a broad term that psychologists use to describe how difficult it can be to bracket, disregard, or otherwise un-know information that we know (or think we do). In life, the curse of knowledge leads us to assume that other people share our knowledge and beliefs; in literature, as Tobin points out, it can lead us to assume that characters have access to all the information that readers do, even when some of those details were introduced through third-person narration. Similarly, readers may be ready to accept a partial or false answer to an unresolved narrative question when it seems confirmed by something they already "know," even when the story's true reveal is yet to come.

From the vast and sometimes overwhelming field of documented cognitive biases, Tobin skillfully identifies those that have the most potential for authorial exploitation and narratological analysis. *Elements of Surprise* pays special attention, for instance, to failures of source monitoring that lead us to misremember or simply forget the origin of a piece of information. Apart from accounting for the bane of every literature teacher's existence—the readiness with which students attribute a character's statements to the author of the text— imprecise source monitoring blurs the boundary between narration and diegetic dialogue or between one character's account and another's, an effect that can be heightened, Tobin tantalizingly suggests, by "the experiential texture of narrative" (83). Ambiguities regarding the reliability of a text's narrator, or indeed whether a diegetic narrator exists at all, account for many of Tobin's readings, and she devotes two full chapters to tracking these dynamics as they unfold over narrative time (chapters 6 and 7, 202–69).

Elements of Surprise is at its strongest, though, when it moves from relatively broad and familiar narratological concepts (like the unreliable narrator) to implicature and inference at the level of the sentence. Tobin has published widely in cognitive linguistics, and chapter 4, "The Naming of Things," mobilizes that expertise by using insights from pragmatics—the branch of linguistics concerned with the contribution of discursive context to meaning—to unpack the subtle ways that authors introduce semantic content without stating it. Such smuggled information is often introduced through presuppositions, "proposition[s] whose truth is taken for granted by some utterance" (127), which can in turn be activated by specific lexical or syntactic forms. Tobin offers a rich catalogue of these forms: from factive verbs that subtly presuppose the truth of their complement (like *know, regret*, or *realize*) to implicative verbs that presuppose a prior condition for their complement (*succeed, fail*) to change-of-state verbs that presuppose that some state of affairs was already or not yet happening (*begin, stop*); from cleft sentences like "It is Zelda who wants a drink," which presuppose that "some entity exists that fills the variable set up by the subject," to definite descriptions like "the queen of Russia" that presuppose some individual that meets that description (127–30).

Presuppositions possess the special power of being unaffected by syntactic embedding or even negation: the proposition that Leon has been drinking coffee, as Tobin shows, is presupposed not only by the sentence "Leon stopped drinking coffee" but also by "If Leon has stopped drinking coffee, I'll be very surprised!" or "Leon hasn't stopped drinking coffee yet" (138–39). This unusual feature, which makes presuppositions particularly handy for introducing seemingly true propositions that will later be disproved, derives in part from a principle central to pragmatics: in most circumstances, speaker and hearer (or, Tobin's analysis implies, writer and reader) try to work together to produce a successful utterance. If presuppositions are "a sort of precondition for . . . felicitous utterances," as Tobin frames it, then those preconditions will be "accommodated by the cooperative reader" in order to keep the narrative running smoothly (144). If *Elements of Surprise* has its own presuppositions, perhaps the most important is the idea that writer and reader work together (or "collude," in one of Tobin's favorite terms) to produce meaning and that surprise occurs when this collaboration is at first encouraged and then violated—when an author structurally encourages a presupposition that turns out to be false. While we are perhaps used to seeing reading as a kind of cooperation on a semiotic level (as in Barthes's *S/Z*), Tobin's attention to the structural requirements of this coproduction of meaning is indispensable and holds much promise for close reading. "The Naming of Things" will make both an excellent primer on pragmatics for literary theorists and a useful tool to help undergraduates in introductory literature classes focus their attention on the profound implications of small discursive choices.

While the application of pragmatics to literature is, in this reader's opinion, Tobin's most significant methodological intervention, *Elements of Surprise* also offers a refreshingly realistic theoretical perspective on the role of cognitive science in the humanities. Tobin's confident command of current research in psychology and neuroscience makes her willing to take aim at some concepts that have been accepted uncritically in past works of cognitive literary studies. In distancing herself from evolutionary psychology, for instance, Tobin reminds us of the prohibitive difficulty of "reverse-engineering" behaviors and cognitive processes, noting that such teleological claims confuse "selection pressures, which can be temporary, local, strange, and obscure, with 'purposes' that are easy to divine in retrospect" (79)—a useful corrective not only to just-so stories about the evolutionary function of storytelling or art but also to hasty narratives of *cultural* selection for particular aesthetic forms. Tobin is hardly the first to question the conclusions of evolutionary psychology, but her critique is pithy, clear, and, crucially, grounded in the episteme and practices of the sciences.

Similarly, while an innate theory-of-mind capacity has often been taken for granted as a cognitive prerequisite of the novel, and perhaps of narrative itself, Tobin is skeptical of attempts to draw a firm boundary between typical and atypical social cognition. Instead of representing theory of mind as absent or broken in autistic people, for instance, she sees the latter group's struggles with mind reading as continuous with flawed reasoning patterns that neurotypical people often share. "Rather than thinking of social cognition as something characterized primarily by the presence or absence of a working theory of mind," Tobin argues, "it may be more accurate to think of both adults' and children's ways of thinking about other minds as reflecting shared tendencies and biases" (76). Insofar as this reframing resists the reification of cognitive faculties or modules and instead represents cognition as a field of situation-dependent strategies, it models an approach to the mind—one open to the "temporary, local, strange, and obscure"—that will prove generative and useful to cognitive literary theorists. The latter will also benefit from the example set by Tobin's rigorous analysis of experimental methods: rather than simply make use of a study's conclusions, Tobin shows a subtle grasp of how decisions about experimental design can impact one's findings, bringing critical reading and reasoning skills to scientific studies in a form accessible to (and imitable by!) humanists.

In these respects, *Elements of Surprise* improves upon and adds to existing scholarship in cognitive literary studies and cognitive humanities more broadly; what shortcomings the book has are largely shared by other works in this subfield. A literary critic will notice the cultural and historical flatness of many of Tobin's claims, which tend to treat "surprise" as an experience with a consistent definition, cultural valence, and set of prerequisites. (Nor does Tobin typically reach for ideological explanations of the phenomena that interest her; this is not necessarily a problem, but it makes the text's few references to cultural critique—for instance, an invocation of D. A. Miller's *The Novel and the Police* [52]—feel rather jarring.) This sweeping generality can be invigorating but may not be sustainable in a discussion of cultural artifacts—not least because many of the heuristics that lead us to ignore or fixate on particular pieces of information in a text are grounded not in cognitive universals but in expectations about genre and form. The interaction between relatively stable cognitive heuristics and cultural formations that script particular reasoning patterns makes a rich and promising field for cognitive literary studies, one for which this book lays indispensable groundwork—but, for better or worse, does not tackle itself.

It may seem unfair to criticize *Elements of Surprise* for neglecting a domain that simply lies outside its scope of concern, but an attention to cultural difference and historical change in cognitive habits is not simply necessary for useful readings of literary texts; it will also be crucial to any truly reciprocal relationship between cognitive science and the humanities. Tobin suggests more than once that fictional narratives provide a "laboratory" for cognitive investigations, manipulating our inferential processes in a way that makes them easier to see (15, 55). For this to be more than a figure of speech, however, it would have to be possible for literary findings to disconfirm, or at least call into question, a hypothesis derived from psychology: a laboratory that only produces positive results would quickly and rightly fall into suspicion. If literature is to move from the status of illustration to that of evidence in cognitive studies, cognitive literary scholars will have to demonstrate that texts can reveal patterns of thinking, and interdependencies between cognition and culture, that tend to escape the scope of experiments or large-scale surveys—in other words, that literature can help us *generate* new hypotheses about the workings of the mind. This might happen by many different means, but one possible route would be to emphasize rather than downplay cultural and historical variation, using texts to investigate cognitive models to which we might not have experimental access (whether because of historical distance or because of their radical individuality or context-dependence).

In the process, cognitive literary studies might well end up moving away from the fascination with biases that arguably dominates current psychological research. One of the odder consequences of cognitive psychology's focus on the situation-specific bias is the implicit assumption that human cognition is a faulty machine capable, in principle, of being optimized—to what end is never quite clear ("information processing"?). If this end does exist, though, how does it relate to the ends of literature? Tobin, like other narratologists before her, views plot dynamics as a balance between frustration and satisfaction—and notes the aesthetic virtues of the former, a "perhaps higher and more sophisticated object" (159). Like many literary critics, I *do* believe "withholding or thwarting expected resolutions" to be one of the more aesthetically interesting and valuable things literature can do (ibid.), but I have little justification for this belief, and Tobin's book provides a thorough and convincing window into the truly complex machinations involved in constructing even the most clichéd "twist." After reading the novels that most matter to me, as Tobin suggests, I am especially aware of my own cognitive frailties and their potentially pleasurable effects. Still, these texts also leave me especially uncertain of the purpose from which these "curses" are supposedly diverting me. That uncertainty is often less pleasurable, but it may be one with which empirically minded humanists are no less obligated to reckon.

HANNAH WALSER, *Harvard Society of Fellows*

*   *   *

HANNAH WALSER is a Junior Fellow at the Harvard Society of Fellows. Her work focuses on the literary history of cognition. She has completed a book manuscript, "Thinking with Strangers: Theories of Mind in Nineteenth-Century American Fiction," and is currently at work on a history of the homunculus as a metaphor for mental faculties in literature and science.

Cultivating Time

JESSE MATZ, *Modernist Time Ecology* (Baltimore: Johns Hopkins University Press, 2018), pp. 320, cloth, $54.95.

Jesse Matz's *Modernist Time Ecology* is a book brimming with ideas. It analyzes a wide array of cultural objects, from canonical modernist works to contemporary novels and films to the It Gets Better Project. The list of authors covered is impressive. Charles Dickens, Marcel Proust, William James, Henry James, Thomas Mann, Virginia Woolf, Willa Cather, William Faulkner, and Ralph Ellison all have substantial walk-on parts. Chapter-length discussions are given to E. M. Forster, J. B. Priestley, and V. S. Naipaul. Henri Bergson is shown to be compatible with Mikhail Bakhtin, while the time philosophy of J. W. Dunne is rescued from (partial) obscurity. All of these authors are discussed with the subtlety and expert close reading that readers of Matz's previous work on Impressionism and the modernist novel have come to expect. And yet the metaphor at the heart of the book is a problematic one, threatening—as Matz to his credit acknowledges in many places—to obscure as much as it reveals, since "it shifts the focus away from the material environment," which, at the present moment, seems in much greater need of reparation than the temporal one (4). But it would be a mistake to entirely disentangle them. Clearly the ecological crisis that looms represents a shocking suspension of our temporal horizon, a crushing realization, in a different register, of Lee Edelman's *No Future* thesis, about which Matz has many illuminating things to say. Thinking about time, then, has transparently real consequences in the world. But if the admirable goal of this book is to create "a space for a new form of activist scholarship with real potential to change our sense of what temporal representations might do," it would need a richer account both of the current ecological crisis in which we find ourselves and of how the temporality of capital has brought us here (6).

Matz sums up his project clearly and succinctly at the beginning of chapter 2: "Ecological texts are pragmatic but also visionary. Their project is to cultivate our temporal environment. They respond to perceived threats to the temporal manifold and model ways to conserve or enrich temporal possibilities, to reclaim the temporal landscape and husband its critical resources. And they *do so* while also *saying so*" (48). The point, then, is not only about content but also about form, and Matz is particularly good at drawing our attention away from, for instance, Hans Castorp's foolish, inchoate thoughts about time to Mann's formal skill at showing us what Castorp fails to understand. "*The Magic Mountain*," Matz concludes, "is about its own forms for temporal reckoning, which, posed against simplicity, propose to redress it" (58). Mann, in other words, seeks not only to outline a dilemma about time but to offer us ways to solve the problem. Proust, too, is shown to have a public aim for his work. "Subjective discovery is part of it," Matz claims, "but the larger project entails provision of public measures" (94). Modernist time ecology thus brings together two well-known facts about modernism: that it was preoccupied with time and that it evinced an exceptional faith in the power of the aesthetic to shape the way we live our lives.

Given, however, that these facts are so well known, it is hard to see exactly what is novel about the claim that modernist works want us to understand time in a new way or that, with a concept as abstract and vexing as time, a new understanding might, in turn, have effects on the ways we live. Most attentive readers of Proust, Mann, Woolf, and Joyce will have felt as much even if they have not used the ecological metaphor to describe this process. Indeed, one of the paradoxes of the book is that, though rooted in the modernist period, its readings of canonical modernist texts—Proust's *À la recherche du temps perdu*, Woolf's *To the Lighthouse*, Cather's *My Ántonia*, Faulkner's *The Sound and the Fury*, and Ellison's *Invisible Man*—are less compelling than those of the other cultural objects it addresses. Not that Matz has nothing helpful to say about these works. No one working on Woolf will fail to admire the succinct elegance with which he summarizes the way her fictions "show duration to be not just the pattern of true experience but the problem of our lives—the element within which life wastes away, but also perpetually creates new possibilities for human thriving" (76). Nevertheless, though it is clear that *The Sound and the Fury* "presents itself as an alternative to watches," it is hard to find any particular optimism in Faulkner's work, and it is not surprising to read that Ellison "proposes a narrative power that might restore some of the ritual elements lost with bebop as well as the capricious realities of racism" (103, 108).

The virtues of the book lie elsewhere. The chapter-length readings of Forster's *Maurice*, Priestley's time plays, and Naipaul's *The Enigma of Arrival* are excellent, as is the comparison of Edelman's and Dan Savage's, on the face of it, mutually hostile projects. And the book develops two distinct, if overlapping, theoretical resources that will certainly aid new scholarship in these areas. The first is the depth of its engagement with various time philosophies—not only the obvious instances of Bergson and James, about whom Matz finds new things to say, but the less well-known work of Dunne and the more recent ideas of the Tutzing Time Ecology Project. The second is its development of a set of narratological claims that will be of particular interest to the readers of *Novel*.

These two often overlapping theoretical interests are developed in the book's introduction and first three chapters. Time, Matz argues, "does not come naturally to us" but is a matter of "active, deliberate performance" (31, 24). Drawing on cognitive psychology, Matz shows that "time in the mind is naturally incoherent," only arising as a kind of "cognitive supplement" or "remedial representation" when our relationship to our environment breaks down: "In other words, time happens when tuning fails. We implicitly, automatically tune to our environment, but when something disrupts the process—when there is conflict among bedrock temporal processes or automatic processes are inadequate to the demands of new environmental conditions—we become conscious of the process, and time results. . . . Time is the purposive reparation of broken adherence to natural temporality" (30). Here we see both the grounds for understanding how narrative can intervene in our sense of temporality—since it is, by its very nature, a cognitive structure—and the often nostalgic or pastoral dynamic that comprises what Matz refers to as the "ideological fantasies" of much modernist time ecology (246). For what exactly is a "natural temporality," and how can it be captured by the necessarily intentional structures of aesthetic form?

There is no easy answer to this question, and what can initially seem an incoherence in the book actually emerges as one of its strengths. If modernist time ecology names a desire to "save the temporal environment," what that means is endlessly various, dependent on medium, artistic temperament, and historical moment (3). Matz does not force his aesthetic objects into one set of theoretical coordinates but allows them to persist in their ideological diversity. Proust, for instance, offers alternatives to "contemporary temporalities, especially those that block the past or disallow slow focus on present experience," while Gaspar Noé's *Irréversible* suggests that "all times exist all at once" (95, 213).

The flexibility of Matz's reading practice is best seen in the two chapters that discuss queer temporalities: the chapter on *Maurice* and the extended comparison of *No Future* and *It Gets Better*. The reading of *Maurice* is a tour de force, turning what many readers view as the text's "escapism" into a "richly generative" rewriting of the "laws of sequence and tense in such a way as to afford [Forster's] gay friends time-schemes that could, for the time-being of the mid-twentieth century, sustain them" (112, 113). Matz builds his case by drawing on the Cambridge time theorists contemporary with Forster, for here was a critique of that cherished object of modernist time ecology: time as becoming. Often pitched against "[c]onventional time-schemes—atomistic, linear, and logical forms of time" (119), *becoming* is understood by the Cambridge time theorists as itself fundamentally conventional, tending as it does to "identify our experiences with present-tense judgments about them."[1] Tenselessness, on the other hand, imagines the existence of "different cultural moments simultaneously," allowing Forster to "detach judgment from the tyrannically moving present" (120). Arguing that all elements of time are "equally real," tenselessness pitches itself against the irrationality of the theory of becoming (120). Tenselessness imagines itself, in other words, as a rational theory of how time really works.

This theory, then, is used to outline why Forster—despite seeing the potential incompatibility of narrative and homosexual desire—nevertheless "sticks with narrativity for the sake of what narrative might yet afford of queer temporality" (133). A set of distinct temporalities emerges in the text, and it is the uneasy co-presence of them all that distinguishes the queer temporality Forster seeks to cultivate. Matz summarizes these temporalities in the following way: "The temporality of *Maurice*, then, bears these relations to sexuality and produces these narrative results: it sees the false becoming in conventional heterosexual life and ironizes it through excessive linearity; it sees a bad alternative in aesthetical homosexuality and shows it to be more of the same; it denies modernist epiphany for similar reasons and allows Maurice to express authentic desire only once he becomes tenseless" (132). Linearity and tenselessness coexist in a text that seeks to preserve the possibility of a queer future for characters denied any meaningful expression of their subjectivities in the debased present.

A similar wish animates Savage's It Gets Better Project, which offers videotaped messages from adults speaking to queer youth about how their own lives have improved over time. Initially this would seem flatly to contradict Lee Edelman's *No Future* thesis, which Matz claims "makes narrative temporality largely responsible for the political futurity [it] would oppose" (225). And yet, "[i]f we uncouple narrative temporality and teleological futurity, we may discover that the former can subvert the latter in the spirit of queer oppositionality itself" (227). Matz locates just such an uncoupling in Savage's project, and he does so through its particular form of narrativity, which is determined by the narratorial presence speaking in the videos: "[W]hen a narrator testifies to the sequence entailed in a narration, the relationship between that sequence and the narrator's temporal position undoes any simply linear procedure" (233). He elaborates: "What may seem to be a linear imposition—the innocent child will become the experienced adult—is in fact a rhetorical proposition: learn how to think futurity as yourself-to-come speaking to yourself-today. Because this proposition not only sidesteps linearity but reorients futurity as Edelman defines it, it also functions as a queer form of cultivation" (235). The end result is nothing less than an upending of

[1]   D. H. Mellor, "Thank Goodness That's Over," qtd. in Matz 120.

the relationship between narrative normativity and heteronormativity. "Queer temporality," Matz concludes, also "obtains in forms we take to be conventional—forms of narrative engagement, which respond to temporal aporetics in such a way as to innovate queer time-schemes" (238).

Here we arrive at what I think is the book's most compelling methodological intervention. Matz refuses the simplest type of ideology critique, which tends to draw a straight line between aesthetic form and political position. The redemptive temporalities of Priestley's time plays are distinct from those of Naipaul's *The Enigma of Arrival*. Naipaul's faith in the power of the aesthetic must be distinguished from Proust's. None of these conceptual structures can be considered outside the contexts in which they are mobilized. If the diversity of these works threatens to overtake the conceptual coherence of this book's central term, that is a price worth paying for the close attention Matz pays to the specificity of his cultural objects.

PAUL STASI, *State University of New York at Albany*

*   *   *

PAUL STASI teaches twentieth-century anglophone literature at SUNY Albany. He is the author of *Modernism, Imperialism, and the Historical Sense* (2012) and coeditor (with Jennifer Greiman) of *The Last Western: Deadwood and the End of American Empire* (2013) and (with Josephine Park) *Ezra Pound in the Present: New Essays on Pound's Contemporaneity* (2016). His current book project, tentatively entitled *Remainders of Realism*, traces the persistence of realism's defining concerns—sympathy, sociality, class—into the modernist period.

Modernity and a Day

PHILIP SICKER, Ulysses, *Film, and Visual Culture* (Cambridge: Cambridge University Press, 2018), pp. 276, cloth, $105.00.

Upon finishing Philip Sicker's delightful book Ulysses, *Film, and Visual Culture*, the reader is left with the image of a dark stage full of illuminated optical devices. It looks like a sorcerer's workshop or like a museum of popular amusements. Mutoscopes, cameras, stereoscopes, zoetropes, magic lanterns, microscopes, and telescopes are displayed on shelves and tables. Someone inspects each device in turn, a man who can hardly see in the customary sense of the word, whose domicile is among the glorious and trivial corridors of human idiosyncrasy. Is this a stage? A screen? Everything is a dynamic palimpsest, the effect of double—triple, quadruple—exposure, unembarrassed by metamorphosis and noncommittal about its ontological affiliation. "Goldhaired" girls twirl around him as morning, noon, and twilight hours, their gestures carving out a most spacious day. June 16, 1904. Tormented by thorny thoughts, a young man contemplates the dioramic view from the Martello tower—both a panopticon and a rotunda (*how can one be sure of one's eyes?*); in the middle distance, someone is hanging from Nelson's Pillar "by his eyelids," no doubt mercifully punished by a lover safely kept out of sight. Boisterous voices on the street bring the writer to a window that opens onto a *serata* of January 12, 1910. Joyce shakes his head, chortles, muttering under his breath: *Futureless futurists* . . . then pats a poster on the nearby desk, tracing with admiring fingers the spokes of printed text in a mesmerizing spiral. *Very clever, that one*: Carrà's Interventionist Demonstration; *could be Bloom's ad in the "Lotus Eaters."* He lies down, floating among the lights turned stars, transfixed by the moonlit skeleton horse pulling a carriage through the night sky. The ultimate spectacle. *Yes yes yes* . . . he whispers in the voice of Mrs. Breen, or perhaps it is Molly's. *Yes*, he would purchase that 16-millimeter camera with the money from the Random House edition of *Ulysses*. *Yes*, he will allow that Russian fellow Eisenstein to make a film out of the novel. *Yes*.

As this collage of images from Sicker's book suggests, he delivers much more than the argument summarized on page 2: "*Ulysses*, composed as Joyce's vision deteriorated a decade later, is his ultimate act of capturing and preserving the eye's encounter with reality, a transaction conducted via the gazes of Stephen and Bloom and through a multitude of refractory lenses." The book modestly announces itself as an intervention in a now dated conversation, mostly from the 1990s, that challenged the idea of modernism as something "insulated from the cultural world into which it was introduced" (Michael North, qtd. in Sicker 18). Building on North's *Reading 1922* (1999) and other studies by Stephen Kern, Thomas Richards, Tim Armstrong, Laura Marcus, Garry Leonard, and Sara Danius that have focused on the ways technology and modern perception bear on modernist literature, Sicker reads closely Joyce's multidimensional engagement with vision in *Ulysses* in conversation with Victorian and Edwardian visual technology, medieval theology, Enlightenment philosophy, twentieth-century existentialism, phenomenology, and ethics as well as film theory and psychoanalysis. This multilayered theoretical and philosophical scaffolding, which informs two chapters on Stephen (1 and 2) and two on Bloom (3 and 5), also supports what, to this reader, are the most exciting chapters of the book (4, 6, and 7), where Sicker brings futurist painting and the early cinema of Georges Méliès to bear on Joyce's narrative art. These readings represent a contribution to intermedial modernism, that endlessly fascinating approach to the ways modernism integrates multiple art forms consecrated by the work of Daniel Albright. Although Sicker does not seem to worry about the New Modernist studies, the latter's emphasis on bridging high and low genres is echoed in the interweaving of philosophical discourse and the nineteenth-century culture of popular amusements. Finally, the argument that emerges fully in the last chapter reads like an unacknowledged engagement with the rethinking of community in twentieth-century continental philosophy around relationality, singularity, and exposure: Sicker reads *Ulysses* as a modern epic narrating a quest for the right distance—between oneself and the world, God, and the others—that ends in "Ithaca" with a sort of carefully choreographed, if fragile, compromise between solipsism and the comfort of human bonds.

The first two chapters focus on Stephen's ways of seeing and his fraught awareness of being seen, while it also sheds light on the dioramic narrative framework of *Ulysses*. A protocinematic device, the diorama is a theatrically illuminated recreation of a landscape that delights viewers with its hyperreality, only to compel them to deconstruct the fabricated harmony, thus generating epistemic confusion and doubt about the reliability of sight in general. Sicker argues that the late reveal of Stephen's visual impairment toward the end of the day (in "Circe") similarly sows doubts in readers' minds about what they took for a realistic representation of the world through Stephen's eyes. Ontological uncertainty is thus brought into high relief, as it also dominates Stephen's optical experiments, which replicate and modify thought experiments central to philosophy, from Aristotle, Descartes, Berkeley, and Diderot to William James. Sicker revisits these, singling out Locke as the less consciously acknowledged Enlightenment philosopher in the walk-experiment in "Proteus," which in Sicker's original reading also deconstructs the functioning of the stereoscope, a popular entertainment based on Charles Wheatstone's 1833 invention. Highlighting the binocular disparity caused by the 2.5-inch distance between the eyes, the stereoscope creates awareness of the process of optical convergence that humans perform unconsciously. Marking a shift from the Renaissance monocular perspective invested in depth-representation to a self-conscious emphasis on the functioning of our embodied optical apparatus, the stereoscope, Sicker argues, also operates narratively in *Ulysses* as a way to merge philosophy (Berkeley's assertion that distance is added to our apprehension of the world rather than inherent to visual perception) and the nineteenth-century culture of popular amusements. Because Stephen's optical experiments fail to yield certainty about the material existence of the world, Sicker pursues the route of ontological investigation by examining Stephen's awareness of himself as an object in the eyes of others.

Referring to the double fear of being judged by others and of not being seen, Sicker describes "a complex dread" with psychosexual, political, and religious implications, which drives Stephen's quest for a more benevolent alterity that would see him in a nonthreatening way. Sicker invokes Sartre's analysis of the complete metamorphosis of one's worldview under the gaze of an other to diagnose Stephen's "shame," and he invokes Foucault's elaborations on the resonance chambers of power, whose workings are most obviously successful when subjects have internalized the watchful eyes of authority and participate in their own policing. Stephen's Dublin has all the characteristics of Jeremy Bentham's panoptic model of surveillance (1791), doubly exercised by the British Empire and by the Roman Catholic Church. Stephen can only feel "imprisoned by the self-perpetuating nightmare of surveillance itself" (83); it is therefore in his own head that he "must kill the priest and the king." Sicker insists on making a distinction between Stephen's derisive and dismissive view of the Catholic clergy and his more conflicted aggression against God, identifying the source of Stephen's view of a constitutive divine gaze in Nicolas de Cusa's 1453 *The Vision of God*: "[T]he sense of objectified existence that Stephen both craves and dreads resides in his fitful awareness of the divine gaze as Cusanus describes it" (97). Echoing the longing for the self-actualizing experience of a woman's touch following Stephen's inconclusive ocular experiments, the solution to the fear of an omniscient God that he cannot intellectually accept is a religious chant performed "not as a priest ascending the altar, but as a man descending into a '[s]treet of harlots'" (3.366). In Sicker's apt formulation: "Craving and fearing, inviting and disdaining the gaze of the ultimate Other, [Stephen] strives, through defilement and profanation, to perform before the outraged eyes of Divinity an agonizing yet enlivening rite of resistance" (99).

Although Stephen's observational practice generates epiphanic moments, it is Bloom who inherits the "role of the epiphanic flâneur" (107). Dublin might deprive him of the anonymity enjoyed by his earlier European counterparts, but, as a colonial capital, it offers him an ideal balance between the "local traditions and vestigial customs of an earlier epoch" and the "dehumanizing hallmarks of high capitalism" (111). Readers of Baudelaire and Walter Benjamin will likely remember that this originally Parisian figure, whom urban modernization changed from "a botanist on the asphalt" into an arcades dweller among commodities, eventually became an anachronism whose role of noticing fascinating, fugitive details was replaced by photography in the mid-nineteenth century. Building on the work of Susan Sontag, Roland Barthes, and Henri-Cartier Bresson as well as other Joyce scholars, Sicker argues compellingly that Joyce updates the flaneur by bringing photography to bear on Bloom's peripatetics and ways of engaging visually with Dublin. Extending Garry Leonard's characterization of Joycean epiphany as "a snapshot of a world permanently in flux," Sicker argues that it offers "not only an apt epistemic metaphor but a portal for an extended investigation of the role of photography in shaping Bloom's epiphanies and his flânerie in general" (125). Noting that the structure of Constantin Guys's long day, around which Baudelaire constructed the artist's portrait, is in many ways similar to Bloom's, Sicker draws a parallel between the figure of the flaneur, a "human palimpsest," and the dialectical image of photography as "a photographic double exposure" (133) that superimposes an old image upon a contemporary one. Indeed, "Joyce demonstrates that photography can function as a conceptual framework for registering and interpreting the modernist flâneur's most luminous moments of perception" (125).

Just as the memory of the diorama informs Stephen's visual experiences throughout the day, Bloom fondles mentally the pornographic images he enjoyed through the mutoscope. Rigorously attentive to details of Joyce's biography and correspondence around the time he wrote *Ulysses*, and to the cultural history of the optical devices he reviews, Sicker points out that William K. L. Dickson's 1895 invention anticipated the silent film projector used in the Cinematograph Volta inaugurated by Joyce in Dublin in 1909. Chapter 5 draws a compelling parallel between Bloom's erotic scopophilia in "Nausicaa" and "Circe" and the gendered models of film spectatorship elaborated by Christian Metz and Laura Mulvey (175). Analyzing minutely the ways Bloom "configure[s] Gerty as a mutoscopic spectacle," Sicker identifies in this episode "psychological affiliations between voyeurism and cinema viewing that [Bloom] grasps only fleetingly but registers subliminally" (179): the fantasy of reciprocal desire, the rich satisfaction of the woman's cinematic objectification, subtly calibrated through her avoidance of the male viewer's gaze, the controlling distance that ensures the preservation as much as possible of the "source of the scopic drive" (184), a "primordial *elsewhere*, infinitely desirable [but] never possessable" (Metz, qtd. in Sicker 185). Gerty will of course escape from the scenarios of innocence and eroticism projected on her by Bloom by turning from displayed object into voyeuristic subject in "Circe," an episode driven by an entirely different scopic regime. Sicker contrasts here Bloom's dread of the castrating female gaze and the "psychological instruction" (190) derived from the gaze of other males, even when negative. As in the second chapter, where Sicker traces correspondences between Stephen's fraught relationship with God and Joyce's own theological ruminations, here Bloom's fetishes are paralleled by Joyce's own fantasies, as illustrated by his letters to Nora.

"Painting Motion" and "Mirages in the Lamp Glow" argue that Joyce owes important principles of visual representation to Futurist painters and the trick cinema of Méliès. Trieste, where Joyce resided, was one of the three capitals of the futurist movement, along with Paris and Milano. The Irish writer could not have missed (at least the noise around) their *serata* as he returned from Dublin in January 1910, just as he was likely aware of discussions of Futurist art by Huntley Carter, John Cournos, and Wyndham Lewis in the very issues of *The Egoist* that serialized *Portrait* in 1914. Sicker's elegant reading of the "Wandering Rocks" alongside a great number of paintings by Boccioni, Gino Severini, Giacomo Balla, and Carlo Carrà compellingly paints Joyce's episode as "the visual equivalent of a Futurist canvas." Not only does it portray Dublin as "a vast automaton of a myriad interactive systems" (148), in line with the Futurists' fascination with the machinery of urban civilization, it also incorporates principles of simultaneity, perspective, motion, and symbolic analogies, the analysis of which enlists readers as Joyce's collaborators in the work's "architectural environment" (Boccioni, qtd. in Sicker 174). Chapter 6 documents closely Joyce's opportunities to watch Méliès's films on his sojourns in Dublin, Paris, and Trieste. Equally comfortable with film analysis, Sicker delves into the screen fantasies of Méliès (the illusionist-turned-filmmaker made 500 films between 1896 and 1913, 173 of which were released in 2006), showing that "Circe" owes these films its visual style, hybrid structure, and self-reflexivity: its phantasmagoric effects mimic those of theatrical magic shows, and the episode employs "cinema fakes," substitution tricks (including gender conversions), stop-motion techniques, and effects reminiscent of Méliès's multiple exposures (images recorded directly over others, generating ghostlike transparencies). Finally, Méliès's 1907 experimental dream film *Tunneling the English Channel* inspires Sicker's analysis of "Eumaeus" and "Ithaca," where Stephen and Bloom share visual engagements where their respective anxieties meet and are eventually—if temporarily—alleviated. Drawing on the phenomenology of Edmund Husserl, Maurice Merleau-Ponty, and Emmanuel Levinas, the final chapter offers an insightful reading of "conjoined vision," or "intersubjective perception," in which visual perception is entwined with epistemic, emotive, and bodily experiences that grant Stephen and Bloom a "convergence that accommodates separateness and difference" (249), an "epiphany of expressive sight" requiring no verbal translation.

Strikingly, three or four times in Ulysses, *Film and Visual Culture*, Sicker refers to the optical devices and visual art he analyzes as "portals" that give access to a different understanding of Joyce's novel. The metaphor aptly conjures the multidimensional narrative space of a capacious day, in which the optic technologies of modernity, be they surveillance networks or media-infused subjectivities, conspire to design a literary spectacle that expands the imagination in new, fascinating ways. Joyce readers, students of futurism and cinema, scholars of philosophy and literature, and more generally those who have made modernism their intellectual home, are likely to appreciate the fine prose of Sicker's book, its delightful insights, and the rigor that sustains it throughout.

CORINA STAN, *Duke University*

*   *   *

CORINA STAN is associate professor of comparative literature in the English Department at Duke University, where she teaches modernism across the arts and courses at the intersection of literature and philosophy. She is the author of *The Art of Distances: Ethical Thinking in Twentieth-Century Literature* (2018) and of articles published in *Comparative Literature Studies*, *MLN*, *The Journal of Postcolonial Writing*, *Arcadia*, *English Studies*, *Critical Inquiry*, and others. She is currently at work on a book project on the "end of the West" and the European refugee crisis.

Homelessness Revisited

PAUL BUCHHOLZ, *Private Anarchy: Impossible Community and the Outsider's Monologue in German Experimental Fiction* (Evanston: Northwestern UP, 2018), pp. 242, cloth, $99.95.

In *The Theory of the Novel*, Georg Lukács famously described the poetics of modern prose fiction as "transcendental homelessness" (Lukács 41). While never explicitly cited, this descriptor resonates strongly in Paul Buchholz's engaging monograph *Private Anarchy*, which focuses on novels that introduce "outsiders" who cannot feel at home in the world they inhabit. Buchholz analyzes a group of twentieth-century pieces of prose fiction in terms of alienation, solitude, and their abstract longing for "impossible community." For both Lukács and Buchholz, the concept of alienation is limited not only to a lost relation to an estranged *physis* but also to what Lukács calls second nature—all the features of community that seem to define the human habitat, its traditions, rituals, social orders, and manners. Succumbing to the task of being autonomous beings, modern subjects sense the oppressive force of these cultural environments. Novels tell the stories of their restlessness, disorientation, and lost utopias. Buchholz pushes this perspective to a new extreme. He is interested in prose texts that both formally and thematically engage in literary forms of radical solitude.

Although the topic of the outsider who opposes society and simultaneously longs for it may strike us as an extension of Lukács's trope of homelessness, the literary forms in which Buchholz expresses this angst reach beyond the traditional forms of the bildungsroman and later realist fiction. As a result, we must regard the novels he subjects to concise close readings as "experimental fiction," as indicated by the book's subtitle. These novels share the narratological feature that Buchholz identifies as "the outsider's monologue" (4), a radical form of first-person narration that is for the most part "antimimetic" (209n1), nihilistic (5), and anticommunicative, as in "characters who talk only to themselves" (6). He devotes a chapter to a novel by each of four experimental authors, novels that together cover the long twentieth century. Gustav Landauer's *The Death Preacher* (1893) and Franz Kafka's early story "Description of a Struggle" (ca. 1910) serve as examples of early and high modernism, while three novels from the middle to late postwar era represent the latter half of the century. One is an early set of drafts by Thomas Bernhard synthesized under the title *Leichtlebig* (ca. 1961); the others Wolfgang Hilbig's dark stories "Old Rendering Plant" (1990) and "The Lore of the Trees" (1992).

Buchholz's claims are neither primarily formal nor fixated on literary and communicative nihilism. Quite the contrary, his main objective is to show how "the fiction of private anarchy" (24) subverts nihilist tendencies in order to expose new forms of community. In these novels, sociopolitical negativity, or what Buchholz calls "verbal voiding," "becomes a necessary step in opening up space to imagine a togetherness that transcends ideas of the sovereign self as well as the bonds promised by traditional kinship ties" (24). This signature claim relies on two central concepts: the impossible community and the outsider's monologue.

The outsider's monologue is, as I have suggested, a special instance of soliloquy that "writers of the nineteenth and twentieth centuries frequently utilized . . . as a showcase for extreme and unwanted solitude" (3). Buchholz draws on Victor Erlich to argue that the twentieth-century monologue differs from earlier forms that provided markers of individual

Novel: A Forum on Fiction 53:3 DOI 10.1215/00295132-8624733   © 2020 by Novel, Inc.

distinction. A new, radical disconnection from any social sphere is therefore an important feature of this form of monologue, the historic origin of which can be located in Dostoevsky's *Notes from the Underground*: "The Underground monologue projects a vacuum onto the surrounding world by referring to social relations that *could* exist but do not, addressing listeners who might hear but do not . . . " (11). Like Erlich, Buchholz ties this shift to the alienating effects of modern life, which renders human relationships increasingly abstract. Literature expresses this experience by highlighting "a lack of communication and community, an imprisonment within the self, or sequestration within some segment of a social hierarchy" (3). These topoi characterize the "'lonely crowd' of modern society, where mass social integration coincides with abjection and alienation" (4). The book's focus on individual estrangement as the result of collective alienation provides the basis for one of its central claims. According to Buchholz, the solitude expressed in the outsider's monologues is no individual fate but that of a multitude of human beings who experience isolation from one another. Although expressions of extreme solitude afford only small glimpses of utopia, they are responsible for the social implications of this study.

Working with and expanding on Jean Luc Nancy's notion of "negative communities," Buchholz wants to show that each of the novelists he considers "developed their own distinct ideas of negative community prior to, or apart from, the discourses of poststructuralism" (7), ideas that are not accomplished by pure monologue alone. Those outsiders' monologues are accompanied by a moment of metalepsis, or slippage between different levels of narrative discourse. He argues that metalepsis in twentieth-century fiction should be read as a relational technique that weaves together different textual layers as well as diegetic and extradiegetic levels to create bonds between—to give just one example—protagonist and implied reader: "In other words, metalepsis *is* community. It is literature's way of declaring community against what may seem to be an inescapable isolation" (14). Buchholz contends, however, that the novels he has selected push this idea still further. "I will show," he explains, "that experimental German prose . . . tends to employ metalepsis for the imagination of community in contexts where community has become otherwise unimaginable" (14). In *Private Anarchy*, metalepsis emerges as the central trope of twentieth-century German fiction, a symbiosis of its poetical distinctions and political inclinations. This general setup prefigures the structure of Buchholz's close readings. The formal analysis of a text's monologism culminates in a moment of metalepsis, a moment that transgresses the formal and thematic isolation of an individual's mind and allows for a glimpse at new forms of community, impossible or not. All four close readings follow this basic pattern.

This similarity in structure ties the texts together aesthetically. By working within a predetermined structure, each of Buchholz's four analyses inadvertently strengthens formal aspects that prove his point while downplaying those that deviate from his framework. The most egregious case of this misplaced emphasis occurs in chapter 4, in which Buchholz offers a reading of Bernhard's *Leichtlebig*. In a circular argument, the interpretive framework determines the outcome of the analysis. The problems with this chapter are twofold; for one thing, the interpretive framework forces Buchholz to overgeneralize his analysis, downplaying the particular variances that we generally value in a work of literature. Second, he makes the status of the novel in question less than clear. Neither a finished nor a unified draft, it is accessible in Bernhard's estate only in "four separate portfolios" (134). Where other critics stress that "it would be virtually impossible to reconstruct a readable edition of these drafts," Buchholz promises to "reconstruct the narrative trajectories of this lost novel, as well as its remarkable experimentation with forms and ideas" (134). Because Buchholz never deals explicitly with editorial questions related to the highly problematic status of the text, the reconstruction of the novel simply happens without much, if any, discussion, leaving us with a set of unanswered questions: Where did he find the excerpts on which he bases his reading? Which parts of the story were composed and arranged by Bernhard? Which, on the other hand, are the results of Buchholz's reconstruction?

One reason Buchholz regards this fragment as such a powerful illustration of his ideas is a striking moment of metalepsis, which transforms the roles of protagonist, narrator, and even the implied reader. Here, metalepsis serves as a far more powerful concept than the outsider's monologue. The (reconstructed) text consists of a dialogue between a young railroad worker with political ambitions and his recent vacation acquaintance, an obscure academic known only as "the Doctor." When at one point of the conversation the Doctor tells Leichtlebig, the railroad worker, very personal details of that worker's own youth, the young man is baffled but acknowledges that what the Doctor has to say is absolutely correct. Since the narrator has never mentioned most of those details, the novel makes it clear that "each character is capable of swallowing the other character's world" (157), thereby creating a bond between the two individuals who otherwise remain isolated from each other. If we take into account the frequency of their discussion about the classic authors of anarchist literature, this bond "aggressively subverts the available social and political positions of the postwar era" (158). While the community thus envisioned is, as a literary one, politically impossible, according to Buchholz, it is also "the only [alternative] worth writing about" (158).

While this novel, if such it can be called, makes it clear that metalepsis, as a formal feature, is far more important to Buchholz's project than the outsider's monologue, *Leichtlebig* is nevertheless a dialogue and, as such, works counter to the principle of monologic speech. Had Buchholz acknowledged the relationship between monologue and dialogue in this novel, he would have noted that the decisive moment of transgression, the moment when the doctor suddenly turns into an auctorial narrator, is inherently dialogical. One cannot help but think that hidden in the rift between dialogical and monological dimensions of the novel there might be an even stronger sense of literary community than the bond created by metalepsis. Rather than insist on the *impossibility* of these communities, Buchholz might have stressed the possibilities inherent in their contradictory yet dynamic organization.

To offer an account of the novel from 1893 through 1992, Buchholz has to single out four works, a rather small sample that cannot be seen as a single coherent literary movement. The problem is not only that the historical and sociopolitical environments of the four writers are so different but also that there is a gulf between Bernhard and the novelists preceding him, Landauer and Kafka. Kafka's "Description of a Struggle" was composed around 1910 and is followed by two world wars, a culturally decisive interwar period, and the first decade of post-1945 Austrian history. Does Buchholz stress the formal similarities between these novels simply because their historical relationship is so difficult to justify? Not if these similarities prove convincing.

This is especially the case in the chapters on Landauer and Hilbig. Landauer seems like the author who best fits Buchholz's interest in the crossroads between experimental fiction and anarchic political visions. A leading anarchist of fin de siècle Berlin, Landauer was an activist, a theorist, and a writer of fiction. Focusing on Landauer is so intriguing to Buchholz's project because the progressive line of his deeds and writings, while perfectly fitting Buchholz's interest in progressive political imagination, is at odds with the nihilist writers that he identifies with the outsider's monologue, most significantly Arthur Schopenhauer, Friedrich Nietzsche, and Fyodor Dostoyevsky. The tension between the poles of misanthropy and social utopia drives this chapter. Buchholz identifies the 1898 novel *The Death Preacher* as Landauer's most significant contribution to the literature of private anarchy, and rightly so. The story of "the tortured intellectual" is at the same time an attempt "to both document and *harness* this 'chaos' [of fin de siècle culture] and stage a productive collision between decadent aesthetics and socialist ideology" (73).

The novel adopts the basic structure of a bildungsroman, its hero evolving through self-altering intellectual passions along with the historical conditions of the period in which the story is set. The monologues that capture Buchholz's narratological interest are variously nihilist and socialist sermons that Starkblom composes throughout his life, the last of which is a fiery call to revolution. As Buchholz convincingly shows, it is precisely the fact that nothing gets destroyed and nobody is hurt by the monologues of his tortured individual Starkblom that best demonstrates literature's ability to imagine impossible communities. Landauer violently voids all traditional ideas about human identity, but he does so "only *virtually,* that is to say *verbally*" (102). He does so not to incite violent upheaval but to enable the imagination of utopian societies: "This vocal insistence on the possibility of all community becomes the precondition for alternative forms of togetherness that are yet to be written or realized" (102). Here one of Buchholz's central arguments achieves its clearest expression. A radically negative, highly experimental work of fiction erases traditional images of community in order to imagine alternative future ones: "The language of impossible community is actually the *preview* of a community that could emerge in another possible world" (102). Elegantly, this chapter shows how a novel can combine literariness with a political perspective without subsuming either into the other. The novel neither turns literature into a vessel for political agitation nor turns the possibility of political change into mere imagination.

While this logic defines the outcome of each close reading, the last of the four is perhaps Buchholz's best example. Experimental and abstract though they may seem, Hilbig's prose narratives directly address the historical conditions of the late German Democratic Republic. Hilbig himself immigrated to West Germany during the 1980s, when he was known as a poet. He wrote his most important works of narrative prose during or shortly after German reunification. In a fifth chapter, Buchholz takes a closer look at some of Hilbig's longer stories, allowing Buchholz to address issues that go well beyond the formal considerations that preoccupy the other chapters. These stories engage contemporary political debates over such problems as the environmental pollution devastating large areas of the GDR. As Buchholz explains, "Hilbig's negative communities are always adorned with grotesque material remains of nature that has been nullified by human industry—celebrating precisely the images environmentalists used as warning signs. Hilbig's stories experiment with the unsettling idea that living as a mass of talking slime, or underneath a pile of garbage, would be preferable to the status quo of the 'false environment' of socialist East Germany" (166). Hilbig's reliance on metaleptic effects and his obvious intertextual references to Joyce and Dostoevsky as well as his own aesthetic reflections make his work perhaps the most powerful example of what Buchholz means by "the literature of private anarchy." In the transformation of the monological *I* into a polylogical *we*, he most clearly reveals a particular brand of monologism as becoming the "monologue of the many . . . which conjure[s] another world" (187).

It goes without saying that none of the novels of "private anarchy" gives rise to a concrete positive alternative to a radically alienating world. These novels are simply too intent on expressing the alienating and enraging effects of their particular historico-political environments to establish formal continuity with their predecessors. What therefore holds Buchholz's argument together is his persistent concern with metalepsis and monologue, which sometimes seems to strangle the novels (as in the case of Bernhard). *Private Anarchy* nevertheless convinces me that novelistic expressions of transcendental homelessness, even in their most radical form, are also expressions of hope. Buchholz's success in identifying these glimpses of optimism in some of the darker works of the German-speaking twentieth century is the major achievement of this book.

CHRISTOPH SCHMITZ, Duke University

*   *   *

CHRISTOPH SCHMITZ is pursuing a PhD in the Carolina-Duke Graduate Program for German Studies at Duke University and the University of North Carolina at Chapel Hill. In his dissertation project, he investigates the role of disembodied voices and audio recordings in contemporary German novels.

Work Cited

Lukács, Georg. *The Theory of the Novel.* Trans. Anna Bostock. Cambridge, MA: MIT P, 1971.

Lines of Fracture, Lines of Flight

LYNDSEY STONEBRIDGE, *Placeless People: Writing, Rights, and Refugees* (Oxford: Oxford UP, 2018), pp. 244, cloth, $34.00.

How should we write the literary history of modern statelessness? Lyndsey Stonebridge's remarkable book *Placeless People: Writing, Rights, and Refugees* locates the answer to this urgent question primarily in the lives and works of six major writers: Hannah Arendt, George Orwell, Simone Weil, Samuel Beckett, Dorothy Thompson, and W. H. Auden. What unites this somewhat oddly assorted group is less a convergence of style or topic, still less of genre—since their output includes novels, poetry, journalism, political philosophy, and theology—but rather what Stonebridge shows to be a broad concern with the politics of human suffering, loss, and exile. As with her previous monograph, the award-winning study *The Judicial Imagination: Writing after Nuremberg* (2011), *Placeless People*'s historical center of gravity lies in the late 1940s and early 1950s, and each book takes the international political settlement with which the Second World War closed as a source of unfinished business that continues its impact upon our turbulent present. But whereas *The Judicial Imagination* shows the ways in which the attempt to construct a brave new era of global justice failed to measure up to the depth and sheer scale of the profoundly traumatic crimes that were among the conflict's defining features, *Placeless People* sets its sights on the limited ability of a refurbished concept of human rights to ameliorate the problems of displacement that were inseparable from the very aims of the war. Differences of focus aside, however, these volumes are closely intertwined and best read in tandem.

Of the six figures chosen by Stonebridge, only Arendt and Weil could accurately be identified as refugees, Beckett's predicament being more complicated since he never really managed to leave France. Despite being a citizen of a neutral country, he had been a committed member of the Resistance, and although he escaped arrest, he would certainly have faced imprisonment or execution had he been captured during his fugitive existence in Vichy France. And one must also add the name of Yousif M. Qasmiyeh to the list, a contemporary Palestinian poet born in a Lebanese refugee camp, whose work is briefly contrasted with that of Auden at the end of the book. Almost all the writers on whom Stonebridge concentrates are linked either by their proximity to refugee communities or by their active support for the innocent victims of war, and sometimes both, as in the case of Beckett's work for the Irish Red Cross at St-Lô in Normandy in 1945 or Thompson's campaigning for Palestinian refugees between 1949 and 1951. Yet it is ultimately Arendt whose powerful presence is felt most strongly throughout *Placeless People* and to whose work Stonebridge constantly returns in order to anchor and assess her other chosen writers and texts. And rightly so, for not only did Arendt's middle years coincide with the remaking of the global political order, but, having witnessed these events from the standpoint of a refugee, she became the sharpest of critical observers.

Arendt's importance for Stonebridge's project is twofold. First, Arendt offers some essential methodological cues, in part because of her impatience with conventional disciplinary borders, an irreverence that sat alongside a traditionalist's disdain for the deterministic excesses of contemporary social science. For Arendt, stories, images, and poetic language were indispensable in grasping and judging the world around us, and she always refused to compartmentalize history, literature, and philosophy—which is why a book like *The Origins of Totalitarianism* (1950) is simply unclassifiable. Thus over a long career, she turned to Franz Kafka again and again, praising his ability to unsettle his readers and regarding him as a writer who was good to think with, comparing the substance of his aphorisms to the philosophy of Friedrich Nietzsche and Martin Heidegger in her final, posthumous study *The Life of the Mind* (1971).

Arendt (and her mother) became stateless in 1933 by taking refuge in a house literally built on a borderline, entering from the German side and exiting by the back door into Czechoslovakia. Stonebridge appropriately describes this transition as "Kafkaesque," stressing that Kafka's depiction of an arbitrary world in which human lives are governed by the vicissitudes of chance played a vital part in Arendt's classic account of how becoming stateless effectively removed countless unwanted individuals from any legal right to protection or redress, denying them any rights whatsoever (29). This is the second reason for Arendt's pivotal role in *Placeless People*: her prescience in recognizing "that the 'refugee crisis' of the mid-twentieth century was not a one-off tragedy that belonged to other people, but marked the beginning of a new kind of refugee history that would set a pattern for future tragedies" (33). In short, this is a story of dislocation that has become a form of world history, one that touches all our lives. Today, the questions of who is to be judged stateless and who has the authority to make that fateful decision remain deeply contested issues, notwithstanding the growing importance of a postwar international legal agenda to tackle precisely these issues. The ruling that no one can be deprived of their national identity if there is no other state jurisdiction to which they can apply has a special significance here. Nevertheless, governments are still often tempted to sidestep difficult cases by revoking the citizenship of problematic or potentially dangerous men and women and turning them into stateless persons rather than put them before a public court or under state care—as controversial decisions from Britain and the United States have recently demonstrated. Arendt would have understood these developments all too well. To be "denationalized," as the Jews were under Nazi rule, means that those who are ostracized from the nation-state immediately risk being regarded as somehow less than human, as someone undeserving of what she famously called "the right to have rights" (57–61).

Notwithstanding its clear historical roots, this phrase necessarily operates at a high level of abstraction: in *The Origins of Totalitarianism* Arendt used it as a synonym for "human rights" in general. However, she staunchly believed that only through membership of a specific nation-state could such universalizing notions become politically viable, since however desirable "human rights" might be in theory, they were unenforceable in practice. Against Arendt's tough-minded stance, critics have argued that protocols of international governance like the 1948 Declaration of Human Rights did make a difference in enabling individual nations to be called to account. But as Stonebridge emphasizes, this attempt to internationalize human rights was always in conflict with and undermined by another "part of that same package," namely "the self-determination of peoples," and as a result, "little could be (or was) done to prevent new generations of people being expelled, pushed, or driven from their homes" (2). In other words, the new rights and responsibilities that were part of the definition of what it was to be a nation-state after 1945 were inherently contradictory and inevitably had the most devastatingly perverse effects.

Whatever position one holds as to the current overall health of the nation-state project, it is undeniable that from the mid-century onward the continuing breakup of old empires side by side with the creation of new imperial power blocs put the postwar global order under considerable pressure. One common response among the writers examined in *Placeless People* was to intensify that pressure, to question the nation-state's ethical standing, to expose its bad faith—a necessary preliminary to the work of imagining "a different politics of belonging" (21). Hence their preoccupation with the daily experience of totalitarianisms large and small, from George Orwell's omnipresent "Big Brother" in *Nineteen Eighty-Four* (1949) to Weil's purist critique of representative democracy for having its own inherently authoritarian dynamic in her *Note sur la suppression générale des partis politiques* (1943). And, per contra, one also finds an impatient dismissal of a facile humanitarianism, an ineffectual counterweight to governmental realpolitik that ignores the political etiology of human misery. Perhaps the most powerful staging of the ineffectuality of rights and political philanthropy is to be found in the first few pages of *Nineteen Eighty-Four*, when Winston Smith starts a secret diary with an account of a war film he had watched at the cinema the previous evening. In her outstanding reading of this episode, which turns on the bombing of a refugee ship in the Mediterranean, Stonebridge focuses upon the close-up of a Jewish mother trying to shield her child from a hail of bullets—an action that the totalitarian regime aims to eliminate from the hearts and minds of its subjects. When the "jewess" interposes her own body to save her "little boy," her spontaneous movement is the exact opposite of Winston's terrified cry at the novel's denouement as his tormentor is about to release the starving rats on to his face: "Do it to Julia! Not me! Julia!" (74–75, 90).

Of course, these are two contrasting kinds of events. On one hand there is the saturnalia of the cinema, where the crowd greets the horrific massacre with unrestrained hilarity, except for the outraged reaction of a solitary proletarian woman; on the other is the secrecy of the torture chamber, where no one will ever know what happened. When Winston privately records his pleasure at the cinematographic virtuosity of the film, it is as though this serves as a screen memory initially blocking out the perilously ambivalent feelings he had experienced at a compulsory Party ritual known as "the Two Minutes Hate" earlier in the day. In these short, intense collective outbursts, Winston and his coworkers are obliged to publicly revile the so-called enemies of the people—especially the notorious (and notoriously Jewish) renegade Emmanuel Goldstein—by shouting imprecations at images on a large television set. Paradoxically, Winston's troubled evocation of these visceral nationalistic exercises is what turns him into a "thought-criminal," a traitor who repeatedly writes the slogan "DOWN WITH BIG BROTHER" in his diary (Orwell 18–24).

By returning the figure of the Jew to the center of *Nineteen Eighty-Four*, Stonebridge is rereading the novel in the context of Orwell's 1945 essays "Antisemitism in Britain" and "Notes on Nationalism." In the second of these two pieces, Orwell suggested that the English intelligentsia tended to be on the side of the Jews on the question of allowing boats carrying Jewish refugees into Palestine without being stopped by the British Navy—the inspiration for *Nineteen Eighty-Four*'s depiction of Jewish blood being spilt in the Mediterranean—while also insisting that antisemitism was commonplace among all the English social classes at that time. And could it also be found within Orwell himself? This question continues to dog the writer's reputation, and Stonebridge commendably recognizes that because Orwell understood that he had to search for the wellspring of antisemitism among his own thoughts and feelings, including his own colonial past, he was at least aware that he did have "a problem with Jewish people," one that he came to see as integral to "the psychopathologies of nationalism," whether in its totalitarian or its democratic form (88–87). One of the pressing challenges still faced by readers of *Nineteen Eighty-Four* is to find a way to identify with the scapegoats in the boats yet also to resist the seductive brutality of state power. The American journalist Thompson, who championed European Jewish refugees in the 1930s and later argued for Palestinian rights as the new state of Israel was coming into existence, faced another version of this same dilemma. In each case her work was attacked and vilified, simply because of public hostility to the groups she was supporting. Worse still, the treatment of the Palestinians represented an unprecedented nadir in the history of human rights, for such was the power of Middle Eastern nation-states that only those refugees who renounced their right to citizenship could make a valid claim to receive UN-sponsored humanitarian aid (152–53).

The Palestinian example once again raises the question of the relationship between nationalism, militarism, and the fate of the refugee. Winston Smith's homeland in *Nineteen Eighty-Four* is depicted as an unremittingly aggressive armed camp where the merciless pursuit of external and internal enemies displays two sides of the same coin. Of all the writers in the book, Weil comes closest to Orwell in her grasp of the unsurpassable destructiveness of modern warfare as it drives toward annihilating civil society and overcoming the least threat of military opposition, always just one step away from implementing totalitarian rule. In an important sense, Weil had a far more uncompromising critique of human rights than Arendt, because she thought they were ultimately dependent upon "force." If this reifying violence turned people into objects, she asked, then how could it support the demand for justice from those who had become *déraciné* or displaced? (99) For Weil the refugee's plight epitomized the horrors of modernity, which had to be seen as the culmination of centuries of cruelty, with Adolf Hitler as Julius Caesar's fearsome progeny. Stonebridge sees this bleak diagnosis as a kind of trap, leading to a life that we can only "learn how to live tragically" (113). In an attempt to envision a way out of this impasse, Stonebridge turns, via a complicated series of moves, to a reconsideration of the Italian neorealist director Roberto Rossellini's early films, films strongly influenced by Weil's writing and in which the Swedish actor Ingrid Bergman is typically cast as an outsider (113–18). Taking up an argument developed by Jacques Rancière, Stonebridge cannily transposes his identification of a disruptive "foreigner's gaze" in Rossellini's *Europa '51* to the earlier film *Stromboli: Terra di Dio* (1949), where a female refugee who finds herself stranded in a remote island fishing community points the viewer toward a new ethical truth. Stonebridge opens up a fascinating line of approach to Weil's legacy, yet this encounter with Rancière seems curiously incomplete. What this chapter elides is any discussion of Rancière's own very different analysis of *Stromboli* in a companion piece from his collection *La fable cinématographique* (2001) in which he suggests that Bergman partly represents the invasive presence of Northern Europe in a still-pagan Christian South, arguably a stark allusion to the skewed wartime relationship between Germany and Italy when Rossellini's own film career was just beginning. More positively, Stonebridge's inventive account of Rossellini does chime productively with her later characterization of Qasmiyeh's poetry as articulating "a memory that has yet to settle into a future," just as Auden's did for an earlier historical moment (182).

Placeless People consistently provides fresh insights and reveals new connections that widen our field of vision. But not all of them are explored in the same depth. One is left wishing that more could have been said on the involvement of Auden, Orwell, and Weil in the Spanish Civil War (1936–39), for example, since this was crucial in making them the writers they became. While their exposure to the din of battle may have been partial and sometimes brief, these experiences indelibly colored their ideas about politics and armed struggle in the years that followed, though they seldom drew the same conclusions. Orwell's criticisms of Auden's poem *Spain* (1937) is an instructive example of how fraught these political and aesthetic commitments could be, to such an extent that the poet later removed it from his collected works. Indeed, 1937–42 was the key period in Auden's ongoing revision of his early writings. His dissatisfaction was to prove particularly fateful for *Look, Stranger!* (1936), a book that pitted "truth" and "heart" against "the external disorder, and extravagant lies/The baroque frontiers, the surrealist police" in its dedication to Thomas Mann's daughter Erika, whom Auden had married in order to furnish her with British nationality and guarantee her escape from Nazi Germany. As Stonebridge aptly notes, Auden "understood the intimate relation between the making and breaking of poetic form and the mass politics of displacement that surrounded him better than most" (176–78). But it is also worth remembering that his stringent editorial hand eventually cut some fourteen poems from the volume's original total of thirty-one, a sign of how conflicted and vulnerable his responses were in these formative years, an issue Stonebridge overlooks.

No author was more stringent than Samuel Beckett in his willingness to pare down and rework his postwar writings. In the finest chapter of an exceptionally illuminating, not to say moving book, Stonebridge very convincingly gives a new priority to three of the four novellas written between February and December 1946, immediately after Beckett's contract with the Irish Red Cross in the Normandy town of Saint-Lô had ended, bringing to a close his participation in the French war effort. The story of Beckett's sudden switch from English to French is now almost as well-known as the distinctive mode of interior monologue that he initiated, an inner speech that was as unplaceable as it was implacable in its suspicion of any conclusions that might be drawn about a life, even of how a life might end. Stonebridge writes this writerly transition into the space of rightlessness, from which Beckett's voices tell of being evicted from hospital or home, drifting from "door to door, cave to cowshed, ruin to ruin," and struggling with the shriveled humanitarianism of grudging handouts, indifference, and closed doors but always refusing "the terms of a bogus humanity" with rancor and humor but also despair (120–22). And so the barriers faced by each lone figure—ingrate, exile, or refugee—are precisely set out, in a world where "charitable institutions protect themselves with all the ferocity of a sovereign nation state" (129). Return is of course impossible—small wonder, then, that the narrator of *La Fin* (Beckett's first novella) should finally envision himself aboard a leaky damaged boat, attached to it by a chain, floating out to sea. Throughout, Stonebridge attentively teases out the complex sociopolitical resonances of the French and English vocabulary in these spare but astonishingly rich texts, noting, for example, how the French verb *refouler* in *La Fin* can mean "to turn away" or may refer to the discharge of sewage, while the noun *refoulement* is both a legal term for sending migrants back to their country of origin and the word used to translate the Freudian concept of "repression," the holding back of thoughts, images, and memories from the conscious mind (130).

Yet Beckett's novellas were not quite the clean break that Stonebridge's excellent analysis implies. After completing *La Fin* in May 1946, Beckett spent more than three months writing *Mercier et Camier*, his first complete novel in French, a text that in style and content was closer to *Watt*, the novel that he had worked on during his clandestine years in Vichy, than to the novellas or his later writings. *Mercier et Camier* (unpublished until 1970) has found scant favor among Beckett scholars and is usually positioned as a dry run for the cross talk in *Waiting for Godot*. But in fact, this novel complements Stonebridge's reading of the novellas due to the way in which Beckett addresses the afterlives of war in this neglected text. As Phyllis Gaffney has argued, *Mercier et Camier* thematizes the "dislocation of expatriate soldiers" who die as strangers in a foreign land with only the most minimal of markers, barely visible from the high road (Gaffney 231). Moreover, toward the novel's close, the fate of heroes who fall from grace and are abandoned or destroyed by the *patria* is linked to madness when Watt—the eponymous protagonist from Beckett's previous novel—makes a surprise appearance and explains to an irate police constable that Mercier and Camier are crazy but basically harmless. Why, says Watt, the smaller of the two cannot even be sure who he is and "hésite entre Jules César et Toussaint Louverture [*sic*]" (Beckett 196). In early modern usage, when a state had become corrupted or murderous, it could be called "a stateless state"—that is to say, a state beneath contempt, not worthy of the name (Greville 133). It is a phrase that seems ready for a contemporary revival, to be placed alongside the more familiar late-modern inflections of "statelessness" that Lyndsey Stonebridge tracks so brilliantly in her landmark study.

DAVID GLOVER, *University of Southampton*

*   *   *

DAVID GLOVER is emeritus professor of English at the University of Southampton. His books include *Vampires, Mummies, and Liberals: Bram Stoker and the Politics of Popular Fiction* (1996) and *Literature, Immigration, and Diaspora in Fin-de-Siècle England: A Cultural History of the 1905 Aliens Act* (2012).

Works Cited

Beckett, Samuel. *Mercier et Camier*. Paris: Minuit, 1970.

Gaffney, Phyllis. "Augheim, Flanders, Ladysmith, and Other Sites of Memory in Beckett's *Mercier et Camier*." *Cultural Memory: Essays in European Literature and History*. Ed. Edric Caldicott and Anne Fuchs. New York: Lang, 2003. 225–40.

Greville, Fulke. *Selected Writings*. Ed. Joan Rees. London: Athlone, 1973.

Orwell, George. *Nineteen Eighty-Four*. 1949. London: Penguin, 2000.

Rancière, Jacques. "La chute des corps: Physique de Rossellini." *La fable cinématographique*. Paris: Seuil, 2001. 165–85.

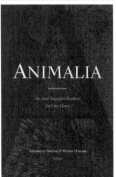

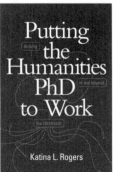